PRAISE FOR *LAW OF ZERO*

"It is often difficult to remember that every single one of us is divine. *Law of Zero* beautifully illuminates the path to graciously embracing our whole selves, unlocking the balancing power of perspective, and recognizing our collective intrinsic worth. Hardy's profound insights into nonjudgment, acceptance, and interconnectedness, coupled with his candid discussion of personal challenges and triumphs, provide essential guidance for anyone seeking personal growth and self-discovery."

—Glenn Ostlund, podcaster at *Infants on Thrones*, author of *Bathing with God*

"*Law of Zero* centers one's soul and soothes one's aching heart in times of crisis. It provides a pathway to the inner serenity we all seek as we cope with the intolerance of others and the complexity and chaos of daily living. Author Chad Hardy shares his own life journey, highlighting his quest for solutions in the face of profound situational and spiritual challenges. *Law of Zero* counters the negativity of others even as it shines a bright light on the wisdom of embracing a solid moral compass, expressing kindness to all, and endeavoring to fulfill our individual dreams. A 5-star read!"

—Laura Taylor, award-winning author, veteran editor

"An inspiring LGBTQ tale of bravery and transformation, *Law of Zero* is a compelling call for embracing radical self-acceptance."

—Fred Karger, author, activist

"*Law of Zero* is an essential read for anyone on a journey of self-discovery and empowerment. It provides invaluable insights for those navigating their path to authenticity and balance."

—David Meltzer, legendary sports executive, speaker, author, investor

"For anyone grappling with the intersection of sexual orientation and religious beliefs, *Law of Zero* offers an affirming and insightful guide. Written by an author with deep personal experience, this book is an empowering and moving account for the power of Zero."

—Dr. John Waldron, CEO of the
LGBTQ+ Center of Southern Nevada

"Finding your true path; here is a book worth reading."

—Julie Newmar, author of *The Conscious
Catwoman Explains Life on Earth*, winner of Tony and
Golden Globe awards, inventor and entrepreneur

"An LGBTQ journey of courage and becoming that will resonate far beyond its pages, *Law of Zero* is a rallying call for radical self-acceptance."

—Sal Osborne, Hulu's *Mormon No More*, *Peace Out* podcast host

"Inspiring and actionable, *Law of Zero* has something that will help everyone, no matter what stage of life you may be at."

—Jamie Roy, actor

"*Law of Zero* is a remarkable fusion of heartfelt memoir and practical self-help. With its candid storytelling and relatable advice, this book offers the gentle push that countless individuals require to liberate themselves from their burdens and truly embrace life."

—Pete Kotzbach, *The Travel Wins* podcast host

LAW OF
ZERO

THE JOURNEY TO AWAKENING YOUR
AUTHENTIC SELF, UNLOCKING YOUR
INFINITE POWER, AND TAKING
CONTROL OF YOUR LIFE

CHAD MICHAEL HARDY

GREENLEAF
BOOK GROUP PRESS

Published by Greenleaf Book Group Press
Austin, Texas
www.gbgpress.com

Copyright © 2025 Chad Michael Hardy

Distributed by Greenleaf Book Group

For ordering information or special discounts for bulk purchases, please contact Greenleaf Book Group at PO Box 91869, Austin, TX 78709, 512.891.6100.

Design and composition by Greenleaf Book Group
Cover design by Chad Hardy and Martin Cohen

Publisher's Cataloging-in-Publication data is available.

Print ISBN: 979-8-88645-257-0

eBook ISBN: 979-8-88645-258-7

To offset the number of trees consumed in the printing of our books, Greenleaf donates a portion of the proceeds from each printing to the Arbor Day Foundation. Greenleaf Book Group has replaced over 50,000 trees since 2007.

Printed in the United States of America on acid-free paper

25 26 27 28 29 30 31 32   10 9 8 7 6 5 4 3 2 1

First Edition

To all whose hearts are in search of mending, and to those journeying toward their own Truth, this book is crafted for you— with hope, with healing, and with the promise of discovery. May you find what you seek within these pages.

And to my dear family and cherished friends, thank you for the life lessons and boundless love. This book is a tribute to the profound impact you've had on my journey.

CONTENTS

FOREWORD

**By Monique Soltani,
mother, journalist, dreamer**

When I look at where I am it's hard to imagine where I've been. The unrecognizable self transformed into the authentic self. There is pain in the past, any past. Grief work dictates there is no hierarchy in suffering; irrespective of your rank, the misery will continue to be real until you are still. Struggling for what was before surrendering to what is.

Chad's journey into Zero aligns with my journey into accepting my after life—a road we traveled together rising and falling in unison while the principles of Zero remain neutral. Our friendship made of magic twenty-two years ago inspired many master plans, most notably our multi-million-dollar idea. It was 2005, our BlackBerries blinking red while visions of creation danced in our heads. It was that day, brunching in downtown LA, where we gave birth to an innovative platform to harness the collective power of the people. We called it Sponsor Moi, a website designed to crowdsource funds to donate money to struggling artists. We often credit ourselves (not our LinkedIns) with inventing one of the world's first crowdsourcing platforms. The practical realities of building a tech startup from scratch weren't in the stars for us. Engage Power was still twenty years away from taking on its present form.

It is August 2019, the skies are pink, my heart is shattered, less than thirty days since I lost my forty-seven-year-old husband to colon cancer. Our twin daughters, who turned four a few weeks before, play in the pool, a taste of a happy hour in what has come to be our darkest hour. Chad is elated and animated as he rattles off another brainchild delivered to him in a dream. He calls it the law of Zero. I am deflated and shattered. I can't hear him. I've lost my ability to listen. Hijacked back to a life out of grasp but still within reach. Lost in the past, still longing for the future I thought was guaranteed.

Time loiters by, not jaunting like I need it to, and then the text from Chad: I've just discovered there are five entry points to Zero: Find Awareness, Secure Alignment, Take Ownership, Release to Receive, Engage Power.

Secure Alignment sticks to me. Emotional control, something I've searched for since I broke hairbrushes struggling with homework. As I tiptoe into my after life, my ability to hear is starting to clear and Zero is resounding and resonating. I absorb it as a logical, balanced solution to the unbalanced, illogical realities of life. The disappointments, the disillusionment, the day-to-day imperfections that beat us down, my resolution becomes my new rallying cry: "Don't let the worst of life get the best of you." I would spend the next few years digging deep, and deeper, putting the principles of Zero into practice as I begin to rise again.

It is August 2022, another text. What are the five entry points again? For some reason I can always only remember four. Chad: It's the one you can't remember that you need to work on the most, Take Ownership.

I walk, the beach by my side, yellow Notes in my palm as my opposable thumbs hunt-and-peck, attempting the impossible. I write—

Take Ownership: Until you see how you created it you will keep repeating it. Once you realize you created it, it is then that you are finally in control. You had the power all along, Dorothy. When you are managing a situation that is not in alignment with your truth, think of it as a fire that you think you are pouring water on to but no matter how much water you pour the fire grows larger. You can't understand why and then you look down and see you are holding lighter fluid. The only way to put the fire out is to let it burn out. Channel that energy into a fire that sets your soul on fire in search of your authentic self. Trust in your truth. Creation grows where energy flows. There will always be more work to do, but remember creation starts with you!

The life-changing principles that Chad came up with are tools you can use to take control of your life, reveal your authentic self, and ignite your core power. Your Sponsor Moi is somewhere out there, not over the rainbow but inside of you. You are more powerful than you know. Your journey into becoming the person you were born to be begins beyond this foreword.

It is October 2022. I write—

October Sky: I'm better, I can't believe this day has come. I never imagined this would be possible. Never forget who (Chad and yourself) and what (Zero) got you here.

INTRODUCTION

Blessed are the pure in heart: for they shall see God.

—Matthew 5:8, New American Standard Bible

The Sanskrit word *anahata* means unstruck, unhurt, and unbeaten. Further, anahata "symbolizes overall balance between all modes of consciousness and the ultimate potential for individual and global transformation."[1]

This concept ties to the understanding that common ground can be found among most religions. The term "universalism" embraces the idea that all faiths seemingly point to the same truth despite their differences.[2] My traditional Mormon upbringing disputed this because Mormons find universalism heretical.[3]

This, I dispute. I dispute this because I have learned that there is a place and state where this concept of anahata can be fully experienced. It can be experienced by anyone. It is a place where one can find perfect balance and peace despite all hurt, pain, grievance, suffering, fears, and faults.

This is where you can find yourself not just unhurt, unstruck, and unbeaten but whole, complete, and valued—just as you are. And beyond that, it is a place of sacred power and infinite possibilities—the place and the Source of *all* creation.[4]

This is Zero.

Every person can reach this pure, balanced, divine creative place. Every person has the right of entry to its power. It is accessed through each person's unique state of being and is known in our world by many names. It can be discovered through various rituals, is embraced in numerous cultures, and is claimed in some form by virtually every religion.

Zero is a neutral state and balanced power of Source governed by the universal law of Zero, and it holds all who seek it accountable. Zero is completely available and utterly universal; no one is restricted from accessing Zero.

But I will issue a word of caution. You *must* Zero responsibly. Once you understand how to access its power, you will be accountable for everything in your life—the good, the bad, all of it. Zero does not discriminate. Zero simply *is*.

And without the fear of sounding cheesy, the best way for me to describe Zero in one word is *magic*. Yes, magic. Not the Disney kind, but the real, tangible, life-changing variety. When you find Zero and align with it, your energy is perfectly balanced, and creation freely flows toward its desired destination. This is when the magic happens.

You might ask, "How does this relate to me? How does this relate to *my* life?"

That, my friend, is what this book is all about. It is about you and your life as seen through the lens of my life experiences. I found Zero through a Cracker Jack box of pain, joy, rejection, humor, trauma, and forgiveness. This book describes how I found and reclaimed my sacred power through Zero. More than this, it is about how you can too.

Take a minute and consider all the ways you work to show up in this world, both authentically and inauthentically. There is a vast difference between the two. When we make mistakes, we unwittingly default to covering them up or sidestepping them altogether. We do this to justify our actions or to avoid the feelings our mistakes create. We concoct little white lies that seemingly hurt nothing and no one to save face and hold tight to what little control we have.

Manage

Maintain

Manipulate

Whatever it takes . . .

We are willing to do just about anything to represent some idea of perfection, to find some semblance of acceptance. Yet, in the end, there is one singular truth that no one really wants to or is able to admit: we are each and all imperfect beings living imperfect lives in an imperfect fashion.

Well, that sucks. Who wants to embrace that?

No one, that's who. As humans, we want to be anything but fallible. Anything but transient, temporary, or finite. Finite is limited, and this scares us. To be finite eventually leads to the end, and the truth is that mistakes, particularly big ones, can lead to the end of all that we know to be true, all that we know to be real.

As such, in a real way, finite can equal death.

Perhaps this is why religion exists. Almost every world religion has one thing in common: they all package some version of eternity and paint perfection into the story of what's possible while holding a someday version of infinity just out of reach.

You see, even after contending with the inner workings of my family's religion, after overcoming insurmountable odds in my own spiritual walk, and after learning to find solace in Zero—again and again—I *still* try to avoid the reality of my fallible nature. I imagine that you might do this too.

Yes, our imperfect, finite selves can easily become tripped up by something as seemingly insignificant as coffee shop gossip, but we can also just as easily recorrect. We can find alignment and conjure our paths to Zero in a moment's breath. We can then fill our place amid all that is and all that's meant to be.

Accessing Zero by calling upon Source energy is the key to unlocking the sacred power of human potential, releasing pain and trauma, and experiencing unconditional love. If you're ready for this, it's time to gather your strength and prepare yourself for all the possibilities that reside beyond your current perspective, belief systems, and understanding. This is what it takes to grow, mature, and rise into your highest self. This is what it takes to find your alignment with Source.

If you recall, I told you no one is restricted from accessing Zero. This is true. However, there is one prerequisite to entering the place and state of Zero: your will. The human will is born of the mind and adheres to each moment. Each moment in time is grounded by a decision—and every decision is anchored in choice.

As of this particular moment, you are *willing* to read these words, one after another. As of now, this is a decision you've made among the various options you have available for using this moment in time. Thank you for this. You see, I've navigated some rough waters in my life, both figuratively and literally. Yet, there was always this part of me that knew, beyond all doubt, that there was purpose—even in the pain.

On some level, I always knew that something beautiful would come of all the ugly. It may have taken forty years of living, endless research, a massive amount of meditation, and my fair share of therapy, but eventually, I found my way into it. I found my freedom. I found Zero.

Free will is your greatest gift. It is the impetus behind your ability to have and harness your own choices in life. It not only assumes that you are free to choose your behavior, but it also grants you the capacity to be self-determined.

Ultimately, free will empowers us to choose our own way, despite all external influences, past experiences, and future unknowns. In short, free will means you and I both have the power to release anything that does not serve the life we most desire to live.

Free will empowers us to release ego, pain, suffering, and trauma—that which we've inflicted and that which has been inflicted upon us. It all begins with one's will.

I've used my free will to find Zero. In turn, Zero found me. I've used Zero to release trauma and create miracles and magic in my life. And on the flip side, I've also used Zero to create dysfunction and turmoil in a rinse-and-repeat cycle.

Remember the "Zero responsibly" warning?

The practice of navigating Zero has gifted me a newfound presence and a massive amount of perspective—it has helped me to heal, create, and live. Now, my greatest desire is to share my story and more so that you may learn, grow, and heal with the Truth of Zero too.

I'm not perfect. I make mistakes. I make them every single day. I struggle with ego, pride, shame, anger, fear, and insecurity—but I no longer allow these things to impede me. Zero helps me manage all of it.

I no longer allow myself to be accosted (or overwhelmed) by that pervasive sense of uncertainty that we all know too well. I wake up every day with the desire for Zero. I desire balance, peace, harmony, and joy—true joy. I desire to be one with Creation—to know Source, to feel Source, and to channel Source. This is my will at work.

For the stories and strategies in this book to guide you to your sacred power, you must be a willing participant. You must choose to engage with a desire to pursue all that's possible. And with that, you must also be willing to take ownership of everything Zero presents to you.

Be willing to submit yourself to the endeavor of exploration here and now because where there is a willing heart, there is always a path to Zero.

1

INTRODUCING ZERO

Lord, we know what we are
but know not what we may be.

—William Shakespeare, *Hamlet*

I had just returned from taking my small team to Disney World in late February 2020 to celebrate record-breaking first-quarter sales. Fifteen years of hard work had paid off, and I was sitting on top of the world. Two weeks later, if you remember, everything was a dumpster fire.

The calendar read March 13th, 2020. Just that morning, COVID-19 had been declared a national emergency. Two days prior, the World Health Organization had transitioned COVID-19 from a global health emergency to an official pandemic.

A text message from my business colleague popped up in all caps, "IT'S OVER! WE ARE DONE!"

My company, AdVenture Games Inc., had produced in-person corporate team-building events since 2005. How could I help companies build interpersonal relationships when coworkers couldn't be in the same room? If this pandemic planned to stick around, all I'd put into building this company would be nothing but ashes.

Monday morning, after the stay-at-home order came into full effect, I awoke to the eeriest form of silence. There was no traffic noise from the nearby freeway. I looked out my window to see the parking lots all but deserted. For the first time in two decades, I didn't have a single email to respond to. No phone calls to make. Nothing remained but my thoughts. I felt utterly alone.

The next day, I was one of three passengers on a flight to Florida. Life was falling apart. The perils of my current situation kept replaying in my head: I have no business, I have no staff, I have no income.

For the next month, I lay on a pink inflatable raft in the middle of my swimming pool. Time no longer existed by counting minutes and hours but rather by clouds and sunsets.

One day, while I watched the leaves dance in the trees, I started to reflect on what my life had become. I realized I had pushed so hard for so long that I had forgotten to just exist. To just be. I had forgotten my power, my magic. It's easy to do, particularly when things are status quo, even more so when distracted by chasing what doesn't matter.

I realized I needed to get out of that pool and make a plan. But first, I needed to get to Zero.

I closed my eyes to reset my mind. I allowed myself to be completely aware of my current situation and all the effects of what had transpired. I then imagined everything working itself out as needed. The business, my staff, my finances, my home, my happiness. Everything would be—no, everything *was* in perfect order.

"How was that the case?" you might wonder. How could everything be *in perfect order* when the world whirled on its axis in a state of chaos?

The truth was that no matter what was occurring around me, I was in control. No matter what, I was whole, complete, and valued. Nothing could take this from me. Nothing could take away my power. I was connected to Zero, the Source of all Creation, whether I wanted it or not, knew it or not, or felt it or not.

Once I took my ego out of the equation, I acknowledged and accepted the situation that had brought me to this place of awareness. Even though the conditions surrounding the worldwide pandemic were out of my control, I still took ownership that this was *my* reality, *my* life, and this was happening to *me*. I saw the chaos as separate from me, and I accepted the circumstances beyond my control.

I allowed my entire body to relax as I recalled a mantra given to me by a friend:

I accept what is given,

I release what needs taken away.

This mantra leans into peace and acknowledges that the energy of surrender is much more powerful than that of control. Also, being receptive and communicative with Source is a necessity for making peace with the unknown. I also reminded myself of the five entry points to Zero.

- *Find Awareness*
- *Secure Alignment*
- *Take Ownership*
- *Release to Receive*
- *Engage Power*

Boom—Zero found.

I relaxed further in the weightlessness that Zero offers. I knew I would remain at peace no matter where my life would take me next. As I continued to breathe and rest in the Truth, the creative muse began to flow to me, through me, and beyond me. Immediately, inspiration emerged. I had the answer.

I needed to expand AdVenture Games by going virtual. There was no rulebook for this, and companies would need help navigating these waters. Virtual cohesion was uncharted territory, but I knew my team could facilitate this space. My programs would be challenging online, but with some creative modifications, it was doable. I knew it was doable because I knew I could trust the Truth found in Zero.

After three months of being shut down by the pandemic, I was back in business. This time, with more versatility and a new capacity. Going virtual allowed me to offer our services to people worldwide, a reality I couldn't have imagined three months prior.

All was well, and all was right with me. I felt calm, collected, and happy. I was in perfect alignment and felt a familiar connection to the wisdom that dwells within. I thanked wisdom for reminding me who I am, what I stand for, and why I'm here.

This is the state in which I'm meant to be.

This is me, at Zero.

NO HIERARCHY IN SUFFERING

Now, I get it. This story of getting to Zero might seem like an unempathetic example in the context of a worldwide pandemic. The world was truly in chaos. Lives were lost, disrupted, and ruined. In light of this, it may seem insignificant to concern oneself with business woes.

Even when the stakes are seemingly small, like a monetary loss for AdVenture Games, the feelings can still be overwhelmingly large, like fear, anger, shame, and ineptitude, in my case. In other words, there is no hierarchy in suffering.

We can deny the Truth of ourselves. We can deny the Truth of our situations. We can do this as a mere effort to get through a day. This is survival mode. This is living small. This is inauthenticity.

The problem that arises here is a rejection of self and/or a denial of self-truth. The most haphazard thing you can do is disregard the Truth of You.

A simple setback can quickly disrupt any given day and result in negative self-talk, disassociation, suppression of feelings, and much more.

I refer to these instances as *"cyclones,"* swirling like emotions in a storm. The infusion of energy mirrors the process of feeding a storm, raising it to greater heights, much like the ascending strength of a cyclone amidst the elements. When we fail, be it big or small, the disaster is less about what happened in the external world and more about its effect (and the effect we continue to allow it to have) internally. Without love, acceptance, and forgiveness in one's life, every negative situation winds up cascading either externally or internally, and oftentimes both—this occurs whether it is acknowledged, made known, or even realized.

You might wonder how I stumbled upon this profound concept of Zero and what makes me an expert. The truth is that I am just an ordinary man who happened to have lived through some extraordinary experiences. The man who can now get to Zero relatively easily and quickly didn't always exist. There's a tale of transformation here. Life threw its curveballs, and I swung with all my might.

There was a time when I felt incredibly insignificant and small, as if I were a mere whisper in the grand symphony of the universe. I was a puppet, controlled by the strings of external forces where my entire identity was determined for me, thus shaping my every step. Yet, within that intricate web of control, my thirst for answers ignited an internal spark, and it set me on a journey of self-discovery, seeking understanding amidst the chaos.

For you to understand how I shifted my course in the face of a worldwide pandemic, carrying with me the confidence that things would not only fall into place but also rise to a level beyond what was before, we must first start with the basics.

UNIVERSAL LAWS

When you picked up this book, you might have asked yourself, "What exactly is the law of Zero, and how does it relate to me?" Believe me, I had the same question. The first time I heard the words "law of Zero" whispered to me from the depths of my own consciousness, I was intrigued yet perplexed. It was an entirely unfamiliar term, and I needed clarification about its meaning. I began scouring the internet, searching for books and articles about the law of Zero. I found nothing. I developed a thirst for answers and spent years researching, comparing my findings with those of other thought leaders, and putting my life to the test to realize that the law of Zero had been a part of me from the very beginning.

So, what exactly is *Zero*?

Simply put, Zero can be compared to the law of attraction,[1] but even more fundamental, like Newton's law of universal gravitation. Zero is the intelligent power that governs everything in our world and beyond, making it the most powerful force in the universe. It's completely neutral and forms the basis for everything in our existence. Every creation originates from and returns to Zero, whether in our thoughts, our bodies, our world, or the universe itself. It's both everything and nothing, a paradoxical essence that is fundamental to our reality. Zero is a balanced state of being. Zero simply is.

During my research, it became increasingly evident that a profound connection exists between the law of Zero and other universal laws that extend far beyond the boundaries of my comfortable modern world. I began to look beyond the constructs of my environment and culture, searching instead for the common ground that exists among various cultures and religions. I found that many aspects of Zero have been identified by numerous people in the world across space and time.

One commonality I encountered was the religious concept beneath nirvana, which refers to the realization of non-self and *śūnyatā* (emptiness).[2] In various Indian religions and philosophies, nirvana is believed to be the state of perfect quietude, complete freedom, and highest happiness, combined with liberation from attachment and worldly suffering. There are qi, chi, prana, and numerous other experiential states that embrace life force, enlightenment, liberation, and harmony—this is the common ground of Zero.

I then dove into this concept of "nothingness," particularly in the context of Zen Buddhism and the teachings of the Kyoto School of Philosophy. This school of thought was more clearly founded in the early twentieth century, but its roots extend to ancient Buddhist teachings. The Kyoto School of Philosophy emphasizes the importance of nothingness in bridging Eastern and Western philosophical traditions.

In this philosophy, nothingness does not connote mere absence, but rather a profound emptiness interconnected with everything. This emptiness suggests that all things are interconnected, and no inherent, permanent self exists. Embracing nothingness, or realizing the intrinsic emptiness of all phenomena, is a central theme in Zen Buddhism. It is believed to be a path to liberation and enlightenment.

By recognizing the impermanence and emptiness of all things, individuals can free themselves from attachment, desire, and suffering. The idea of nothingness challenges conventional notions of existence and non-existence. It invites practitioners to go beyond dualistic concepts and experience reality directly and intuitively.

Perhaps one of my favorite findings is the Japanese *ensō* (円相), a circle that represents freedom, concentration, and attention to detail.[3] The ensō, when drawn, is said to represent enlightenment, limitless strength, or the *mu* (the void). The ensō both lacks nothing and holds nothing in excess. As such, the art of the ensō circle lives not just in the presence of a singular, complete circular stroke but also in the intention, message, and meaning within it. I particularly love the confirmation this offers to what I call Zero, as it confirms these understandings as universal law despite the language attached to it.

From culture to culture, we learn that Zero, known by different names, can be experienced and developed with practice by people who find themselves or can put themselves in a specific position under specific conditions.

Zero embodies the essence of nothingness and everything simultaneously. It's the void; it's nirvana; it is as much nothing as it is everything. When we enter the realm of Zero, we connect with the void that resides within every individual, forging a deep interconnection among us all. This realization has offered me profound comfort as I've journeyed away from the illusions of our world, drawing nearer to the radiant Truth that emanates from within the heart of Zero.

I understand that this may still seem a bit perplexing, and you might still be trying to wrap your head around this. Stay with me, though. Understanding Zero and how it can revolutionize your life will be monumental.

THE MATH OF ZERO

Let's briefly dive into a bit of mathematics. For centuries, philosophers have engaged in a profound debate regarding the nature of mathematics: Is it something we discover or is it something we invent? Those who lean toward formalism view mathematics as its own entity with its own rules, like a game, not necessarily reflecting the external world. On the other hand, Platonists argue that mathematical concepts exist independently of human comprehension.

Regardless, we can't escape the fact that math plays a role in virtually every facet of our existence, both in the natural world and the human world. Math explains human experiences like beauty, evident in the golden ratio found in nature and the symmetry of architectural designs.[4] Additionally, it's the language we use to assign value to money and measure time and space throughout our lives.

Physicist and cosmologist Max Tegmark proposed the Mathematical Universe Hypothesis (MUH), which states that everything in our physical universe is a mathematical equation. This theory suggests that math is not merely a tool for describing the universe but that the universe is fundamentally mathematical. According to the MUH, all physical reality and the laws governing it can be represented and explained through mathematical structures.[5] In essence, the universe is a vast, intricate mathematical entity.

We won't plunge too far into the abyss of mathematical philosophy. However, based on the theory that everything in our universe is math, I want to shed light on an algebra rule related to the law of Zero.

The zero exponent rule is a mathematical rule that tells us that any nonzero number or base raised to the power of zero is always equal to one. In other words, if you have a number, say "A," and you raise it to the power of zero, it will be one, no matter what the value of "A" started as.

It's a bit like magic, but there's a good reason for it. This rule is based on the idea that when you raise a number to an exponent, you're essentially multiplying that number by itself multiple times. For example, when you raise a number to the power of two, it's like multiplying it by itself once (A x A). When you raise it to the power of three, it's like multiplying it by itself twice (A x A x A), and so on.

Now, when you raise a base number to the power of zero, it seems like you're not multiplying it by itself at all. However, to keep the mathematical rules consistent, mathematicians have defined that any number raised to the power of zero should equal one. This definition helps simplify calculations and makes mathematical expressions work consistently in various contexts.

If we take a slightly more abstract look at the zero exponent rule, we discover an important facet of the universal law of Zero. Consider this: if we think of Zero as the primary source of intelligent power, it implies there must be a creator (or a base) to set Zero's force in motion. And when things are already in motion, raising that motion to the power of Zero essentially means that the base is always one.

That base is You.

Consider a challenge you might be facing in your life right now—perhaps a difficult relationship, an unhealthy habit, or a career that doesn't fulfill you. Visualize that issue clearly in your mind. Now, apply the concept of raising it to the power of zero, and what you're left with is simply . . . yourself. This simple yet profound math rule reminds us that, at the core of it all, *you* are the common denominator in your life's challenges and triumphs. You are the base, which means you hold the power to bring about change and transformation in your life. Everything starts and ends with your choices and actions, just like everything starts and ends with Zero. You are the creator of it all.

It's truly empowering to consider that Zero and its Source power are inherent within each of us. Take a moment to ponder this: every idea, invention, beautiful moment, and challenge we encounter all trace their origins back to Zero. It's intimately woven into our very existence and our surroundings.

Perhaps you are familiar with the law of attraction. It suggests that the universe responds to the thoughts and emotions you emit. According to this principle, focusing on positive thoughts and envisioning your desires will attract positive outcomes into your life. Conversely, dwelling on negative thoughts may attract unfavorable experiences. My grandfather introduced me to the law of attraction when I was very young, but as I've journeyed through life, I've come to realize that this law is merely the tip of the iceberg and what lies beneath is the law of Zero.

When you tap into the power of Zero, you're not just attracting a response. You are proactively creating in the direction where your power and energy are focused because Zero operates as a neutral force and moves where it's directed. It doesn't discriminate between positives and negatives, nor does it judge your intentions or worthiness. Think of Zero as the ultimate "Yes Man"—it produces what you feed into it as you actively engage with it to harness its power (your power) and manifest the life you've always envisioned.

Picture this: You're gripping the end of a fire hose as water gushes out with tremendous force. You have complete control over directing where that water goes. Now, imagine releasing your grip on the hose.

What happens next? The hose behaves like an angry snake with water wildly surging in unpredictable directions, possibly even splashing right back at you.

Zero does not distinguish between positive and negative. So, just like releasing a high-pressure fire hose at full throttle, as much as you can create joy and magic in your life, you can also unwittingly direct Zero to behave erratically and steer your life in ways that are entirely undesirable to you. This is where accountability comes into play.

Zero is not simply wishing on a star or posting daily affirmations on social media. It demands willpower, like taking hold of that hose and steering it in your desired direction. With genuine effort, Zero allows for an authentic space deep within yourself to align with its power, granting access to the source of everything. This formidable force ignited within you can accomplish seemingly impossible feats—from parting metaphorical seas to shifting monumental obstacles. It can even lead you to that soulmate or dream job you're meant for. Think of Zero as a threshold, that liminal space, bridging the gap between where you are today and where your future self awaits.

As you learn to access and live in a state of Zero, you'll realize that the power to chart your life's course lies at your fingertips. Despite your past, the traumas you've faced, or the mistakes you've made, when Zero aligns with your journey, there is no limit to what you can achieve. Even if you are happy where you are in life, Zero simply can help you manage your day-to-day experiences and emotions, making everything you do that much easier.

Regardless, you must train yourself to harness its power in your desired direction. Zero doesn't just create harmony. It creates *everything*. You must do the work and put in the effort to connect with Zero so you can control it. Like a beacon, you must carefully guide it, especially during your darkest moments when it seems like your world is crumbling around you. It's precisely in those times that you need to harness Zero the most.

FIVE ACCESS POINTS TO ZERO

How do you connect with and access Zero? It all begins in your mind. Everything starts with a thought, which then leads to action.

Now, this might sound a bit like science fiction, but here's how I like to visualize Zero. Picture it as a circular portal located at one end of a wormhole. Surrounding this portal are five distinct entry points, positioned just like the tips of a five-pointed star. When all these access points are unlocked, illuminated, and remain open, your pathway to Zero will be clear.

What are these entry points, and how do you unlock them?

I mentioned them briefly earlier, but as we journey through the pages of this book, I introduce each of these five points of entry and explore how to access them. I share my personal experiences of discovering each point at various crossroads in my life. And I reveal the incredible transformations that unfolded once I became a master at harnessing the power of Zero and using it to my advantage.

It's important to note that the path to Zero is not linear, nor is it a rigid step-by-step program with a fixed order to unlock the five entry points. The key is to ensure that each is activated and remains open, regardless of how you get there. To make things easier to follow, I introduce them in a flow that mirrors the natural progression of the discovery process.

Find Awareness

If I were to place one entry point to Zero as an initial checkmark, it would be *Find Awareness*.

Awareness comes in layers—self-awareness, awareness of others, and awareness of the world around you. While there are multiple layers to explore, self-awareness is the most pivotal on your journey to Zero. It's a jumping-off point into recognizing your trauma, acknowledging your shortcomings, identifying your aspirations, and, above all, understanding your authentic self, the Truth of You.

There's an age-old saying that comes from the poetry of Thomas Gray: "Where ignorance is bliss, 'tis folly to be wise." Personally, I couldn't resonate more with such a profound notion. So much of my life has been spent running from my traumas and undeniable imperfections, pretending everything was "just fine." And I know I am not alone in this. Many of us don't want to face the gritty, raw pain that lives inside. We often fiercely resist acknowledging our inherent imperfections and past traumas, which is particularly true for those raised in highly controlled environments. In such cases, facing your authentic self can be daunting, especially when it contradicts the carefully constructed image of who you believe you should be.

Paradoxically, our efforts to escape this pain or conceal our authentic selves often tether us even more tightly to it. If we live in a state of ignorance, unaware of our trauma, we cannot break the chains holding us to it. To successfully unlock the awareness entry point to Zero, we must actively seek to understand, accept, and heal the wounds entwined within us. This journey involves embracing the unvarnished Truth of You.

Additionally, we must activate our discernment skills to become aware of the world surrounding us and its long-lasting effects on us. Consider the people closest to you that influence your life. Are they uplifting you toward a higher version of yourself, or do they tend to anchor you in the struggles of their own existence? Are you consciously choosing activities, jobs, and habits that align with the goals you have set forth for yourself, propelling you in the direction you wish to go? Or have you settled into believing that what you desire is unachievable and life can't get any better?

Awareness is not an easy journey; it can be quite arduous and downright heart-wrenching. The reality is that we humans have an innate aversion to pain, which is why blissful ignorance can seem like an attractive escape route. Knowledge and self-awareness can be far more difficult to grapple with than simply coasting through life unaware. But the catch is that the bliss of ignorance is a fallacy; it's nothing more than a comforting illusion. You see, you can't outrun your trauma because it has a way of catching up with you.

In her book *Feelings Buried Alive Never Die*, Karol K. Truman delves into this topic brilliantly.[6] When you ignore your traumas, it's like building roadblocks and scattering spikes on the path to your health, happiness, and success. You won't find Zero in its fullness until you confront those haunting demons that bring you pain or make you feel unworthy. It's a harrowing journey, but it's the only way to break free from the chains of limitations holding you back from the life you want and your genuine happiness.

Secure Alignment

Now, let's dive into the next entry point on our journey to Zero: *Secure Alignment*.

Much like finding awareness, the path to securing alignment is a multifaceted undertaking. As you begin your journey of self-discovery, you will gradually pull back the layers of your life to uncover your authentic self, setting the stage for aligning all aspects of your being. This discovery process can be quite startling. The more you uncover, the more you'll come to a profound realization of the degree to which you are in alignment or out of alignment with your True Self and your deepest desires.

This alignment allows you to fully grasp the profound potential that Zero holds for you, tuning you into the correct frequency for your journey. To stay on the superhighway of creation, your heart, mind, and soul must align with your authentic aspirations. Think of it like this: If you're in Los Angeles and want to reach San Diego, you must take I-5. Jumping on I-10 will lead you to Phoenix, which, while appealing to many, isn't your intended destination (not to mention it lacks a beach).

Beyond aligning your destination, you must proactively do the work to shape your life and surroundings to foster an environment that supports your desires. It's like physically taking the wheel of your own car. Your desires won't come to you through mere wishes, and focusing your energy elsewhere won't steer you toward your intended destination.

As you establish intentions for your future, it's vital to identify and pinpoint any potential roadblocks that could knock you out of alignment and hinder your progress. If you question why something isn't working, revisiting the awareness entry point might be necessary. Taking an active role in discovering and maintaining alignment with your desired outcomes is paramount to ensuring the alignment entry point remains activated and open.

It's important to understand that alignment and awareness are inseparable companions on the road to Zero. These two entry points also form the foundation of the law of attraction. This powerful law suggests that you paint vivid mental pictures of your desires by creating a vision board or repeating daily affirmations. Furthermore, it emphasizes the importance of having faith and genuinely believing that your desires will manifest. By doing this, you align yourself with the outcomes you seek.

The law of attraction offers the bare minimum for those who aspire to lead a life that's genuinely fulfilled and actualized. However, when we venture into the realm of Zero, we're presented with a whole new spectrum of steadfast and long-lasting possibilities.

You cannot expect to do the minimum to reach Zero and still unlock its full potential. In essence, Zero demands more from both you and me. You will be required to aim higher, dream bigger, and prepare to give more of yourself to attain a life that surpasses your wildest expectations. You must push beyond your comfort zones and explore uncharted territory in your personal growth and development. So, while the law of attraction provides a fundamental starting point, to reach Zero, you must assume accountability for every aspect of your life.

⟨⟩ Take Ownership

This leads to the third entry point: *Take Ownership*.

As you unravel the tapestry of your life to become more aware of the threads that serve and hinder you, you must take ownership of each one. Owning your failures and traumas as well as your successes allows you to prevent them from owning you. While not every trauma you have experienced is your fault, you must take responsibility for the role you played in it. You are the sole authority on how events and people are allowed to affect you.

This is not to say that your feelings of pain or hurt are invalid, or that you were not truly victimized. Your feelings are valid; your story is real. You are allowed to grieve a loss and nurture the wounds inflicted upon you.

However, taking ownership becomes a choice that determines how you enable or disable the impact of various traumas or negative experiences that affect your life as a whole. When you fully take ownership of your circumstances and experiences, you empower yourself to gain control over them. They become entirely yours, no longer subject to external influence or control. Once you're in the driver's seat, you have the agency to take action.

This entry point to Zero is one that I have struggled with repeatedly. It is difficult to admit the amount of control we have over our lives when it feels like the world is against us. It's so easy to point blame away from ourselves. When we feel wounded by those we love or even strangers, we naturally gravitate toward desiring revenge and wallowing in the comforting embrace of the gloriously ominous feelings of victimhood and self-pity.

Picture this scenario: I show up at your doorstep with a truckload of the foulest, most repugnant trash you can imagine. I gleefully dump it all over your meticulously manicured lawn, spreading it out evenly to cover every square inch. To add a little parting touch, I leave a polite note on your front door that simply says, "You're welcome."

Now, I'm pretty sure this would trigger just about anyone. You might give me a call, unleash a few colorful words, and demand that I return to clean up the mess. But here's the kicker—I'm not going to do it. Nope, I gifted you that trash, even though you didn't ask for it.

As I persistently refuse to take responsibility for the mess, you might resort to calling the authorities and reporting a case of vandalism. And when it seems they won't lift a finger to help, you begin recounting the tale to anyone who will lend an ear. You tell your friends, your family, and even unsuspecting strangers of the grievous act I committed against you. It consumes every conversation you have as I unwittingly become the leading character of your life.

But then, a lightbulb moment hits you: I'm never going to come back and clean up that mess, and no one else will do anything about it. You're tired of staring at the trash just as much as you're exhausted from talking about it. Suddenly, it dawns on you that, unwanted as it may be, that trash now belongs to you. It's entirely yours. And the only person who will clean it up is, well, you.

So, you roll up your sleeves, armed with a shovel and a stack of hefty trash bags. One by one, you pick up that garbage and haul it away until your once beautiful lawn is pristine again. My friend, this is how you take ownership of your trauma and life experiences. You become the Zero Hero of your story, the one with all the power. You're the sole survivor in this showdown with the trash when you take ownership and raise all of it to the power of Zero.

Taking ownership, like every entry point to Zero, is a practice meant to be used again and again. None of these points I am bringing you are one-and-done actions. Life will persistently challenge us and shake our resolve. When we fall off the horse, we are not meant to stay down in the dirt; we must get back up to continue our charge into greatness. Each time we practice reaching our place in Zero, we will gain new clarity and precision, so much so that Zero can be accessed instantaneously.

⦂ Release to Receive

The fourth entry point to Zero is *Release to Receive*.

If you decide to completely redo the design of your living room space, can you do that with all of your old furniture and decor still in the room? No. You must remove or *release* everything in your living room that does not align with your new vision and clear out the space before you can receive the new furniture and decor. This metaphor can be applied to yourself.

Release to Receive is arguably one of the most formidable Zero entry points to tackle, mainly because it necessitates stepping out of our comfort zone. Letting go can be an uncomfortable process, whether it involves forgiving long-held grudges and amicably parting ways with a toxic relationship or breaking free from harmful habits and changing personal beliefs that are inadvertently detrimental to our authenticity. Our natural tendency is to hold onto the familiar, to cling to what provides comfort. If the thought of letting go scares you, it's likely because you're addicted to the status quo and the illusion of safety it offers, even if it no longer serves your personal growth. It's like clutching for dear life to a life vest when you're safely on land.

Much like our loyal canine companions, humans are creatures of habit—habits built on the careful constructs of our lives. This explains our tendency to be drawn to romantic relationships that echo the same patterns of love, even if they're harmful, which we might have learned during childhood. It's not that we enjoy these patterns, but rather, we find familiarity—"Better the Devil you know than the Devil you don't." We often choose to gravitate toward perpetuating cycles and patterns that we're accustomed to and understand.

Release to Receive asks us to disrupt recurring cycles, opening the door to harvest Zero's abundance. We must be willing to let go of anything incongruent with our authentic selves to give voice to our deepest desires and aspirations. It calls for releasing everything to the power of

Zero to create a clean slate. This will free up space within ourselves and our lives to welcome the future we genuinely deserve.

Always remember, you are the base, worthy of the life you aspire to live, but it requires creating space for it to manifest.

Engage Power

The final entry point that will unlock the portal to Zero in its fullness and shape the future as you desire is to *Engage Power*.

More specifically, *your* power. The power of Zero is inherently yours; it's a blazing force that resides within you. Engaging your power isn't a passive act. It's the act of staking your claim on the vast potential of your existence. It is setting things into dynamic motion through deliberate action void of fear. Think of it as your noble birthright. It's the unwavering belief in your inherent birthright that shines like a beacon of light within you and pierces through the darkness of doubt and uncertainty like Excalibur.

Picture this inner beacon as a towering lighthouse perched at the core of your existence. Its luminous, irresistible signal shines so intensely that it reaches the farthest corners of possibility. This beacon serves as a magnetic pull, compelling the cosmic vessels carrying your true desires to race eagerly toward you.

Fully engaging your power means taking the necessary steps to become aware of your authentic self, and releasing everything that doesn't serve you. Only then can you receive more truth and wisdom into your life. This is how you create a life aligned with your Truth and unencumbered by the ways of the world. This is how you get to Zero with past, present, and future trauma. Ultimately, this is how you get to Zero with yourself. When you begin to trust in the power that dwells within and your consistent capacity to get to Zero with anything, you can extend grace and forgiveness to yourself, others, and situations as an active force of love in daily life. In actions such as this, Zero becomes a continuous facet of your state of doing and being.

THE JOURNEY STARTS

As much as I'd like to tell you that these five points of entry to Zero are all it takes to live your life as a beacon of all things joy and abundance, it's unfortunately not that easy. It's not easy because we are still very human, and the state of Zero responds consistently to our human nature. As I mentioned earlier, Zero is the power that governs everything. It is a primordial Source power that merely exists to breathe life into *all* creation. I want to reiterate that just as you harness Zero to manifest harmony, you can also employ it to create mayhem. You must remember that Zero is inherently neutral, devoid of distinctions between right and wrong.

Life is messy, stressful, and riddled with dysfunction, pain, suffering, and trauma. This means that you *will* be pulled out of alignment. It is inevitable. But if you are willing to do the work and continue to be accountable for everything you create—and I mean all of it—you can hone the capacity to reach Zero again and again. Much like traumas, you can't evade Zero. It's been actively shaping your life since your inception and remains in motion even as you read these pages. You must harness the power of Zero to work positively in your favor and take control of your destiny, or it will take control of you.

Embracing Zero as a practice means that you can get to Zero repeatedly, and it will become easier to recognize when you are out of alignment with Self and Source. Furthermore, each and every time you realign, you will grow your trust in both Self and Source. This trust will grant you further capacity for developed truth and understanding of the world in which we live.

Connection with Zero is a journey. It is something to be contended with daily and something that will need attention and readjustment as time goes on. Know that your Truth will change just as you will; this is a beautiful thing—certainly not something to shy away from. Discovery is the forerunner to growth, and growth is the foundation of all that is to be. Rest in the knowledge that Zero *is* worth your time and attention. Appreciate the progress you have already made by picking up this book.

If you're finding all of this a bit too abstract or perhaps deceptively simple, I extend a heartfelt invitation to embark on an extraordinary journey—a journey that begins in the depths of my earliest life experiences.

Steve Jobs famously said: "You can't connect the dots looking forward; you can only connect them looking backward. So you have to trust that the dots will somehow connect in your future.[7]

Once I discovered Zero, I could easily connect the dots backward to realize Zero had always been a force in my life. My story is a tale of struggle, resilience, and the pursuit of a more profound understanding—a reflection of the very essence of the human experience. While our individual stories may differ, there will be common threads that hold a mirror to your life, where you can connect the dots backward to realize that Zero has always been at work in your life too.

Jobs continued: "You have to trust in something—your gut, destiny, life, karma, whatever. This approach has never let me down, and it has made all the difference in my life."

I ask you to trust yourself as we explore the depths of transformation and self-discovery through the transformative law of Zero.

2

FIND THE MAGIC

*Love, work, and knowledge are the well-springs
of our life. They should also govern it.*

—Wilhelm Reich, *Character Analysis* (1933)

When I was a young boy, my family lived on a desert hillside far on the outskirts of Palm Springs, California. The view of the valley below surrounded by snow-capped mountains made for a spectacular daytime wonder, equally complimented by the nighttime sky filled with unmeasurable stars and galaxies. The distance from city lights made the evening sky mesmerizing, with a clear view of the enchanting Milky Way.

I was a curious boy filled with belief in all things magic, so on moonless nights, I would lay on our front lawn nestled between a pair of olive trees and stare into the heavens, imagining what possibilities were out there. The vast number of stars made me feel insignificant and disconnected from the universe, yet at the same time, I had this innate sense that what was out there was part of me. Looking back, the magic of the universe was calling to me; I was just too young to comprehend its message.

My belief in magic stemmed from my upbringing as a Mormon and was highly influenced by my grandfather. He believed in a form of magic that existed in the power and free will of the mind. He was a Renaissance man in every sense of the word. My grandfather was an adventurer—an explorer of the mind, body, spirit, and world. He was an objectively intriguing man, the man whom my childhood self wanted to emulate most.

Whenever I was sick or injured, my mom took me to my grandfather's house. It was a haven of healing and safety. He was a chiropractor by trade and, by many standards, a pioneer in his field. He went to chiropractic school at a time when any form of healing without drugs was considered the enemy of organized medicine or, at the very least, quackery.

My grandfather held a strong belief that, in many ways, the human body possesses the capacity to heal itself, healing made possible by an interrelation between the scientific world and the metaphysical world. Yes, he was certainly a man before his time. He placed within me a foundation that would prove to be unshakable.

He did not see healing as an either/or affair but rather as a both/and construct. He leaned into his spiritual convictions while working to develop innate understandings through various forms of alternative medicine, including kinesiology, acupressure, electrical stimulation, energy healing, meditation, and faith. Just as he lived his life, my grandfather built his practice with great intention and careful decisions. He seemed to find an innate balance within his chiropractic philosophies rooted in naturalism, magnetism, and devout Mormonism.

MIND OVER MATTER

At the age of four, I was diagnosed with celiac disease, long before it was a commonly known illness. Naturally, this diagnosis resulted in regular trips to the doctor and my grandfather's house. My grandparents lived in a modest suburban home in Riverside, California, that they designed and built themselves. Their seafoam-green home on the corner of a tree-lined street felt like something from a storybook. Upon arriving, you were greeted by a mass of precisely pruned rose bushes that strategically surrounded their beautifully manicured home.

I don't recall ever entering the house through their picturesque front door or spending any amount of time in the front room, for that matter. Instead, we always entered through the breezeway into the kitchen. The front room was reserved for company and was kept in accordance with what felt like both needed and necessary appearances. Such careful appearances mirrored my grandmother's persona, which was packaged in lovely fashion by pastel pink outfits that seamlessly matched, right up to her earrings and down to her shining shoes. She was an immaculate woman.

A standard Sunday afternoon meant a trip to Grandfather's house, which always resulted in a curious adventure. More days than not, a visitor would encounter my grandfather's current work or most recent invention in progress. Belle's father (from the Disney film *Beauty and the Beast*), a crafty, tinkering man, might be a good visualization for you here. My grandfather was a man who built and flew his own glider, built a homemade ham radio connecting him to truck drivers and other hobbyists across the country, and even made a ukulele out of a coconut.

What was most mesmerizing about him was that his creative work extended beyond the physical realm into a deeply spiritual one. In fact, his belief in the law of attraction[1] was so strong that when he and my grandmother decided to retire and move to Provo, Utah, in the late '80s, he wrote on numerous pieces of paper, *this* house, located at *this* address will sell on *this* date for *this* price. *Cash.*

He taped these notes all over the house and committed to speaking *this* into existence daily. When we entered the house, he would encourage us to declare it aloud with the fervent nature of a praise-filled prayer. I believed him wholeheartedly. And when the goal date approached for the house to be sold, it did—for the full asking price, with a cash offer.

Anytime my grandfather spoke, it was easy to listen. He would say,

"Chad, my boy, all you've got to do is read the scriptures to know the power of words. Words spoken with great intention and belief hold power beyond our wildest imaginations." His words of wisdom were like living water born of love, bringing life and health. My grandfather's gifts and my grandmother's confidence, combined with the depth of their faith, were a beautiful testament to living a life of freedom within chosen constructs. My grandmother was very active in the Church of Jesus Christ of Latter-day Saints and firmly set in her own ways, yet this did not keep her from supporting my grandfather in his.

She was a mindful woman with a keen sense of awareness about herself. In fact, she did the research when I experienced extreme dietary troubles and connected my symptoms to celiac disease. When I was six, she was the first to notice the peculiar way in which I ran. My feet would turn inward, and my arm would come up in a foreign fashion. After observing this a few times, she and my mother took me to our family doctor, who ran a gamut of tests. The resulting conclusion was that I had a spastic muscle disorder. This diagnosis came with a warning that I would most likely experience progressive muscular weakness as I aged. This weakening would make daily activities more difficult. As my arms and shoulders became more affected by the disorder, I would eventually lose my ability to walk. They were told that I would be wheelchair-bound by my twentieth birthday.

My mother (being her father's daughter) and my grandmother (being filled to the brim with the power of her faith) quickly saw beyond this diagnosis. They never gave any energy to this prognosis. They didn't ignore the diagnosis or the information they were given, but they immediately went to work, hoping to counteract such a future. My family collectively believed with complete faith that there was a solution beyond what was offered. They believed that power existed beyond the here and now and that they had direct access to it.

My mother, Cynthia, who truly is the Queen of Light, instilled within me perseverance and ignited my fire to never give up, not to mention my sense of humor. She taught me to stand up for what I believe in. Leading by example, she often became involved in local and state politics, making signs and marching at the Capitol. She never took "no" for an answer.

She also taught me by example to be independent and to take care of myself. I vividly remember her teaching me how to do my laundry when I was tall enough to reach the washing machine controls while standing on a stool. Our nightly prayers always included a special request from God to have the spirit of discernment. Even though I had no idea what that meant, I prayed for it anyway. With that, she taught me the importance of being a critical thinker and to not be afraid to question and challenge things. She always said the best way to win an argument is to not tell someone they were wrong but to simply use the phrase "well, that is not necessarily so."

Everyone loved my mother. She embodied it all: kindness, stubbornness, unwavering faith, and an indomitable will. She could have also given Mrs. Field's Cookies' cover girl a run for her money with her sugar-coated, sweet-as-pie smile. On the flip side, she had a sharp wit coupled with an Irish temper that moved faster than a leprechaun chasing a pot of gold. When she was happy, she was like a walking sunshine-and-rainbow dispenser. But when she got mad, oh boy, duck and cover from the brewing storm! If they gave out Academy Awards for phone performances, she'd have a shelf full of them for her sweet "hello?" when just two seconds earlier, she could be heard screaming bloody murder at us.

Her powerful duality ultimately led me to a path of healing. She also deeply believed in magic, in the idea that a power greater than myself could heal my physical body. Through her wisdom, I learned that this magic, this extraordinary power, resided within me and was capable of creating miracles. I learned that no one and nothing else had enough power to keep me from reaching my greatest potential. She drove me every week for years to see my grandfather.

My grandfather, who was already treating me for celiac disease by having me visualize my villi (the small fingerlike projections that line the small intestine) as growing strong and impermeable, began new and varied treatments. He applied all his wisdom to training my mind to be positive and my body to function. I learned about what I believed was magic, sprouting from a great deal of trust, faith, and personal power.

At the time, my family didn't tell me about the diagnosis. I was told that, because I was having trouble running, there were things we could do to help my body heal itself. My family said that we were going to do these things together. I remember my grandfather saying, "If your spine is in line, you will be fine. Alignment is the goal."

One of the many aspects of my treatment plan included refining my fine motor skills. Some curious exercises made no sense to me, like crawling around my house on my hands and knees. Generally, I just did whatever my grandfather instructed, as I was accustomed to his unique way of doing things. I also followed suit because I genuinely believed that the magic would work. I trusted my grandfather implicitly, and I was practiced in responding to his gentle, confident instructions. However, this request felt silly and embarrassing at the big-boy age of seven.

"But why? Why do I have to crawl everywhere when I can just walk?" I asked.

He replied, "Because often we must take a few steps back to find the needed step forward."

In the LDS Church, it is believed that anyone who engaged in healing arts was either ordained to heal (through proper church channels) or in cahoots with darkness or black magic. As such, my grandfather's beliefs regarding energy healing created some unspoken conflict. His beliefs and practices were not agreeable with the constructs of the church. These aspects of his life were often discussed by others with a sideways glance or conditional whisper.

Even though my grandfather's work was not aligned with darkness by any stretch of the imagination, our family seemed to work collectively to overcompensate in every way. We walked our own collective narrow road along the very edge of acceptance. Step by step, we journeyed in his shadow as he walked with one foot in the path of devout Mormonism and the other in the practice of new-age natural health.

When I was a child and even a young adult, I maintained that my grandfather had it all figured out. Now, I don't believe that was the case. In fact, I don't believe anyone has it all figured out. We are all just doing our best, bumping and bruising along this road we call life.

I know that my mother benefited greatly from my grandfather's unique form of faith, and her sister, my Aunt Cherylee, followed in his professional footsteps. She became a chiropractor, aiming to bridge the gap between Western medicine and new-age health practices. Thankfully, times have caught up a bit, and Cherylee's practices are more readily accepted than my grandfather's were in his time.

As I've ventured through life, I've learned to grant myself the freedom of an open mind and broadened perspective. This has allowed me to join my grandfather and Aunt Cherylee in the ambition to be an explorer of the mind, body, spirit, and world. Only in doing this was I able to honestly acknowledge my experiences, address my own feelings, and leverage my innate wisdom.

In place of missing answers, I have evidence born of behavior and observation. Over time, my grandfather's knowledge blessed me, as did the results of my mother and grandmother's faith and persistence. Through our collective work, my celiac disease became manageable, and my muscle disorder miraculously disappeared by the time I was in middle school.

OVERCOME LIMITATIONS THROUGH SACRED POWER

There comes a time in every person's life when they begin to ask the real questions.

Who am I?

What do I desire?

Why am I here?

I asked these questions a lot, staring up at the star-filled skies in my youth. And they are not idle questions. They are, indeed, the catalyst for igniting life's journey and they hold an important key to unlocking the awareness entry point to Zero.

Our own awareness is the beacon that lights our life's path. It's not merely the knowledge that we exist but the realization that every heartbeat, every thought, and every sensation serves a grand purpose.

Much like Alice whose curiosity sent her down the rabbit hole to Wonderland, the quest for answers is the brush that paints the canvas of consciousness.[2] Awareness ignites the flames that awaken the inner explorer and serve as architects of self-discovery, crafted to provoke, challenge, and inspire. Each question is a step closer to unlocking the gateway to Zero, a step closer to peeling away the layers of inner thoughts and emotions to uncover the authentic, sacred foundation of You. Finding awareness and living the answers to these questions can lead to a happy and fulfilling life. You see, the question is not "What am I doing?" It is "Who am I?"

It's all about your state of being—not your state of doing. If you take note of little else in this book, take note of this: A life lived to the fullest is about being—not doing.

In that regard, the next question is not "What's next?" but "What do I desire?" It's a matter of positioning, asking "Why am I here? What is this all for?"

Questions such as these cannot be answered by the mind alone; in fact, I would venture to say when it comes to self-inquiry, the mind is oftentimes more of an impediment than a help aid. My grandfather's words come to the rescue again: "Alignment is the goal." To find our answers and broaden our awareness, we must go beyond the mind and find alignment in the body and Spirit.

Awareness often manifests as warning signs in our lives. Begin by reflecting on the aspects that cause discontent. Consider recurring sources of complaint or unspoken feelings that lead to internal turmoil. Is there a facet of your parenting, relationships, career, or aspirations that feels incomplete or unfulfilled? Direct your attention there and embark on a deeper exploration. You don't have to tackle everything at once; choose one area. It might involve a bothersome coworker, an elusive career milestone, or something more profound, like finding your ideal life partner. This could even extend to dissatisfaction with your current living situation or the need for a complete life overhaul. The initial step is cultivating awareness and identifying the issue you wish to address.

We must anticipate and expect the answers we seek to be found in communion with our sacred self and our connection with Source. The wisdom derived from here will lead us to the life we are meant to live. Being in one's highest state (at Zero) is a freedom unlike any other, but before one can venture into such a sacred reality, one must free oneself from the limitations of the here and now and tap into the power within.

The truth is that there is so much more to the story of power, particularly the power that dwells within, than most people realize. When you align with power inside yourself, you are granted access to an entirely new level (and nature) of resources. These resources are divine. They're powerful, they're varied, and they're unique. Collectively, they're what I used to understand (with my limited life experience) as *magic*. Wisdom has since revealed it to me as the power of Source manifest—sacred power. I've learned that such power can only be accessed within your sacred self when aligned with Zero.

Yes, the sacred self and the self-interested self are two parts of the same whole, but they're not the same. The self-interested self is a mere mortal. The sacred self is the soul, its consciousness, your highest self. The power that dwells within the sacred self has the capacity to shape more than your day-to-day existence. It has breadth, range, and magnitude—it has amplitude. Sacred power has the capacity to transform not simply your life but also your destiny, your legacy, and your world—our world.

When it comes to sacred power, it is important to remember that our resources are limited when we view life only in terms of the natural world. We have a finite amount of time on this earth. We only have so much energy each day. Our knowledge is limited to what we've gathered up to this moment in time. All we have to work with are the assets that our earthly selves can access, be they material, monetary, or mortal. From this perspective, we are only human. Yet, sacred power is born of the sacred self. It is of one's soul and contains capacities and possibilities beyond our wildest imaginations.

The wisdom of my grandfather resounds when I think of his words: "Often, we have to take a few steps back in order to find the needed step forward."

As your awareness broadens, so too does your capacity for alignment. This act of stepping back offers an opportunity to contemplate the intricate interplay of your actions, values, and aspirations within the larger context of your existence. It allows for the discernment of patterns that might otherwise elude you, and it allows you to recognize the ripple effect of your choices.

When you open yourself up to being over doing, observing over thinking, acceptance over rejection, and embracing authenticity with forgiveness and love, your human self aligns with your sacred, authentic self. This state of communion is what I call divine alignment.

As we discussed in the first chapter, Secure Alignment is one of the five entry points that grant access to Zero. To truly embrace Zero, one must move beyond worldly influences and be present in the moment, unburdened by past, current, or future concerns. Zero represents complete presence, freedom, and harmonious alignment.

To connect with divine alignment, you must immerse yourself in the immediate moment with effortless neutrality. You cannot be in alignment with what you desire if you give energy to an outcome you do not want. Fear has a distinct alignment of its own, and it is the kryptonite of divine alignment. Like a cyclone, entertaining fear and stepping into its path can sweep you away to Oz. However, seeking shelter from fear and aligning with Zero will enable you to love, accept, and genuinely forgive yourself and others. And, in turn, you can align with and create beautiful and harmonious experiences in your life. This self-possessed state of perfect alignment achieves a natural balance similar to syzygy.[3]

Syzygy, originating from the Greek word "conjunction" or "yoked together," is perfectly exemplified by celestial events like eclipses. These rare alignments, when the sun, moon, and Earth unite, symbolize ultimate harmony and connection.

Specific conditions are necessary for these eclipses. The relationship of the sun, Earth, and moon must be perfectly aligned, and the moon should be near a lunar node.[4] Depending on the moon's proximity to the Earth, we see an "annular eclipse" with its characteristic ring of fire or a "total eclipse" where darkness mimics night.

Witnessing a solar eclipse, whether total or annular, is witnessing true syzygy. The distinction between the two types of eclipses depends on the moon's distance from the Earth, affecting how it appears in our sky.

In personal growth, alignment with one's inner power is paramount. For me, this power is channeled through the law of Zero. Recognizing and striving for self-possession, alignment, and intuition is the first step toward harnessing this divine energy.

WE ARE THE STARS

There are many parallels between the celestial bodies governing the sky and the guiding forces within ourselves. In its celestial magnificence, the sun is the source of light, warmth, and life for our planetary system, just as Source is the intrinsic essence that illuminates our soul. Both embody cosmic energy, with the sun's physical brilliance reflecting the metaphysical luminosity of Source. Just as the cosmos revolves around this stellar beacon, our lives are anchored by the profound depth and potential of our inner selves. The Source within each of us is an unlimited well of magic, power, and hope.

In astrological terms, the Earth represents our foundational being, analogous to grounding energy. We can touch, feel, see, smell, and taste the Earth. There is a grounding connection between us and nature. We can know the Earth as it knows us. Therefore, let us link the guiding force of our minds to the Earth. Our logical minds are shaped by the knowledge we've accrued from living on this beautiful, tangible celestial body.

Throughout history, the moon has been inextricably linked with our emotions and inner psyche. Its cyclical phases mirror the ebbs and flows of human experience, casting shadows of introspection during its new phase and illuminating our ambitions in its full glow. Folklore and cultural mythologies have often associated the moon with passion, desire, madness, and intuition. The moon exerts a gravitational pull on the Earth's tides, it draws forth the tidal waves of our emotions, reminiscent of the profound connection between the cosmos and the human spirit. Our internal moon is our emotions, our heart.

Just as a solar eclipse represents nature's purest form of alignment, Zero is the spiritual embodiment of that alignment within us. For us to achieve true syzygy, our sun (Source), Earth (mind), and moon (emotions) must be in complete alignment; then we can reach Zero and unlock our purest potential.

Through the development process of seeking awareness and securing alignment, you are on your way to experiencing Zero. Once there, anahata is found, and your being is unhurt, unstruck, and unbeaten. Creation flows. Wisdom dwells.

3

THE TASTE OF TRAUMA

*Your task is not to seek for love, but merely to seek
and find all the barriers within yourself that you have
built against it.*

—Helen Schucman and William Thetford,
A Course in Miracles

Just as planets have unique gravitational forces that influence each other's orbits, our lives are intertwined with various relationships that influence us, shaping our thoughts, emotions, and actions. Relationships grant passage to alignment, so we must examine our various relationships. This means our relationship with ourselves, others, society, and above all (and intersecting all), our relationship with Source.

Much like the planets in syzygy, when these relationships are in alignment, they can create a sense of balance and harmony. However, when they are misaligned or conflicting, they can cause disturbances in our emotional and mental landscapes.

It is trauma that leads to misalignment and misalignment that leads to trauma, which can impact a person's physical and emotional state.

We have to come to terms with the understanding that trauma is part of the human experience. The sooner we recognize this, the quicker we can develop strategic approaches to contend with our trauma.

Trauma is defined as an incident or series of emotionally disturbing or life-threatening events with lasting adverse effects on an individual's mental, physical, social, emotional, and/or spiritual well-being.[1] We all have wounds; we all have trauma. This cultural universal truth is easy to recognize if you are willing to see things as they really are.[2] Trauma is often born of a scenario when someone is powerless and vulnerable, while someone else is enacting the power they hold to either diminish or control someone else.

CHILDHOOD TRAUMA RUNS DEEP

Trauma breeds fear, anger, shame, and ineptitude. When a person feels unloved or unaccepted, even something deemed a small "failure," something seemingly minute in the big picture, can unravel everything.

As a young child, I not only contended with physical ailments but emotional and relational ones as well. One of the most tangled relationships in my life is with my older brother. My mother says we were best friends when we were little. He was only two years older than me, yet in every aspect, we were as different as could be, right down to our appearances; my pale blonde hair stood in stark contrast to his rich brown locks. As is often the case with younger siblings, I remember idolizing him like a superhero. We embarked on numerous adventures in the desert hills behind our house, riding our bikes along trails and exploring the long-forgotten ruins of abandoned houses. He had a unique, independent spirit, often marching to the beat of his own drum, which sometimes led him into trouble. Regardless, I wanted to be just like him.

One day, after a scuffle with our parents, he decided to run away from home. He packed a small suitcase and walked out the front door. I ran after him, tears streaming down my face, desperately pleading for him to let me come along. He stopped in his tracks, turned around, and gave me a piercing look. The weight of the moment hung in the air between us.

"You're not going with me. You're so annoying. I never want to see you ever again."

His words were like a sledgehammer to my little seven-year-old heart, shattering it into a million pieces. Of course, he came back, but from that moment on, my brother continuously bullied me, often teaming up with his friends to make me feel unaccepted and unloved. He resorted to intimidation and extortion tactics to prevent me from telling my parents. I felt like he made it his mission to make my life as miserable as possible.

About a year later, our family had a wonderful addition—my little sister, Cherylyn. After facing years of heartbreaking miscarriages, my mom finally received the miracle she'd prayed for. I felt a deep sense of responsibility to protect my sister, especially as I continued to endure the relentless bullying from my brother. In many ways, I naturally took on a parental role toward her. Cherylyn became a shining light in my young life as she played a pivotal role in holding the fragments of my broken heart together.

The day after my eighth birthday, I was out playing in the field with a couple of neighbor girls, and we were talking about the difference between boys and girls. Ultimately, they pressured me into flashing my private area at them. Of course, I regretted it immediately as the girls laughed hysterically and ran away. As expected, they told my brother.

Well, my grandmother was visiting that day, and my brother took full advantage of this. He threatened to tell the whole family at dinner unless I gave him my new birthday gift: a 1984 Olympic wristwatch. He knew this watch was my most prized gift—and that was enough.

After I handed over the watch, he got the girls to call me and threaten to tell their parents all about my behavior. Come to find out, my brother had masterminded the whole incident. He had asked the girls to coerce me into showing them my private parts so he could leverage it against me.

He knew how badly I wanted to be included and liked by the other kids, and he took advantage of this every chance he had. I had been fully taken advantage of for the musings of a cruel adolescent prank. I was embarrassed and felt like a fool. This experience left me feeling utterly powerless and deepened the wound of feeling unworthy and unloved.

Another example that lasted not only through my childhood but also into adolescence was my problem with bedwetting. The issue unfolded as another perfect opportunity for my brother to blackmail me. He forced favors out of me and demanded I give him anything I had of value—even non-valuable things that I cherished, all on the premise that he would tell my friends at school and church if I didn't comply. My bedwetting, unfortunately, continued through high school despite every attempt to rectify it.

My parents had various professionals and psychologists working with me to try and understand why I was bedwetting. They went as far as to put a metal pad underneath me for when I wet the bed, it would ring a bell to wake me up, but not even that stirred me in my sleep or rectified the problem. Even my grandfather's treatments could not fix the ailment. Eventually, I started to doubt the magic I held within, feeling helpless and broken. I remember being in high school and feeling such shame. I would ruminate over the idea that, when the time came for me to marry, I would wind up peeing in our shared bed. How would I survive it? How could they love me then? My bedwetting even kept me from earning my Eagle Scout rank. I was one camping merit badge away, but I lacked the necessary nights of camping because I was terrified of wetting my sleeping bag in front of my fellow scouts.

Beyond the bedwetting disclosures, I struggled with weight gain. Mother Nature must have had it in for me. As if my self-esteem that didn't register on the Richter Scale wasn't low enough, as soon as I hit puberty, I gained enough weight to make Ursula the Sea Witch look like a size two. The summer of my tenth birthday, my parents sent me off to an unofficial fat camp with my dad's mother, a health fanatic. Little did they know, this experience would imprint a lasting body image struggle within me, which I carried well into my adult years.

Besides already feeling like I didn't measure up and struggling with self-acceptance, during high school my brother spread rumors around that I was gay. The very idea that I could possibly be gay, as he claimed, was absurd. I had had adolescent crushes on girls for as long as I could remember. I knew from my church that homosexuality was not an option for me—or any Mormon, really.[3] But my brother had somehow befriended every guy in the church and planted that seed to the point that they all turned their backs to me.

Every. Single. One.

Every Wednesday, our parents dropped us off at church to participate in girls' and boys' activities. Of course, I was left entirely out of the boy's activities. They wouldn't include me in any activity, courtesy of the scarlet letter my brother had put on my forehead. He did a thorough job of making sure I was ostracized.

Instead of being able to join the boys, I would sit outside the girl's class and listen to them talk about spiritual things and all the exciting happenings in their lives. When the door was shut, or I feared being caught, I would sit in the common room and play the piano by myself.

The emotional abuse I endured from my brother, compounded by my body image and bedwetting issues, made for a perfect storm in my young life. The treatment I received from my brother and, subsequently, the other boys at my church only heightened my fears that something was indeed wrong with me. I felt ugly and unaccepted, undoubtedly unworthy of love. Because who could ever love someone as disgusting and flawed as me?

At times after I prayed, just as my busy mind would find rest, wisdom would appear to me as a reflection in a mirror. On the other side of the looking glass was not me in my current state but a shadowy grown-up version of my future self, staring at me as if begging me to heed a warning.

This haunting man in the mirror would stand there, void of emotion, poking holes in the paradigm that had been mapped out and consistently set before me. The man seemed confident, self-assured, and attractive. He had an air of freedom about him that seemed like he was tethered to no one, not even the church. There was something about him that felt sinful in my young mind, yet he seemed somehow an inevitability. He showed me that I had my very own Pandora's box, and acknowledging its existence released my worst fear—the fear of Truth. This fear would weave its way in an attempt to expose all of my vulnerabilities. I knew I could become him, which exacerbated the fear of being someone different than what was expected of me. I was both afraid and overwhelmed as my mind would ruminate over all that I innately knew and that much of this did not fit the constructs of what I was taught to believe.

What's wrong with me? Why do I feel so out of place? Why don't I fit in?

I began to have more questions than answers, and my secret desires that I had worked so hard to mask in the daylight would suddenly become transparent. Much like when Adam and Eve became aware of their nakedness, this mirror would be dropped in front of me, and I would see myself for who I was, created to be filled with contradictions. It went against everything my family and church had taught me about the life and future promised to me as a token of my Mormon birthright.

I refused to believe that what I saw in the metaphorical mirror was me. It was a paradox of the happiness guaranteed by my faithfulness. I would reason that, certainly, these things I felt were crafted by the hand of Satan and were the image of what my life would be like if I was *not* obedient.

I knew exactly what to do. I stuffed everything I felt and thought I knew into that box. I pushed it far away until the reflection of what was expected of me came back into view. Pretense was the name of the game; "fake it 'til you make it" became my mantra. The motivational poster from English Class saying "If you can dream it, you can do it!" danced with the Old Testament tenet "Thou shalt not sin."

Fragmented snippets from Genesis, Leviticus, Romans, and I Corinthians twisted their way to me, empowering the ever-present refrain: The unrighteous will not inherit the kingdom of God.

There was safety in not knowing, not questioning, not tuning in. There was security in tuning out. I needed to put my head in the safe and comfortable sand of familial religion with all its expectations. I felt compelled to turn away from the man in the mirror. His freedoms and truths were not meant to be mine. I felt it was the only way, as I knew I would not be accepted unless I remained obedient, fit the mold provided, and hit the mark presented for me. Too much individuality is sinful. Too much personality is ego. To think for oneself or to forge one's own path is to play with fire, and we all know what fire leads to.

"Put your trust in the men who came before you; they know what's right."

"Only approach the approved reading sections, or the world will corrupt your soul."

"He who abides in sin cannot be sanctified by law, neither by mercy, justice, nor judgment. Therefore, they must remain filthy still."[4]

HUMAN STORY CODE

The stories of my life and the stories of your life are not mere individual happenings. Instead, they are each part of a grand interrelated, interconnected saga pieced together brick by brick like LEGOs.

I call this the "Human Story Code."

At its core, our Human Story Code is etched with the impressions of our environment. This code is woven together from diverse threads of cultural heritage, familial teachings, societal norms, religious beliefs, and personal encounters, all converging to sculpt and filter our worldview. The Human Story Code encapsulates the intricate narrative that shapes our individual and collective existence, echoing the very essence of our human experience. It encompasses the fundamental principles and building blocks imprinted upon us since birth, weaving a complex tapestry of identity, values, and purpose.

For example, a person with a code emphasizing self-sufficiency might interpret success as personal achievement. At the same time, someone with a code valuing community could perceive success as contributing to the collective good.

The family unit serves as the first classroom for the Human Story Code. Familial interactions teach us our values, beliefs, and modes of relating to others. Parental models provide us with templates for behavior and emotional responses, laying the groundwork for our self-concept and interpersonal dynamics. Sibling relationships and birth order contribute further to our code, influencing our roles and communication styles.

Religious and spiritual beliefs weave a profound thread into the Human Story Code. Faith offers answers to existential questions, guiding our understanding of purpose, morality, and the nature of reality. Our chosen religious path, or lack thereof, deeply colors how we make meaning in our lives. From the rituals we practice to the ethical guidelines we follow, our spiritual beliefs inform the decisions we make and the paths we pursue.

Formal and informal education contributes significantly to the assembly of the Human Story Code. The stories we hear, the historical narratives we encounter, and the knowledge we gain shape how we perceive and interpret the world. The educational environment introduces us to shared knowledge and societal norms, which, when embraced, become integral parts of our code. However, education also offers the opportunity for questioning and reshaping the code as new information emerges.

Once the foundational elements of the Human Story Code are established, they undergo reinforcement through the lens of our perceptions. This lens, often shaped by the code itself, filters information and experiences in ways that validate existing beliefs and perspectives, allowing us to categorize, understand, and react to stimuli. This confirmation bias reinforces the code, creating a feedback loop that further strengthens its influence.

Confirmation bias is the cognitive tendency to seek out and interpret information in ways that align with our preexisting beliefs. When we encounter information that confirms our code, it reinforces our sense of identity and worldview. This phenomenon explains why individuals exposed to different sources of information can emerge with divergent views, each viewpoint aligned with their respective Human Story Code.

We will continue to build, develop, and reinforce our code throughout our lives, but at the heart of its intricate web lies the profound impact of trauma—a force that can etch itself as an indelible cornerstone within our Human Story Code.

Yes, trauma, both big and small, is real. Mine is real. Yours is real. And trauma is pervasive. We know this, and science knows this. Let's acknowledge that first. No single person escapes life unscathed by the battered and broken world in which we live. For me, the man in the mirror became a perversion of my trauma, and it was just getting started.

The influence of traumatic events and experiences is profoundly far-reaching, multifaceted, and long-staying within the core components of our Human Story Code. Moreover, the effects can continue even decades after the trauma occurred, shaping how we perceive ourselves, others, and the world around us.[5]

Each person's life comprises a combination of small and large-T traumas.[6] The reality is that the mechanics of unprocessed trauma are the same across the board, despite scale. Additionally, small traumas can be compounded by large-T traumas, and vice versa.

Research on the relationship of childhood trauma on later-life health and well-being found that, although adverse childhood experiences (ACEs) are *more* common among some populations, they are still common across *all* populations. Almost two-thirds of participants from one study reported at least one ACE, and more than one in five reported three or more ACEs in their lives.[7]

There is so much emphasis on childhood trauma because the human brain is at a critical stage of development during childhood. During this time, positive experiences can lead to healthy brain development, while negative experiences can promote unhealthy development. Acute and prolonged trauma can decrease the volume of areas of the brain responsible for cognitive functions such as short-term memory, emotional regulation, and higher cognitive functions.

This is a big deal, because it pertains to acute and prolonged trauma, meaning it is not just impacted by large-T trauma but also by a category of small-T trauma. These traumas are anything that exceeds an individual's capacity to cope, thus disrupting function. This disruption is often emotional, but it can be mental, social, relational, physical, or spiritual. Understanding small-T trauma recognizes that a person doesn't have to have a near-death experience or have been abused as a child to collect trauma in their life. The bedwetting I experienced is an example of a physical disruption of function. My system was so overwrought with the trauma I had experienced or was experiencing (much of which I'd suppressed) that my system was literally in a state of dysfunction.

Small-T trauma often produces feelings similar to large-T traumas. These strong and disturbing feelings often abate independently, but not always. A person's range of emotions in response to traumatic experiences can include fear, anger, guilt, shame, and vulnerability.

Additionally, it is essential to note that members of historically marginalized populations have a disproportionately higher prevalence of trauma and adverse childhood experiences than non-marginalized populations. These groups include ethnic and racial minorities, members of the LGBTQ+ community, individuals with disabilities, women and girls, and people living in poverty. It wasn't until much later in life that I fully understood the impact their environment can have on their self-esteem and their capacity for self-love.

The good news is the deep-seated trauma triggers within the Human Story Code are not a static force. You have the power to change it.

Yes. You.

CRAFT YOUR TRAUMA TIMELINE

Cultivating awareness by recognizing its influence is the first step toward healing and reclaiming agency over the code. This awareness begins with your ability to identify the trauma point(s) within your own personal story.

Thankfully, we've advanced enough as a society to know that there are defined pathways to finding one's trauma points. These pathways include prayer, meditation, clinical therapy, somatic movement, and numerous other activities promoting awareness and embracing personal Truth. When I did this work for myself, I sought professional help in unpacking my trauma and the complexities thereof. I strongly advise anyone interested in unpacking their personal trauma to do the same.

Trauma-informed healthcare professionals specialize in various therapies that aid individuals in developing their personal well-being regarding their trauma. Trauma-informed care acknowledges trauma's role across the lifespan and recognizes that unpacking and understanding one's life experiences are vital to delivering effective treatment. This recognition—by both the provider and the individual—can create space for effective engagement and treatment, proper healing, and newfound health for the mind, body, and spirit. If you are not willing to even look at your trauma, you will surely not be capable of getting over it, much less learning from and growing past it.

The most valuable exercise I've done to get to Zero with my trauma was crafting my personal trauma timeline and addressing each point of impact. Plotting your trauma timeline can be painful and difficult, so you must be able to trust yourself. Such an exercise will undoubtedly uncover feelings and emotions previously encountered during episodes of trauma, and suppressed memories can resurface. This process can lead to feelings of confusion and unrest. It may feel like a superhuman effort to separate oneself from the pain and suffering caused by the trauma. You may also find this process heart-wrenching because it could mean admitting to and exploring weakness or wrongdoing caused by yourself or others you care for. But it can be done.

You can heal your trauma. And it is essential to do so in order to fully experience Zero. To do it effectively, you must be willing to encounter your actual adverse life experiences and investigate any associated beliefs, perceptions, expectations, values, and moral understandings. Once you've identified your trauma point(s) and named them, you need to admit to the repercussions that exist—not in the context of the cause, but despite it.

Naming pain, no matter the cause or construct, means you can do something to rectify said pain. Facing such Truth is the scariest part— your mind has shielded you from this knowledge thus far—so it's okay if you're unable to do this right away. Remain kind to yourself. Take the time you need. When you are able, return to the task with a renewed application and self-possession. Continue to do this until you can sit comfortably with the state of your Truth.

Small-T traumas have a unique capacity to accumulate more significant adverse effects as time passes. They can also have a greater impact due to preexisting large-T trauma. No matter what therapies are implemented, nearly every form of trauma work begins with identification. Once the list of known traumas is complete (with all the identifiable signifiers in place), a description for each is written and discussed through various therapeutic techniques.

The interesting thing about trauma is this: no two traumas are the same, just as no two lives are the same. We all journey through this world in accordance with our unique circumstances. Our trauma is part of how we filter our perception of life and our ideas of truth, justice, morality, self, and Source. To know your trauma is to know your story. To reconcile your trauma is to own your story.

Consider the difference between the following questions:

What's wrong with you?

What happened to you?

The first implies judgment. The question itself implies that the person is "wrong." The latter question, "What happened to you," is the opposite. Such a question offers nuance and acknowledges life's happenings—good and bad. It also grants an understanding of external influence, environment, happenstance, and individuality. It emphasizes external factors.

So, when I say that I have learned to acknowledge my own experiences, feelings, and innate wisdom, I am also saying that I now acknowledge context. I can now see how many of the formative influences in my life were just pieces of a greater whole.

Gaining awareness of our story helps us recognize how our experiences of trauma have become integral threads within our personal narratives. This understanding provides us with a bigger-picture perspective, not just for our own lives but for all lives. It acknowledges that every human story is intricately woven with personal growth and adversity's aftermath, naturally encouraging empathy and understanding.

As with my celiac and muscle disorder, I eventually got control of my bedwetting. Although, it wasn't until I was well into high school that my Aunt Cherylee intervened to help me with my damaged self-esteem. Her help subsequently allowed me to release some of the trauma I had been experiencing from the treatment I received from my brother and the others.

Although I still struggled in many ways, Cherylee re-sparked bits and pieces of the magic in me. She taught me how to identify my feelings and address the circumstances behind them. She also trained me to look for other ways to deal with my trauma. Because of her, I learned that there was always something to receive from every experience and that to heal something, you had to work on releasing yourself (and perhaps others) from the circumstances that created it.

Cherylee is someone I would call a cornerstone in my life. I genuinely believe that without her steady presence and guidance over the years, I would not be where I am today. I'm exceptionally grateful that so much of my grandfather's wisdom found its way into my aunt and that she could take hold of it in an authentically applicable fashion. It is easy to see how trauma can be passed on from generation to generation, but sometimes, we forget how belief, faith, and wisdom can also be passed along.

If you need a compelling reason to seek Zero, a reason to behold your own beautiful sacred self and claim your sacred power, here it is: when at Zero, the power trauma has on you is obliterated. The sooner you acknowledge this, the more capable you are of reaching the balance, calmness, and serenity associated with anahata, and the more you can build healthy, happy relationships with yourself and others.

This healing means the power dynamic shifts to you, and your will is activated even further. When at Zero, all possibilities are available to you. There is no such thing as *can't* or *won't* because the creative pulse that powers the pure premise of *can* and *will* is fully available and perfectly aligned.

Once you've learned to embrace Zero, you will be equipped to contend with any of the difficulties in your life, past, present, or future. You will learn to move through the world with a power far beyond your human capacities. You will learn to love fully and compassionately and to seek beauty and light in dark situations. Zero will aid you in honoring the Truth by aligning with the wisdom that dwells within.

I am so grateful I eventually understood that, despite my traumas, my imperfect being is perfectly loved and thoroughly accepted just as I am. And just as you are.

4

DISCOVER YOUR (T)RUTH

Let discernment be your trustee, and mistakes your teacher.

—T.F. Hodge, *Within I Rise: Spiritual Triumph Over Death and Conscious Encounters with the Divine Presence* (2009)

As a child, I had a clear vision of heaven, a repetitive daydream that reflected a beautiful world of grassy green hills, perfectly manicured trees, overflowing flower beds, and a golden path that continued as far as the eye could see. The sky was the kind of vibrant blue only found in National Geographic magazines, filled with enormous, puffy white frosting clouds. When the sun would shine through the clouds, a sea of diamonds would sparkle on my eternally righteous face.

Regardless of my current awkward appearance, I was perfect-looking in my heaven—tall, blonde, handsome, and wearing the most beautiful white bell-bottom suit. This was my Garden of Eden, my own world that I had created and was the god of.[1] It felt good there. Safe.

I was never alone in my heaven. A perfect-looking woman in a long white dress was always by my side. Her beautiful white skin complemented her long, flowing golden hair that sparkled from the sunlit clouds. Her constant smile and the loving, warm squeeze of my hand made me realize that this was my eternal companion—my wife and goddess forever.

At her side were two equally perfect-looking children—one boy, one girl—beautiful miniature versions of us. In that vision of my heaven, my eternal family always stood upon that golden path, hand-in-hand, smiling off into the sparkling white frosted clouds. I couldn't wait for that heaven; I just hoped I would be worthy enough to get there one day.

My day to begin securing my heaven arrived at the ripe, golden age of eight. In the LDS Church, this is considered the age of accountability, the age at which a person knows right from wrong. Most importantly, it's the age at which you are mature enough to decide to accept Jesus Christ as Savior and to officially become a member of the Church of Jesus Christ of Latter-day Saints by being baptized. The best part about baptism is that all sins from birth to that point are wiped away, never to be thought or worried about again—a fresh, clean slate. It's like a new start to a midlife crisis . . . at age eight.

As a young, curious, and sometimes devious child, I looked forward to my sins being washed away, because I truly believed I was unworthy. After all, I had just shown my genitals to the neighbor girls. I didn't quite understand what being baptized meant in accordance with the lifelong commitment to the church that comes with it. I did understand the concept of forgiveness—that through baptism, I would be made clean and whole—and that was enough for me. My baptism was the first step I had to take if I wanted to get to my heaven.

So, there I sat, alone in the office of my bishop—exactly a week after my eighth birthday. The bishop asked a series of questions: Did I understand what baptism was? Did I have a testimony of Jesus, Joseph Smith, and the church?[2] I was told this was an important step in my life, not to be taken lightly. I was excessively excited for this sacred rite of passage, to be included, to belong, and most importantly, to have my grievous sin washed away. Naturally, at eight years old, I completely understood what I was getting myself into. I knew everything.

"Yes, sir, I am mature enough to accept the call."

In reality, I didn't feel like I deserved to be baptized. The constant bullying had left me with deep wounds, festering with a sense of unworthiness and unlovability. I vividly remember a tearful moment in my mother's arms when I asked her, "Why doesn't anyone love me?" She tried her best to reassure me that I was loved, but it was not enough for my fragile heart.

On a warm summer night, sometime after my bishop's interview, I was lying between the olive trees gazing up to the vast heavens, asking God why no one loved me when something remarkable happened—I deciphered a message from the divine. A gentle, almost familiar female voice said, "Chad, you are loved more than you can imagine. Even though you can't see it now, you're going to achieve great and wondrous things in your life and be loved by many."

A wave of profound love washed over me, a feeling I had never experienced before. With newfound assurance, I retreated to my bedroom, my heart brimming with excitement, knowing that God and Jesus were waiting for me with open arms to be baptized.

When the big day arrived, my parents, siblings, grandparents, and even my favorite aunts and uncles were all in attendance. I wore a brand-new suit that my parents had specifically bought for the special occasion. As each person entered, I was presented gifts like it was my birthday. The most impressive one was my very own set of brown leather-bound scriptures with my full name engraved in shiny gold on the front cover.[3] Additionally, I was given a "Book of Remembrance," which is essentially a scrapbook to journal my sacred Mormon lineage and all the important milestones of future church commitments.

The baptism took place at the church in a special baptismal font in the back of the building. It was essentially a large bathtub about four feet deep with a mural of Jesus baptizing John the Baptist on the back wall. Above the water hung a slanted mirror that pointed down, allowing all those in attendance to witness my baptism of full immersion.

Before the baptismal ceremony, we all gathered in another room where everyone took turns telling me how proud they were of me. We prayed and sang worship songs, and my grandmother gave a talk about the importance of baptism. Though she spoke to the entire small audience, her eyes were upon me, smiling through her entire speech. Baptism is the first needed step in this progression of faith and attainment. This was my special day.

When it came time for the baptismal ceremony, my dad took me into the dressing room, where I was given a white jumpsuit to wear that covered my arms and legs. My dad also changed into a similar jump-suit. Standing side by side in the mirror, our only resemblance lay in our matching outfits. My white-blonde hair contrasted with his dark brown hair. While I had a round, bull-chested frame, he was tall and slim with a ruggedly handsome face. The only feature we shared was our deep-set blue eyes.

He took my hand and walked me into the baptismal font filled with warm bathwater. It's tradition for worthy fathers to baptize their children as they hold the Melchizedek Priesthood (the highest level of priesthood power available to worthy male members of the Church). If the words are not spoken precisely as given in the *Doctrine and Covenants* 20:73, or if a part of the person's body or clothing is not immersed completely, the baptism must be performed again.[4]

Once centered in the middle of the tub, my dad firmly gripped my right wrist with his left hand as he raised his right arm, exposing his hand-icap that he always tried to hide. He had lost most of his right hand in a meat grinder accident at age four, leaving just the thumb. The trauma of that, mixed with being forced to become left-handed, caused him to stut-ter, which would become prominent when he spoke publicly.

His shaky voice spoke slowly, but with pride, "Chad Michael Hardy, having been commissioned of Jesus Christ, I baptize you in the name of the Father, and of the Son, and of the Holy Ghost. Amen."

Then I plugged my nose, my dad placed his right hand on my back, and under the water I went. The few seconds I was underwater felt like an eternity. I thought of who I was before this moment: the sins, the shame, the bullying, all of it. As I resurfaced, I felt the most incredible relief. It was as though my past was left behind in the water that had just consumed me. I emerged clean and anew—a fresh start. Everything bad I had ever done was officially washed away in this special water.

I was clean! I was pure!

It was heavenly. I knew that everything would be better now, which was affirmed in the confirmation that followed as members of the Melchizedek Priesthood placed their hands upon my head and confirmed me as a member of The Church of Jesus Christ of Latter-day Saints. I had officially received the Holy Ghost in the name of Jesus Christ.[5]

THE KNOWING BEHIND THE KNOWLEDGE

In the days that followed, I held on to every word of every commandment so as not to tarnish my fresh, clean soul. I remember grieving each time I had a fight with my brother. I would wrestle every impure thought that found its way to me. I wanted so badly to stay obedient, worthy, and somehow keep from staining my beautifully renewed, purified soul.

The ritualistic nature of the church's system reinforced my Human Story Code and allowed me to keep believing that being a bona fide member was the answer to salvation. It was this reality and the bell-bottomed, fluffy cloud vision of heaven that carried me through the formative years of my life. Together, they were my guarantee that no matter how I felt, everything was going to be okay. I was surely on the right track. I leaned into this belief with all the determination I could muster. I turned a blind eye and hardened my heart toward anything that looked, felt, or sounded like opposition to what my family and the church were teaching me. I could stay obedient; I was sure of it. I could do well by my parents and my church. Enough prayer would do the trick.

Please, God, let this work.

It is said that discernment comes out of the renewed spirit. I believe this to be true. I was a very aware young person, almost to a fault. Remember, it was my mother who used to tell me to pray for the spirit of discernment, which I did a lot. I guess you do get what you ask for because discernment was a gift delivered to me and that continued to develop over time.

Despite navigating through my early traumas, nothing I experienced has ever negated my belief that Source is real. And that the presence of Source was with me that day in the baptismal, just as was the case every day before and every day after. I always knew that the Source of all Creation was a far greater, fuller, and more powerful force than myself or any other person or human construct, including the church. The problem was everything else that attached itself to the pure and unadulterated presence of Source kept me living a life of unrest. It kept me spinning in circles of fear and uncertainty.

If we look at communion with Source as divine alignment—then it is not hard to see how religion might adulterate the simplistic beauty of the Source-creation connection. This is not to say that love, joy, peace, patience, kindness, generosity, faithfulness, gentleness, and self-control can't be found in the context of organized religion. Still, religion itself is merely context. Ultimately, religion is a relationship—and it's another type of relationship that can grant passage to alignment.

Unfortunately, our world serves as a grand distraction from accessing Zero. Time and again, we abort our awareness and disconnect from our discernment due to discomfort and fear of the unknown. As I mentioned earlier, fear is the kryptonite of divine alignment. When we do this, we turn our backs on the Truth that is always accessible and available to us.

You see, discernment grants awareness and vice versa; with awareness comes knowledge, and with knowledge, wisdom. It is this collective process that I've come to term "Supreme Wisdom." Supreme Wisdom is the unexplainable innate knowing of things—a knowing beyond knowledge that's found in direct alignment with Source.

(T)RUTH VERSUS (t)RUTH

Unfortunately, what wisdom was attempting to reveal to me in my youth with the man in the mirror metaphor was far more than I could manage, and finding my way into such understanding was just too much for me at the time. And that's okay. It's okay because I was never rejected or abandoned by Source. And something did find a way—awareness. In the quiet recesses of my mind, I became aware of two vastly different kinds of truths: Capital-T Truth and lowercase-t truth—(T)ruth and (t)ruth, if you will.

In the realm of knowledge and understanding, the concept of truth takes on a multifaceted character. At its core, "truth" refers to a correspondence between a statement, belief, or idea and reality. However, this simplicity is often obscured by the intricacies of perception, subjectivity, and the interplay between our experiences and beliefs.

Capital-T (T)ruths are propositions that hold universally across all contexts and perspectives. Truths such as the laws of physics are irrefutable. Even universally accepted moral principles are considered to be objective and factual. (T)ruths remain unaffected by human subjectivity and maintain their validity and universality regardless of personal beliefs or cultural context.

Lowercase-t (t)ruths, on the other hand, are shaped by our personal narratives, experiences, and perspectives. They may hold a sense of truth for us based on our limited vantage point, yet they are not universally applicable. These (t)ruths are malleable, evolving as we encounter new experiences and information. A (t)ruth might be an individual's belief that rainy days bring bad luck—an interpretation based on personal experience but not a universal fact.

One of the intriguing aspects of (t)ruths is their potential to masquerade as (T)ruths, particularly when filtered through the lens of our Human Story Code. Consequently, (t)ruths that align with our code can take on the appearance of absolute, unchanging (T)ruths, when, in fact, they are shaped by our personal perspectives. These beliefs become entrenched within our identities, making them difficult to discern, and even more difficult to repave the way for a more nuanced and accurate perception of reality. These unchecked (t)ruths become your reality, your (T)ruth.

COMPROMISE AND DISCERNMENT

Supreme Wisdom is born of relationship—and that's the piece that so often gets diluted or clouded out by all the ritual, structure, judgment, and control that are born of the laws of man. Furthermore, action born of Supreme Wisdom doesn't just acknowledge a knowing beyond knowledge and thinking beyond thought—it engages it. It's mere responsiveness.

When men claim to know the ways of Source definitively or conclusively, watch out. Find awareness to engage discernment, find alignment, and access the wisdom readily available to you—in its own context. You will quickly see that the ways of Source are far beyond any human's capacity to ascertain. And that's perfectly okay.

When we build a life predominantly around the needs, desires, and expectations of those outside of ourselves, we craft a careful deception. If we are compromising ourselves to maintain the status quo, to fill the role, or to fit in, we are not creating balance. If we must fall into conformity to keep the peace or please others, we are, in truth, deceiving ourselves—our inner (T)ruths be damned.

Compromise is not a bad thing. In fact, it can be a wonderful thing. But compromise is not the same as pretense, denial, or inauthenticity. True compromise is born of compassion and connection. It's important to ask yourself: What does a particular "compromise" ask of you? Is it for you—is it of you? Does it align with you and your highest self?

It is so easy to convince ourselves to live a lesser version of life in order to fit the mold and keep the peace—in order to fit or to fill the needs of those around us. This is often what divorce, midlife crises, burnouts, and breakdowns are made of; a pretense of self, denial of truth, and inauthentic living—all toxic conformity disguised as compromise or compliance.

Such a state is not a spirit-filled existence. It is not born of power, presence, or peace. Ultimately, such forms of compromise, compliance, and conformity are the opposite of peace as they create internal struggles that can easily imbed trauma points. In retrospect, my struggle with wetting the bed for years and a depleted sense of self-worth makes perfect sense when seen in the greater context of alignment or, better put, lack thereof. For many years, I was terribly misaligned. My trauma caused me to turn away from my belief in the magic that once made me powerful and aware. Once I accepted that (t)ruth as (T)ruth, I had little guidance on how to find my way back. Everything I worked to align with was in accordance with another human's interpretation of truth.

The Greek word for the gift of discernment is *diakrisis*. The word describes being able to distinguish, discern, judge, or appraise a person, statement, situation, or environment. Discernment, as gifted by Source, is an active and functioning gift. This means that your human self can push against it. It can willfully remain disconnected from it or even deny its very presence. This doesn't remove its capacity; it just removes one's connection to its capacity.

In simple terms, to engage discernment requires we commune with Source and accept what we receive. Further, stepping into discernment requires divine alignment, and enacting discernment requires sacred power. To engage discernment is not something we do of our own ability. We can deny it of our own accord, sure, but to engage it, there's a requirement: Source at work in us—and us aligned with Source. This means discernment requires us to step into divine alignment and tap the sacred power that dwells within Zero. And that power is (T)ruth.

5

BLESSINGS IN DISGUISE

You may not control all the events that happen to you, but you can decide not to be reduced by them.

—Maya Angelou, *Letter to My Daughter*

To embrace the gift of discernment is to step toward more than the knowledge of this world, more than what can be provided through the wisdom of others or books and scripture. To choose this is to choose the implementation of Source in you through both exploration and experience. The problem is that most people are not taught about the miraculous power that dwells within them, at least not in their formative years. Rather, we are generally taught to align our Human Story Code with a particular religion, theory, culture, or understanding held tightly by those who love us. The human condition and our self-interest desire control, power, and justice.

Human beings want so desperately to be right—to know what is right and to do what is right. That desire quickly overcomes intention, conformity overrides discernment, and everything gets muddled up in ego and systematic control. We can look at virtually any difference that presents itself in the minds of men and find the root belief, "We're right, and everyone else is wrong." This is certainly the case in many religions, groups, and affiliations too.

We've to look no further than America's political divide to get a real understanding of the extremes humans will go to on behalf of their beliefs. There's a reason people say to steer clear of discussing politics and religion in polite company. This is because there is a common thread, a simplistic belief between the two—we're right, and everyone else is wrong.

Even though I innately possessed the gift of discernment from a young age, I struggled for so long to engage that instinct of my own accord. I attribute this confusion mainly to the LDS Church's power dynamic. Its systems of ritual, structure, and control leave little room for the interpretation of personal experience or innate wisdom.

MY PATRIARCHAL BLESSING

One of the many rites of passage in the LDS Church is receiving a "patriarchal blessing." This recorded and scribed prayer is usually given to late teens by the designated patriarch in the area. It can best be described as a one-time psychic reading that maps out the biblical lineage and a life of possibilities that is only valid based on strict obedience to the church. It's considered a glance into an upright future and a personal revelatory chapter from the Book of Life.

This blessing becomes an official document in the church records; meant to be a lifelong compass for the individual. The opportunity to receive my patriarchal blessing appeared early for me. My parents had made an appointment with the local patriarch for my brother, but at the last minute, he opted out. So, at fourteen years old, I took his spot. Boy, was I ecstatic! This was the perfect opportunity to completely cement myself into my faith, securing everything I so badly wanted for myself and my future.

Since you only get one shot at this blessing, the church stresses the importance of being worthy to receive it. If there was ever a time I felt worthy, it was at that moment. I desperately wanted to know what God had in store for me. We went to the patriarch's house one warm and unforgettable August evening. I had fasted all day to spiritually cleanse my body and soul so I would be open to receiving the word of the Lord. I wanted to make sure that the words spoken to me were the most perfect words possible.

After a short meet and greet with my parents, the patriarch started the tape recorder and stretched his large old hands out on top of my head as I closed my eyes. The words poured forth as if the heavens had opened up just for me, bathing me in the shelter of holy acceptance and blessing.

Brother Chad Michael Hardy, by the virtue of the Holy Melchizedek Priesthood and by the office of Patriarch which I hold, I lay my hands on your head to give unto you your Patriarchal Blessing. One that would be of comfort, direction, and an anchor to you throughout your life in accordance with your obedience.

Chad, you served your first estate well and, through your free agency, are here now serving your second estate. You were born of godly parents, and you have been taught correct principles and principles you should adhere to. You are part of a gospel plan that is here in its fullness. A true and everlasting plan that Father in Heaven has placed here for all mankind.

In declaring your lineage, you are a descendant of the House of Israel through the loins of Ephraim, the son of Joseph, who was sold into Egypt. A noble birthright, and one to be proud of.

Chad, as you prepare for your future, you have much to do and much to accomplish. It will be a bright future as long as you remain close to your Father in Heaven. Communicate with the Lord in all that you do, and he will direct thee for good in all things. Continue to prepare, organize, and establish in your life a house of prayer, a house of fasting, a house of faith, a house of knowledge, a house of order, and a house of God.

Continue to seek out your education, and through your education, you will be able to pursue a career, finding happiness therein. Prepare yourself to receive a mission call. Be found worthy to accept the call. You will teach people who have been waiting for you with the bright light of the gospel. You will be instrumental in helping many into the waters of baptism. It will be through your knowledge and understanding of the gospel that you will be blessed to preach and teach the gospel principles to all you come in contact with. You will serve a successful mission and continue to seek out your education on your return home. At the right time, you will be led to a mate that is worthy to take to the holy temple where you can be sealed for time and all eternity. At that time, you will become the natural patriarch in your home and, in doing so, serve in righteousness.

Be humble, be faithful, and be a strong priesthood bearer. Be willing to give of yourself of your time and your talents, and through this, you will develop other talents you never dreamt possible. As you are called on to serve in the Holy Priesthood, always be found with clean hands and a pure heart, serving with faith, hope, and charity.

Seek not so much to be understood but to understand, seek not so much to be loved but to love, seek not to build walls but penetrate them. With the priesthood callings you receive, you will be called to some high and holy positions. The priesthood you hold has much power to it. Always realize the importance of it as there is nothing stronger or better in life that can be achieved or had by any man. The Lord is the giver of all things, and because you have been given much, you too must give. Remember what the

Lord said: "I the Lord am bound when ye do what I say, but when ye do not what I say, you have no promise."

Understand all the laws and commandments of the gospel. Understand the law of the fast, be strict in the payment of your tithing, search out your genealogy, and keep a daily journal. You shall find happiness as long as you remain close to the Lord and remain faithful. The challenges will be great, and I bless you with the pressure of your peers that you will be able to withstand them. Throughout your life, you shall have the happiness you desire. However, remember that happiness is not always pleasure. Rather, happiness is victory, and this victory can be yours through your righteous desires. With the Lord as your partner, nothing is too difficult to accomplish.

Always be an example. Love your family, expressing your love to each of them, taking nothing for granted. Love the Lord, and this you can do by your activity in the kingdom. Go forth, understanding that all can be yours as long as you remain close to the Lord. I bless you that the power of the destroyer pass you by.[1]

This is the word of the Lord to you. Go forth and seek out all that awaits you, and this you shall find through the name of Jesus Christ, Amen.

As the blessing concluded, I experienced a warm feeling of emotion in my heart. This feeling, according to what I was taught, was the Holy Ghost, telling me what I had just heard was (T)rue. I could then trust without question that the Lord had just spoken to me directly through the mouth of His patriarch. I could take the words at complete face value. Considering my life up to that point had been a long laundry list of fears and frustrations, the fact the Lord told me my future would be full of happiness made me feel extremely loved and special. That's all I ever wanted—to be loved, to be special, to be accepted, to be happy.

My promise of happiness came with some heavy strings attached. I knew this every time I read the words "as long as . . ." My pristine future was conditional, only to be obtained by my strict faithfulness to the church. Anything less, and the Lord would not need to keep his promise, and my blessing would be worth less than the paper it was printed on.

My dad always taught us that the first law of heaven was obedience, so it did not come as a shock that obedience was the common thread that bound my Book of Life together. Otherwise, I was destined for eternal misery. After all, I was born of noble birthright. The Lord, by way of my patriarch, had said so. Naturally, that was going to come with a lot of living up to do. I was game and had been granted the necessary tools for success.

My blessing revealed the name of the man in the mirror as the "destroyer." And I would do whatever it might take to sidestep its horrifying warning. When he would come into sight, I would think of the outcome of my life as shown in the mirror. It was a life full of confusion and suffering, a life stripped of my family and the blessings of my birthright in this life and the next. I saw my soul and the light of my righteousness succumb to eternal darkness, lost forever. I was terrified to be anything but obedient.

The promises woven into my patriarchal blessing became my antidote. I would read my blessing to remind myself of the generous promises: the education, the successful career, and the eternal wife. These were the premises of my happiness. There was no other option than pursuit.

I swore to my blessing as a witness swears to the Bible. It became my road map and gave my brokenness hope and comfort. As a result, I shoved everything I felt in my heart deeper still. I steadied myself, understanding that so long as I stayed in step and somehow managed to fulfill my second estate, my heaven was within reach. I consigned my heart to the church and put my head and will to the task at hand.

Manage, maintain, manipulate. Whatever it takes.

I crafted myself into a people-pleasing, hard-working overachiever. I became a young man continually denying his thoughts and feelings in exchange for the promise of a better tomorrow. My ambition to attain my blessing in full transformed me into the stereotypical, perfectly happy Mormon with an eye on the prize. I leaned into the idea that God would protect me from the man in the mirror, who gradually revealed his sly motives as he gleefully mocked my obedience. The more I dared to look, the clearer his true nature became. He seemed adrift, unapologetically flaunting it. His presence became a constant cautionary figure. Anytime I had impure thoughts or desires, I would immediately cast them out of my mind as an act of spiritual warfare. It was nothing more than the destroyer looking to steal my promise.

I formulated the greatest of all resolve. I was determined that my allegiance to my patriarchal blessing, combined with focus and hard work, would eventually grant me the benefit of never again facing the terrifying reflection of myself that my brother had spoken of aloud. As long as I kept that at bay, everything would be okay. So, I kept myself busy. Very busy. And the busier I kept, the less time I had to pollute my mind with destructive thoughts and prove myself filthy and unrighteous. I could remain worthy; I was sure of it.

THE (T)RUTH ABOUT POWER AND CONTROL

The universe is dualistic in nature. Where there is light, there is darkness. Alongside order, we find chaos. Due to the comforting nature of patterns and predictability, the unknown is perhaps the most terrifying thing. It interweaves with the light and dark, interrelating with order and dysfunction.

To cope with this, humans exact what little control we have to manage the potential of the unknown. And we do this by leveraging whatever power is available to us or succumbing to whatever power is enacted upon us.[2]

As is evident with the ritualistic nature of these early childhood experiences, much of my youth was governed by power in a highly controlled environment. Controlling one's environment almost always means one of two things: (1) controlling others or (2) surrendering to the control of others. Both will always be defended as necessary for some higher purpose—justice, order, safety, rules, etc. In truth, the primary reason we seek to control others or to be controlled by others is to fit the agenda. We all have an agenda—an idea of how things are to be done, how things are "supposed" to be. When we enact or conform to control, we align to and work toward that agenda.

An individual agenda may be to bring justice, order, and safety to our lives and the world around us. While that can prove to be a very positive thing, it can also be taken too far. Many great crimes and abuses of power have occurred in the name of societal good.[3] Many small slights and manipulations occur, minute by minute and day after day, all for the "greater good."

The interesting thing about power is that most people want it, if for no other reason than to not feel powerless. The more powerless we feel, the more desperately we chase power and control. We do this because we have an innate need to assert (or reassert) dominion over our own situations and, ultimately, over our lives.

Power leveraged to govern and dominate makes us feel in control. It feeds both the personal ego and the collective ego (the unconscious shared egoic experience of a group). This natural phenomenon exists at every level and layer of society, and it is compounded and exacerbated the further up the proverbial food chain you go. Groups of people with common agendas bind together to gain more power in order to dominate their sphere of influence and exact more control, and then they exert greater influence. Systems are established to bend the world to the will, ideologies, and precepts of the powers that be.[4] Tiny gods playing for keeps.

Why do we let this happen? No one among us is immune to the effects of power enacted to control. Maybe you don't crave it yourself; you crave for someone else to have the power. Maybe you want them to decide for you and tell you what to do. Perhaps you want someone to figure out *what you should do and why,* so you don't have to. This, too, like it or not, is just another way for you to feel in control. As long as someone else higher than you is in control, you will know what to do, you will know your role, and this establishes order. This exacts control.

Allowing others to call the shots in your life means you forfeit your power—your personal autonomy—for the *feeling* of control. Life becomes less chaotic, less disordered, and you think this is how it works: *If I just surrender to the powers that be, all will be okay; all will be set right.* And so the story goes. Power is bought, sold, traded, and stolen to exact control or create a sense of control. Control, order, and man-made power are largely an illusion. They're constructs of our own making—a big fat (t)ruth.

Ultimately, the law of man does not reign supreme in our universe. As much as humankind hopes to exert its dominance on every portion of creation—land, sea, air, and space—the forces of nature quickly remind us of the (T)ruth about power and control of our own accord. We don't have nearly as much of it as we like to believe.

6

NURTURING OUR NATURE AWAY

Knowing yourself is the beginning of all wisdom.

—Attributed to Aristotle

By the time high school rolled around, I was throwing everything into building the life my family, church, and patriarchal blessing claimed for me. In my youthful, people-pleasing mind, this was precisely what I needed to do. Do better—be better—no matter what it took.

Despite being continuously haunted by my internal fears and insecurities, everything looked perfect externally. I'd secured a position in my school's most advanced singing group. My vocal talent landed me a leading role in the school musical. During my junior year, I fell madly in love with the most beautiful girl ever—Karla.

Of course, Karla was not a Mormon, which was only one roadblock seeing as I was not yet sixteen and therefore not allowed to date. So, my undying love for her big watermelon smile, Scandinavian blonde hair, and infectious laugh had to remain a careful secret from my family. I knew the only way my parents would let me hang out with her was if we were "just friends." My painstaking agenda began to take form, all for the greater good.

PROVING MYSELF WRONG

I became great at keeping secrets and putting on appearances. Karla didn't even know how my heart would wrap itself in a knot and explode every time she looked into my eyes and smiled. I would dream about the day she would accept the gospel, enter the waters of baptism, and go with me to the temple to become my forever wife. My vision of heaven shifted as if my mind was experimenting to see if Karla could be the mystery woman I envisioned, holding my hand underneath those sparkling white clouds. Outside of not being Mormon, she was perfect.

When the time came to confess my love, Karla responded that yes, she did love me but was not in love with me. She said I was like a brother to her—a really, really good *friend*. Ouch. The puncture wound in my chest quickly turned lethal as I waved a white flag of surrender to the gaping hole in my heart.

How could this be? We spent almost every lunch break and countless evenings together after school. Every birthday and holiday was accompanied by an exchange of gifts. All our close friends knew how much I was in love with her—it was so obvious. How could I have grossly miscalculated my feelings as being one-sided?

It was so unfair—so cruel. I felt like the biggest idiot and couldn't take any of it back. I had told her I loved her, and she didn't love me. It was final. Game over. It was then, in that moment of truth, that Supreme Wisdom found its way right back to the surface.

The man in the mirror began once again to take form, but this time, it was not a pranky ghost bringing a warning of the doom of my future. It was the present me—the real me, the broken me who had always been there. I hated what I saw and was desperate to smash it into a thousand pieces. But I couldn't this time. Reality hit me like a pie in the face, and not the funny slapstick kind. But it was funny, sort of, that I was such a fool. How long could I have kept up this masquerade? Shame gripped its bony fingers around my neck so tight, I could hardly breathe. Karla had seen the man in the mirror all along. I felt the sting of embarrassment and was deeply ashamed. I wanted to die.

Shards of numbness shot through my neck, down my arms, and into my chest as the grim reality of my existence materialized. *Why was this happening to me?*

Was it because I lied to my family about being "just friends" with Karla? Was it because I allowed myself to have feelings for someone off-limits? Was I being punished for not being completely obedient?

I racked my brain for all the ways I'd been disobedient, everything I had done, large and small, that might result in such a punishment from God. I wanted to crawl into the deepest, darkest hole and disappear forever. I knew that Karla could see the real me. She had always known. *Of course, how could she ever love me if I was really broken, if I was not a real boy?*

From that day on, my other close friend Madison became my arms of comfort. She was not a Mormon, but she was a born-again Christian. I felt safe sharing what I saw in the mirror with her. I could tell Madison anything; she would love me regardless. I knew beyond all certainty that the rumors my brother had spread about me at church and school had some merit despite how painful and humiliating they were.

When I told her I was probably gay and had secretly experienced sexual feelings toward men in the locker room, she assured me that it was not the real me. Certainly, I was displacing the rejection and my broken heart into a justification for confused sexuality. She said if I had feelings for Karla and thought I could have married her, then there was no way I was gay—and she vowed to help me prove it.

The next day, we began the first of many after-school math sessions turned into anatomy lessons to both destroy the image of my fate and mend my broken heart. Madison was two years my senior and more experienced in the body exploration of teendom than I was. She was confident that if she simply showed me the ropes, I'd be cured of any unwanted desires. After a few weeks, it seemed to be working, at least a little. But alas, as I approached my senior year, the man in the mirror continued to haunt me, and my physical attraction to men elevated.

I spent countless hours on my knees praying and pleading with God for these "unnatural feelings" to go away. On the first Sunday of every month, I fasted for a cure. I often reflected on my childhood girl crushes, and one memory in specific. One day, while exploring an old, abandoned house in the middle of the desert, my brother and I stumbled on a stack of Playboy magazines. I had a perfect recollection of my brother stuffing the magazines down a dried-up well in utter disgust while I managed to rip out a picture of a naked woman painted blue and shove it in my pocket. Although I was only seven years old when this happened, it became a memory that I ventured back to often. When we had returned home from exploring, I stashed the picture in a hole in the fence of our side yard and would regularly venture to look at the womanly figure.

The day before my baptism, I retrieved my blue woman and did away with her. I knew the dark secret of keeping her would be washed away in the holy waters, and choosing to keep her would stack the cards of sins against me. Years later, it was the blue woman who gave me ultimate solace. Her memory comforted me that all my unnatural feelings *must* be temporary. The fact that the image was a naked woman and not a man had to count for something.

However, more often than not, I was utterly devastated at the truth of my existence. I knew the way things needed to be. I knew being gay was not an option. I was determined that my strict obedience would eventually conquer this trial. My patriarchal blessing promised a temple marriage if I remained faithful. Yet, after months of internal struggle and seeing no end in sight, I decided that the only way to debunk the rumors and prove to myself that I was, in fact, a straight man was to pay the ultimate price— my virtue. I had to have sex with a woman.

Sure, this was the worst sin next to murder—well, that and homo-sexuality. I understood that having sex outside of marriage went against everything my church taught. I knew it wasn't obedient and could potentially keep me from attending church-owned Ricks College.[1] It would surely be a roadblock to going on a proselytizing mission, but I had to do it. I had no choice.

I had to cure what was wrong with me and shatter the man lurking in the mirror once and for all. I would place my chastity and my virginity upon the altar as a sacrificial lamb for the greater good of my eternal salvation. Somehow, God would understand, and somehow, he would forgive me as this instant cure-all would certainly align me back in view of my heaven and reroute me to the right and faithful way.

LOSING MORE THAN MY VIRTUE

It was settled. Madison and I devised a plan in the electronics department of Walmart, where we both worked. I was about to take a huge step into manhood; this was the answer. I couldn't be more relieved to fix what was broken.

The anticipation of that weekend was exhilarating. No cold feet whatsoever. No guilt. No shame. I was determined to get through it and prove the man in the mirror a fool. I could hardly concentrate at work the evening of our planned affair. The rumor must have gone out over the Walmart intercom, because all the guys kept giving me high-fives throughout my shift.

As soon as we got off work, Madison and I raced to her apartment. We had the place to ourselves, as Madison was eighteen and already living on her own. Once we got settled in, the anticipation of the moment created a nervous twitch in my body that caused me to shake. Thinking that I was cold, Madison invited me into her room, and she turned down the covers on her bed and signaled for me to climb in. I removed my pants and hurried under the covers. She did the same and moved in to wrap herself in my arms. I felt safe, and my shaking calmed.

My hands began to explore Madison's body, which signaled her to aggressively take control. This wasn't her first rodeo so to speak; she knew exactly what went where and how. I lay motionless in the craftiness of her lovemaking. Moments later, the deed came to an anticlimactic end. Immediate guilt rushed through me like a raging wildfire. The reality of what had just happened doused gasoline on the fire now burning my soul. The moment's anxiety pushed me off the edge of the bed, landing on my knees, begging Madison to pray with me to ask God for forgiveness.

I pressed my face into my hands and began to cry, which made Madison cry. She got dressed and delicately joined me on the edge of the bed. I dried my tears, and we prayed for God to forgive our sins. As we both sat on our knees in silence, a warm calm came over me, and my anxiety subsided. Somehow, I knew that God forgave me for the sex—and hey, it was with a woman. I did what I had to do. I looked at Madison and smiled. We embraced each other and determined that everything was going to be okay.

As I reflect on the night I had sex for the first time, I want to reach back and give my young self a great big hug. The amount of confusion I felt at that time in my life was immeasurable, and such a state of confusion created extensive trauma within me.

The balance my grandfather struck between Mormonism and his new-age beliefs was just tolerable enough (with the powers that be) to make it possible for him to express himself authentically and maintain his Mormon identity. Unfortunately, this was not an option for my young self. So, time marched along, and I continued ahead with it, cascading my way further from true desire, authentic self, and perfect peace.

MAN VERSUS NATURE

This is as good a time as any to speak to the nature versus nurture debate. If you've ever taken a psychology or sociology class, you might remember that this debate tended to be very one-sided in the past. The nature side argued that genetics is dominant in determining the facets of an individual's inner being. The nurture side said that environmental variables predominantly influence personality and behaviors. However, in today's age, most experts recognize that both factors play a critical role.[2]

Science now tells us that hereditary and environmental influences intermingle to develop our many traits, including human sexuality. The most extensive genetic investigation of sexuality ever conducted was published in August 2019. This study, led by geneticist Ben Neale, at Massachusetts General Hospital and the Broad Institute, conveyed that there is no singular "gay gene" but rather, the contribution of many small genetic effects scattered across the genome.[3] Therefore, sexuality is polygenic, meaning hundreds (or even thousands) of genes make tiny contributions to the trait.

Interestingly, most human traits are polygenic, and many, like sexuality, are also influenced by the environment. These are called multifactorial traits. Human sexuality is multifactorial. I explain all this to say that even though there is much yet to be explored (and despite what specific groups within society want to believe), there is indeed validation that human sexuality is determined by nature and nurture.

Alongside the discussion of nature and nurture, it's valuable to differentiate between man's and nature's laws. Man's laws seek to order and control individual and social behavior so as to make communal life less risky. Nature's laws are deduced from long-term observation of repeatable patterns and trends.

Natural law is a system of law based on the close observation of human nature and the values intrinsic to human nature. And unlike the laws of man, the laws of nature are not decided upon, written down, and then made public. Rather, nature's laws are inherently known and/or available to all, through mental faculty and innate reason.

The beauty of the laws of nature is that they are not about control. You see, nature simply is. It exists without an agenda, and it functions free of fear. This cannot be said for the laws of man. Interestingly and thankfully, some laws of man have been established because of natural law and natural rights. This is made evident in examples such as the United States's Declaration of Independence and France's Declaration of the Rights of Man and of the Citizen. They are also found in the Council of Europe's European Convention on Human Rights and the United Nations's Universal Declaration of Human Rights. Each of these aligns with the concept that there is such a thing as a natural right and right reason and that these are afforded to all due to the law of nature.

There are specific natural laws that science has confirmed as (T)ruths (often termed scientific laws), such as the laws of physics, biology, and geology.[4] There are also natural laws that science has only embraced to varying degrees.

The law of Zero resembles other natural laws in its free-flowing neutral form. It is neither good nor evil; it simply is. We are always affected by Zero, whether we know it or not. Nurture comes into play when we become aware of our ability to navigate with Zero. We can remove ourselves from the natural state of autopilot, take Zero's wheel, and engage our power to direct our lives.

7

ARE WE WHAT OTHERS SAY?

*Power tends to corrupt and absolute
power corrupts absolutely.*

—Lord Acton, letter to Bishop Creighton

A commonality exists in all studies of personal growth and development: to take control of your life, overcome your current limitations, and step into the life you are destined to live, you must align with the power within. Great, but how?

Many of us have no idea that a sacred power dwells within us, much less how to access it. As a result, when we think about taking control of our lives or overcoming our limitations, we think in the context of our human selves and our human abilities. We function from a place of control or desire for control—viewing power as something we can manhandle. After my fateful night with Madison, I believed I had taken back control over my desires, but my true sacred power was still untouched within me.

Madison and I never had sex again. We didn't have to. Beyond the guilt I carried, I fully believed it had cured me. I was back in the driver's seat of my life, and the man in the mirror was nowhere to be seen. I had got the fix I needed and knew there was only one way forward: strict adherence to my religion.

I was prepared to take on the next stage, and I knew it would necessitate nothing less than obedience. I was ready. When raised in a devout religious structure, your entire Human Story Code is shaped according to the ideals and expectations of your religion. There is little acceptance for anything outside the path deemed your right and faithful way. I knew as long as I stayed obedient and held to my gold engraved scriptures, I, too, would be golden.

THE STATUS OF CONFORMITY

My parents met at Brigham Young University, so attending a church-owned and operated college was at the forefront of my ambitions to stay on course with my patriarchal blessing. I had my eye on Ricks College (currently renamed BYU-Idaho). The school was rich in Mormon history. It was originally established as a schoolhouse in 1888 and began including college courses in 1915. Approximately 99 percent of its students are members of the LDS Church, and a significant percentage of the student body serves as missionaries.[1]

School at Ricks was like stepping into a scene from *Leave It to Beaver*. Everyone was so pleasant and perfect-looking. Passing a stranger on the sidewalk meant smiling and saying "Hi." It was strangely more awkward *not* to say hello. At first glance, it seemed like the perfect Utopian society I'd always dreamed it would be.

I remember my first real social encounter at college. A huge welcoming social event was held on the baseball field outside my dorm. My cousin and I decided to attend since neither of us knew anyone yet. As we introduced ourselves to some of the single ladies and engaged in conversation, I quickly realized that Mormons outside of California spoke a totally different language.

"Are you a RM?"

"Have you met your FHE family yet?"

"Where did you go on your mish?"

"Oh, you must be preemie."

I was so not in the know about this kind of lingo.[2]

It was impossible not to be involved at Ricks College. The activity calendar was abundant, and there was no keeping to yourself. I stayed extremely busy and social between church and school activities. It was all part of the grand design, making me feel righteous being one of the busy bees in the hive. I was even named my Family Home Evening's (FHE) leader or "dad," considered an official church calling.[3] This role meant I was in charge of coming up with the lessons and activities every week.

The goal of many students was to find their eternal companion—their soul partner forever, just like in my heaven. It was a ready topic of conversation socially, in class, and in church. If there were not half a dozen marriage proposals at one of the many social dances, something was terribly wrong.

Because I looked older than I was, everyone assumed I was a returned missionary. Girls even asked me where I served my mission. I would often joke, "I didn't serve a mission, I wasn't worthy." What had happened with Madison presented a somber reality, completely void of humor. The look of shame and judgment on their faces before I broke out in a laugh was enough to realize that if I didn't serve a mission, there would be no way in Mormon hell that I would ever find my eternal companion or be legitimately accepted in this community.

Not serving a mission was the ultimate social suicide. It signaled that there was something less-than, or something morally wrong. On the flip side, successfully serving an honorable mission was the golden ticket. Getting my Returned Missionary (RM) badge of honor would instantly make me a good husband, father, and steward. I would not just have validation but proof of my undying love of the gospel and my expressed commitment to the church, which would award me the promises made in my patriarchal blessing.

The harsh reality was, I did have something morally wrong with me. I was still harboring the weight of my serious transgression on my soul. I knew I needed to take care of it with my bishop, but I was afraid of the punishment.

A well-produced short film by the church that I watched in religion class amplified my fear. In the film, a very attractive blonde woman was getting ready to get married in the temple to the love of her life. It showed images of her and an equally attractive dark-haired and handsome man madly in love. Her family shared in the joy and excitement of their engagement.

The next scene showed the attractive woman in the bishop's office, going through the routine worthiness interview in order to be granted permission to enter the temple to be married. During the interview, she was asked if she was sexually clean. The woman became quiet and then admitted that while her fiancé was on his mission, she had sex with an old boyfriend. The bishop told her he would not be able to grant her permission to enter the temple until she went through a lengthy repentance process.

The poor girl broke into tears and pleaded with the bishop to have mercy—the wedding plans were set, and invitations had already gone out. She explained that the incident happened a long time ago. She begged him to please grant her permission to get married in the temple.

He refused her pleas. The following scene showed this broken woman having the embarrassing task of telling her fiancé she could not get married in the temple. He looked at her in disgust and walked away, leaving her alone in tears.

Then came the music cue of a heart-wrenching song as the singer whined about the pain of being unworthy. The final scenes showed her at school, passing her ex-fiancé in the hall as he coldly brushed her off when she tried to talk to him.

It was awful. The film's attempt at a happy ending came as the woman spoke in an interview. She had been working through the repentance pro-cess one day at a time and was finally at peace. But it was apparent the damage was irrevocable.

This film caused the inner foundation of my soul to shake. Having to go through the gauntlet of rejection and shame called the "repentance process," as shown in the film, frightened me to the core. The possibil-ity of getting kicked out of school also worried me. But confessing my sin was a necessary evil to become clean in the eyes of the Lord, to be worthy to serve a mission, and to reap the rewards promised in my patri-archal blessing.

THE DARKNESS IN ME

Making the appointment to see the bishop was the hardest thing I had ever done. I needed to get that horrible guilt-ridden video out of my mind. I fasted and read scriptures the entire day before my appointment, seeking solace. I wanted to come before the bishop with a meek and humble heart. I truly felt God had already forgiven me, but I needed my bishop to give me the all-clear.

As I entered his office, I felt at peace. The Spirit was with me. The bishop seemed friendly enough, and since we didn't know each other that well, he took some time for chit-chat. As the small talk ended, he suddenly shifted to a serious tone and asked me what I came to talk to him about. It was as if he already knew I was guilty of something.

I cracked open my book of secrets and spilled my guts. Not only did my sexual transgression with Madison come up, but I also confessed to lying about being sexually pure when going through the application pro-cess for the school. I wanted to be completely free from all the guilt I had harbored. It was such a relief to get it all off my chest.

The bishop thanked me for having the courage to come forward with my past. He was surprised I could harbor the guilt for so long—like the shame should have pushed me into confession long ago. He must have seen that film too.

Since a significant amount of time had passed since the incidents, and I displayed sincere remorse for my transgressions, he would not report it to the school's Honor Code Office, which could have resulted in expulsion. He also instructed that the repentance process would be shorter than usual.

I sighed with enormous relief. He explained that he would meet with me every couple of weeks to help me through the repentance process. During this time, I could not take the Sunday sacrament (which consisted of a hand-torn speck of bread and a Barbie-sized cup of water) until he'd determined the Lord had fully forgiven me. On top of that, I could not partake in any priesthood duties such as giving a blessing, saying prayers, or speaking in church. I would also be released as FHE leader, as a "disfellowshipped" member cannot have a church calling. I agreed to the sentence with great relief. I literally thanked God that it was all over. I was back on track to receive my patriarchal blessing promises.

Just as our conversation ended, the bishop paused momentarily, cocked his head to one side, and squinted his eyes slowly toward me. In his next breath, he solicited another confession. "Brother Hardy, is there anything else you need to tell me?"

His accusation confused and frightened me. "No, Bishop." I gulped so loud it beat against my inner eardrum. "I have told you everything."

Even though I came clean with everything I'd done, a small panic erupted inside me as if I hadn't. He hesitated slightly before he replied, "I just feel like you have not told me everything." He paused. "There's something dark about you, Brother Hardy."

His words sent shivers down my spine like a visit from the destroying angel. Could he also see what wisdom had shown me? Could he see the man in the mirror? That was impossible. I had smashed that mirror over a year ago—it no longer existed. Even so, there was nothing *dark* about me.

My intentions had always been good, and my heart had always been in the right place. I had strived to do everything right—always. I never smoked, did drugs, or drank alcohol. I was active in and had a strong testimony of the church. I was kind to people and got good grades. I chose to distance myself from my past to attend a church college to be the best obedient person possible. I was the model Mormon, damn it—couldn't he see that?

"Like I said, I've told you everything," I grunted.

I could tell my answer did not satisfy him as he stared at me with a look of intimidation. Guilt was his last resort to force a confession out of me. When I didn't budge, he promptly stood and offered his hand to me with a crooked smile. I shook it and walked out the door. The warm feelings of peace I felt entering the meeting froze over. I was angry and confused. Under what authority did this guy have the right to tell me I was "dark"?

I was raised to believe that ordained bishops were called into service through divine inspiration from a higher supreme spiritual leader in the theocratic church government. I also believed these men were granted superhero spiritual powers of sorts from God to speak on behalf of Him. These credentials explained why I needed his wisdom to know when I had been forgiven. However, this experience pulled back the curtain. I saw an ordinary man with ordinary gifts, not one of laser beam discernment. This short-circuited my faith in the validity of religious hierarchy. After all, I had lied straight-faced to one bishop about being sexually pure to satisfy my worthiness requirement to attend a church-owned school, and he couldn't detect my dishonesty. This bishop practically called me the spawn of Satan after I had come to him with a pure heart of repentance. If God called these men to their sacred duty to be a mouthpiece for Him, why were they lacking discernment?

Thanks to my mother, discernment was known to me. It was the very gift that granted me unsolicited wisdom to see things I wasn't prepared to see and to know things I didn't want to know.

I told no one about this—I couldn't. Over the next few days, I repeatedly played the bishop's accusation in my mind. His traumatizing words planted themselves as seeds in my soul, feeding the fast-growing weeds of paranoia that invaded the garden of my wisdom. The "what ifs" were incessant. What if he was correct? What if he really had the gift of discernment, and there really was something dark and perhaps evil festering within me?

The following Sunday at church marked the first time I had to publicly pass up the sacrament tray of bread and water. This ordinance is reserved only for the worthy members who are obedient to the church rules; it allows the opportunity to publicly demonstrate their willingness to follow the teachings of Jesus Christ. I was no longer considered worthy. Therefore, I was forbidden from taking this ordinance until my bishop deemed me worthy. The old-fashioned public display of punishment—the stripping away of privileges—seemed a bit counterintuitive. I felt that if there was ever a time I needed to take the sacrament, it was that very moment.

My heart began to beat faster and faster as the tray made its way down the aisle toward me. With each change of hands, the scarlet letter of unworthiness closed in on me. I clenched my eyes shut as the sweat began to form around my white collar.

I felt a slight tap on my shoulder. My eyes opened as the tray suspended in front of me. The aroma of stale bread filled the air as it seemed all eyes were on me. I could feel the weighted stare from the bishop. I glanced up with the tray in hand, and our eyes locked. He was carefully watching me.

I quickly passed the tray to my neighbor without snagging a piece of bread, hoping I moved so fast that no one else noticed. Without looking back up, I buried my face in my scriptures, pretending to be reading them as my mind replayed the tray pass repeatedly.

My bishop's riveting words screamed in my head: "There's something dark about you."

TRUST IN SUPREME WISDOM

What happened next can only be described as a divine awareness superhighway opening up like a space portal from a sci-fi graphic novel. It granted me a macroscopic view of my genuine (T)rue Self, revealing to me my inherent value and personal power. In my next breath, I began to feel an all-encompassing calm, a depth of understanding, and love that I now know to be no other than Supreme Wisdom.

I felt a great power rush through my body, revolting against the fear and shame that had engulfed me moments before. Immediately, I looked up from my scriptures, sat tall in my seat, and locked eyes with the bishop, who was still looking directly at me. I knew beyond all certainty that this man had no authority concerning my soul. His soul? Yes. Not mine. He was just an ordinary man behind a wooden podium, drunk on wielding his power and control over me.

I suddenly became aware that what I encountered in the bishop's office on through to that moment was nothing more than the result of a grand expression of control enacted by a very specific person in a secure position of worldly power. And it had absolutely nothing to do with the Truth of me.

And just like that, I was entirely at Zero. I felt directly aligned with Source power. It wasn't aggressive or judgmental but rather forgiving and completely *neutral*. It was peaceful and void of all hurt. Instantly, I felt empathy for the bishop. He was doing what he believed was right, based on his personal testimony of his world and religious view, fulfilling his duty to his own Human Story Code.

His words, "there's something dark about you," had no hold on me. I could feel the direct availability of my Creator. This access had nothing to do with the church's repentance process or the sacrament tray. Was repentance warranted? Yes, I felt it was, but I had taken care of that long before I entered the bishop's office.

So much freedom came from this experience at Ricks College. I was miles from perfect—nobody had to tell me that. I could find rest for my soul in Source power no matter what the bishop, or anyone else, for that matter, thought about me. In that moment Supreme Wisdom revealed to me I was not dark or evil, and above all, God knew the real me—the broken, confused, rebellious me. He loved me and found me beautiful as is. God, the very Source of all Creation, loved the perfect imperfection that was me.

In retrospect, this experience was my first explicit, tangible encounter with the transformative effect of Zero and the immediate shift born only of full, unadulterated trust in Supreme Wisdom. But my journey to Zero was just beginning. The real adversities were yet to come.

8

WHAT TO DO WHEN EVERYTHING CHANGES

They are the chosen ones who have surrendered . . .
Once there were particles of light now they are the radiant sun!

—Rumi, "The Privileged Lovers"

Deep in the core of our being lies an intrinsic drive—an inherent need to fulfill our duty to our Human Story Code and live by its principles. It's as if it were a pact made with our very existence. This profound urge to align with our blueprint emerges from the intricate interplay of nature and nurture. There is safety and comfort within the narratives woven into our story as they provide a sense of truth, purpose, and belonging.

However, the pursuit of fulfilling this duty has its complexities. The same code that guides us can also confine us, because we subconsciously surrender our control to its governing aspirations. It can inadvertently lead us to make choices that echo the past, even when they might not serve our present or future selves.

My commitment to honor the threads of my Human Story Code drove me to accept the duty of serving a full-time mission for the Church of Jesus Christ of Latter-day Saints after completing my first year of college. I always knew I would be a missionary for the church, because that's just what you do as a young Mormon boy. I always thought of it as exciting and adventurous.

However, I was more excited about it when it lay in the distant future. As the day approached, I felt like I was standing on the tracks of a speeding train that would bring an end to my current reality and submerge me in a spiritual twilight zone for two years. Missionary service was necessary to fulfill my responsibilities to my church, family, and social life at college, and receive the blessings of happiness promised to me.

Even though I loved adventure and the thought of going somewhere foreign was euphoric, my feet were beginning to freeze. All the girls at school, who promised to write to me while I was away, were encouraging. The anticipation of the mission was a heady mixture of fear and excitement of the unknown, fulfilling my perceived destiny, and a sense of obligatory responsibility.

Following a series of personal worthiness ecclesiastical interviews, my church leaders affirmed my readiness to take the next step by submitting my mission application. This moment was infused with enthusiasm and restlessness as I eagerly awaited the arrival of my mission assignment from church headquarters in my mailbox. I felt like I did as a child waiting for our family Disneyland trip, boundlessly excited but ever impatient for the day to arrive.

MY FIRST MISSION

The day finally came when I heard a familiar engine roar through the cul-de-sac of my parent's home. I glanced out the window; the red flag on the mailbox had been lowered. My feet did all the thinking as I ran outside and sifted through the pile of newspaper ads and bills. Beneath the mailbox rubbish was an envelope addressed to me, Elder Chad Michael Hardy.

The LDS Church logo was printed on the upper left corner of the white envelope. It looked so glamorous, so corporately official. I held the golden ticket in my hands as my heart pounded loudly in my throat. *My mission call is here!*

I had fantasized about this moment my entire life in what I believed must be how some adolescent girls dream about their wedding day. All I wanted was to tear open that envelope with my teeth and see where God wanted me to serve as a missionary for the church for two years. But that would have been selfish. It's tradition to have all your friends and family gathered when the seal was broken, and the letter read aloud. The letter taunted me all day from the kitchen table while everyone cast their best guess as to where the Lord would have me go. Of course, everyone was hoping for a great destination, maybe somewhere adventurous like South America or France. My vote was for the Sunshine State. I had long felt like Florida was the place for me.

The reveal was to occur at my grandparents' home in Provo, as all the family gatherings took place there. As soon as everyone was circled up in the living room and my dad's parents were on the phone, I carefully opened the envelope and removed the thick packet of paper. I tried to keep my eyes from skipping ahead as I read the form letter from the Office of the First Presidency:

Dear Elder Hardy, you are hereby called to serve as a missionary of The Church of Jesus Christ of Latter-day Saints. You are assigned to labor in the California Roseville Mission. It is anticipated that you will serve for 24 months.

You should report to the Missionary Training Center at Provo, Utah, on Wednesday, 13 September 1995. You will prepare to preach the gospel in the English language. Your mission president may modify your specific assignment according to the needs of the mission.

You have been recommended as one worthy to represent the Lord as a minister of the restored gospel. You will be an official representative of the Church. As such, you will be expected to maintain the highest standards of conduct and appearance by keeping the commandments, living mission rules, and following the counsel of your mission president. As you devote your time and attention to serving the Lord, leaving behind all other personal affairs, the Lord will bless you with the increased knowledge and testimony of the Restoration and the truths of the gospel of Jesus Christ.

Your purpose will be to invite others to come unto Christ by helping them receive the restored gospel through faith in Jesus Christ and His Atonement, repentance, baptism, receiving the gift of the Holy Ghost, and enduring to the end. As you serve with all your heart, might, and strength, the Lord will lead you to those who are prepared to be baptized.

The Lord will reward you for the goodness of your life. Greater blessings and more happiness than you have yet experienced await you as you humbly and prayerfully serve the Lord in this labor of love among His children. We place in you our confidence and pray that the Lord will help you become an effective missionary.

You will be set apart[1] as a missionary by your stake president. Please send your written acceptance promptly, endorsed by your bishop.

Gordon B. Hinkley, the president of the church—the Prophet—had signed the letter.[2]

My mission calling was to my home state, not just my state, but the area where I was born. No one could have guessed that. I only had a few weeks to get everything on my checklist: a half dozen white shirts, ties, two suits, a bicycle—but most importantly, to prepare to take on the greatest of all church covenants. I was to go through the temple for the first time to receive my endowment and make promises to the Lord to keep for the rest of my existence in this life and the next. This also meant it was time to exchange my Fruit of the Looms for the strangely curious Mormon undergarments.

Everything was going according to plan.

BECOMING A WORTHY MORMON

There's a catchy little tune, "I Love to See the Temple," that every young child in Sunday School learns to sing. It's about one day being able to go to the temple and connect with God. Well, that day had arrived. It was time to go to the temple, and I can honestly say there was little taught in Sunday School or within my own home that could have ever prepared me for the events of that day.

Most people know that Mormon temples are not typical religious sanctuaries where anyone off the street can enter to find presence and feel closer to God. Only Mormons in good standing who maintain obedience to the commandments, attend church meetings, pay their 10 percent annual income tithe, obey the word of wisdom (abstaining from alcohol, tobacco, coffee, etc.) and keep themselves morally clean are allowed to hold a valid temple recommend card.

Several sacred ordinances occur in the temple, including highly sacred and secretive happenings. They include the endowment[3] (which I was about to experience), marriage and sealing[4] (which was what my patriarchal blessing had referred to), as well as sealing to parents.[5] Perhaps the most interesting of ordinances is a saving ordinance that can be performed on behalf of the dead.[6] This particular ordinance, baptisms for the dead, often made for intriguing and mysterious discussions among Sunday School children. They'd share accounts overheard of people seeing the smiling spirit of the dead person, who had just been baptized by proxy, standing alongside the baptismal font. These visions affirmed that the dead person had accepted the gospel in the spirit world and was ever so grateful to now be sealed into Mormon lineage and afterlife benefits.

I remember being envious of these dead people. The post-mortem sealed person got to live their entire lives without a lurking man in the mirror strangling them into compliance and the subsequent trauma that I endured. Without all of that, they *still* got a golden ticket to the Celestial Kingdom to rub elbows with the likes of Jesus, Moses, and Joseph Smith. These "lucky" ones still would become God-like even though they weren't born into a Mormon family like me.[7]

There are countless stories about people not being able to witness their child, friend, or loved one get married inside the temple because they were not Mormon, or maybe even worse, they were Mormon but not in good standing. That was perhaps the scariest thing of all, to be Mormon, but not be in good standing, and as such, to be deemed unworthy of one's rightful connection and communion with God.

To enter the temple (and go on my mission), I had to go through another round of personal worthiness interviews. At this point in my life, I was somewhat accustomed to private life interrogations. Interviews were required annually after receipt of the Aaronic Priesthood at age twelve— but no matter how many times I found myself sitting alone with a bishop or other church leader behind closed doors, such intimate questions never got easier.

I had already gone through the standard series of questions with my bishop, but since this was a big deal interview—my temple recommend interview—I had to go through the series of questions again with my stake president. The president is the only one who can officially issue and sign a recommend.

I had been interviewed by my stake president once before in preparing to submit my missionary paperwork. He was familiar with me and quite supportive of my decision to go through the temple. After some chitchat, he pulled out a reference booklet and began the interview. After answering a standard series of questions, the stake president closed his book and pulled out from his desk the small off-white official temple recommend document. Removing the cap from his pen, he wrote both my name and his and signed the document. He then slid the recommend and pen across the desk for me to sign. Signing my name meant I honestly answered the questions, was committed to the Lord, and that I was worthy of the privileges granted to those who hold the recommend. I was about to sign and be on my way when he looked me square in the eyes, indicating this conversation was not yet over. I was caught in his trance.

"Brother Hardy, one who goes into the house of the Lord must be free from homosexual or any other unclean, unholy, impure, or unnatural practices. Would there be a reason you may feel uncomfortable or perhaps even dishonest to the Lord if you were to sign your own temple recommend?"

My heart sank. I suddenly realized I had been holding my breath while he spoke. I tried to calm my nerves as he went on. The stake president continued, "Would you like a little time to get some very personal things in order before you sign it? Remember, the Lord knows all things and will not be mocked. We are trying to help you. Never lie to try to obtain a call, a recommend, or a blessing from the Lord."

I held the pen in my hand, shaking as my mind slipped to my previous bishop's words: "There's something dark about you, Brother Hardy." I began to regress into some post-traumatic stress as wisdom left the room. The man in the mirror came into view, dancing around me, wearing nothing but a devilish grin. Could *this* man see him? Was he aware of my past? Was there a scarlet sheet in my membership file that outlined my previous transgressions and brokenness? I shuttered for a moment but then quickly manned up. I deserved this recommend. The only way for me to fulfill my patriarchal blessing and receive my temple marriage was this recommend. This was my rightful and faithful path; this was my way to my heaven.

I took a big, brave gulp to clear my throat. "I have no reservations or doubts regarding my worthiness in receiving this recommend. I am ready to sign," I affirmed to the stake president.

My hand steadied, and I signed my name. It was official. I was officially a card-carrying Mormon. The next step was to receive my endowment at the Temple in Provo, Utah. I was nervously excited about finally getting to see what went on behind the veil of this mysterious temple. No one was allowed to discuss what went on inside without risking consequences.

THE CEREMONY

One short month later, there I was at the steps of the Provo temple, decked out in my new missionary suit. It was late summer, and my parents flanked me as we walked up the stairs. I could tell they were proud to take their first child through the temple. I was overjoyed at being the good son on the rightful path.

As we approached the 1960-does-modern-vogue rotunda, I kept looking up at the golden spire and the angel Moroni trumpeting toward the breathtaking Rocky Mountains; butterflies turned in my stomach.

When I walked through the main doors of the temple, I was greeted by an older lady with a warm smile at the front desk, much like a hotel. She asked to see my recommend. I proudly pulled it out of my wallet, still in disbelief that I had one. She looked it over, smiled, and handed it back.

"Welcome, Brother Hardy," she spoke.

Walking through the temple doors that day would forever change my identity as a Mormon. The understanding of my religion was far more complex than I could ever imagine.

It's human nature to want things to make sense. We often try to fit new information into our currently held beliefs. However, a shake-up happens when that new data goes against everything we believed was (T)rue. I still vividly recall the moment I discovered the (T)ruth about Santa Claus, the Easter Bunny, and all other magical beings. My world as a young child shattered. I began to second-guess the times I saw evidence that these fantastical figures existed, only to realize it was a wild trick of my imagination. That revelation warped my perception of trust and truth. What *was* actually true in my adolescent world if Santa was just a commercialized mall gimmick designed by the Coca-Cola company? The stark reality that this Disney-style magic didn't exist in the real world traumatized me and aided in my diminished belief in the kind of magic that does exist.

As for my nineteen-year-old self, who thought I had seen and experienced it all, blissfully living my (t)ruths, nothing could have prepared me for the Masonic-like rituals that go on beyond the closed doors of those beautiful heavenly temples. This day at the temple felt like when the truth of those childhood fantasies was revealed; a veil was lifted from my naive eyes.

Once I walked past the front desk, I was escorted into a locker room and separated from my family. I was instructed to disrobe entirely and was handed something white to wear that was referred to as a shield. The clothing that they gave me confused me a little. It was a white poncho-like sheet with a hole in the top for my head, but the sides were completely open, with no place to tie it shut. I slipped it over my head and immediately felt uncomfortable. I was utterly naked, wearing a beach towel with a hole cut in the middle.

Uncertain as to why I was asked to wear the shield, I came out of the dressing room feeling awkwardly humiliated. I tried to hold the sides shut to cover my exposed naked body. With each step that took me further away from the privacy of my dressing room, I could hear my heart screaming in my chest, causing a lump-sized grapefruit to grow in my throat.

I sat in the locker room on a cold metal bench, waiting for instruction. Sitting down made it virtually impossible to hold the sides shut, exposing my naked body. There were other young men my age also waiting with me, wearing the same strange sheet. It was apparent I was not the only one uncomfortable. We tried not to make eye contact with each other. Perhaps it was too easy to let your eyes slip, focusing on the nakedness behind the large slits of the shield. I sat there in silence, staring at the ground.

When it was my turn, I was escorted by a male temple worker into a small initiatory room made with draped white curtains. It reminded me of a hospital emergency room cubicle. My hands nervously clutched the sides of the shield together as I walked, keeping my fingernails from digging into my skin. I waited by myself until a silvery old man dressed in a white suit serving as the officiator entered and greeted me. He asked me to release my hands to my sides and state my full name. The shield released, exposing my body on both sides.

The ritual began with a private "washing and anointing" ceremony. I was touched with water by the male officiator who blessed the different parts of my naked body from head to toe with a recited script. At one point, he reached through the shield and touched me inches from my genitals. I froze. I wasn't sure how far this touching was going to go. I was scared, confused, and unsure of what was happening to me. When the ritual concluded, we moved forward through a labyrinth of sheets and repeated the ceremony, this time with oil. It concluded with moving through the sheets into the final room, where I was assigned a new name I could never tell anyone. The officiators assisted me into my new secretive and sacred holy underwear, like you would dress a toddler.

The washing and anointing rite was finally completed. I was escorted back into the locker room and instructed to dress in my temple clothes over the holy undergarments. The temple clothes consisted of white pants, a white shirt, a white tie, and white slippers. A green leaf apron, a pleated white sash, and a white hat that looked like a cross between a baker's hat and a graduation cap would be used later and remained in my little handbag.

Once dressed, I caught my reflection in the locker room mirror. I gazed at myself, a bit awestruck. I looked like I had imagined in my vision of heaven, glowing in white. Glancing down at my feet, I noticed my white pants were too long for my legs. I stood there, trance-like, trying to make sense of what had just happened to me. Holding back tears, I tried to calm the knot bulging in my chest. I felt unprepared and violated. I couldn't understand why no one warned me about what was going to happen once I passed beyond the welcome desk. Why didn't my parents prepare me? Why didn't my church leaders prepare me? I took a few deep breaths to calm the storm of anger festering within me, rolled the bottoms of my pants, and wiped my eyes. I had to remain strong. I was wearing God's underwear now.

I shuffled down a maze of hallways in my white slippers into a beautiful white chapel filled with soft white pews facing a small white organ. A white-haired woman dressed in a white dress sat behind the keys, softly playing church hymns. The atmosphere created a quiet, calming, and reverent space. There, I was reunited with my family, dressed in the same fashion.

My mom looked like a bride, so pretty in her white dress. The very sight of her made me forget for a moment where I was. She smiled at me sincerely, outstretching her arms to hug me. I could tell she was so proud of me. I didn't want her to know how scared and angry I really was. I smiled back, avoiding any eye contact as we embraced.

We sat silently listening to the music. I meditated and prayed to God for reassurance that what I was doing was indeed part of His divine plan, that this was not a crazy cult scheme where I had just been stripped naked as part of an initiation ritual to intimidate me into submission.

I think my mother saw the stress on my face as I sat there with my arms folded, my eyes closed solidly shut. She tried to comfort me by putting her arm around me, gently scratching my back without breathing a word. I wanted her to speak, though. I needed an explanation of what was going on and why I was never warned about what *really* went on in the temple. She knew how much I hated surprises. It was not the time or place to have such a discussion, because talking was highly discouraged in this sacred place of serenity and meditation.

We waited in the chapel with other patrons until our endowment session. Since this was my first time going through the session, I was there to receive my endowment. My parents, who had already received their endowment when they were my age, were going through the session in proxy for a dead person to receive their endowment.

A friendly temple worker approached the front of the chapel and quietly directed us to move down another series of hallways into the endowment room. I entered this auditorium-like space, and my thoughts focused on the simplicity of the sterile décor compared to the beautiful chapel and lobby. It mimicked a small lecture hall with a center aisle that separated rows of theater seats. In the front of the room, a plush white altar monopolized the space. Behind it hung simple white curtains covering what appeared to be another room behind it.

We were directed where to sit with the men on the right side and the women on the left. The usher separated me from my mother like a pacifier being ripped from my gums and had me sit next to my dad. Settling into the relatively comfortable theater seat, I took it all in; I was curious and silent. Quietly, I stashed my handbag with the strange items under my seat.

Once we were all seated, an old man dressed in a white suit serving as the expressionless officiator for the endowment session stood at the altar. A push of a button dimmed the lights. It started the congregational ceremony of interactive secretive handshakes and promises made to God and the church in order to enter the Celestial Kingdom—heaven.

The ceremony progressed, and we were instructed to start putting on the different costume pieces from our little handbags. I became even more terrified that the cult rumors I'd heard for years might be true. I kept looking at my parents, dressed in their temple attire, still wondering why they never warned me it would be like *this*. Not to mention the compliance of my grandparents and all my Mormon relatives whom I loved and looked up to. They had all willingly participated in this for five generations. I wanted to run out as fast as I could. However, the fear of disappointing my family and the embarrassment of it all kept me there.

I did everything possible to calm my mind and force my limited perspective to fit this new narrative. *Perhaps it was so secret because it was so sacred. Perhaps others before me felt this exact same way, and it is all just part of the process.* The final ritual of the ceremony, I learned, was entering the presence of God by moving into another room with the tools. I presented them at a curtain wall in the ceremony room, referred to as the veil, to an anonymous man on the other side. With only his right hand sticking through the curtain, we exchanged the handshakes with their accompanying names one by one.

My mind fanaticized about what would be on the other side as my right hand reached toward the veil for the final time, locking our hands in an embrace. The hand gently tugged, pulling me through the curtain, where I was greeted by a jolly-looking old man who played the role of God. He smiled warmly at me and shook the hand he was already holding in a congratulating fashion. I turned and looked at what was beyond the veil. There was no heavenly messenger, no glorified personages floating above me, and no vision of my perfectly manicured heaven. Instead, my eyes focused on an enormous crystal chandelier that hung in the middle of a beautifully furnished room, named the Celestial Room. This room had remarkable architecture two stories high and was fit for any fairytale princess. By design, it felt much like my grandmother's living room, reserved for only special occasions.

A good feeling was undeniably present in the reverence of the room. I allowed myself to fully feel the emotions that washed over me. When I spotted my mother smiling at me from across the room, I charged toward her. I wrapped my arms around her as if we were reuniting in the afterlife. My heart felt like it might burst as tears of joy rolled down my face.

An overwhelming feeling of love, communion, and connection overtook me. In that moment, I was at Zero with what I had just experienced.

I could feel my heaven; I could believe it all to be possible. The promise of my perfectly manicured future was laid out before me. It was all going to be worth it—so very worth it. I no longer cared that someone had touched my naked body or that I had promised everything I had and everything I would become to the church by doing what felt like some weird hocus-pocus. The idea of being reunited with my family together in the Celestial Kingdom—fully loved, fully accepted—was it! It's all I had ever wanted. Being safe and secure and sealed to my family for all eternity. This feeling right here was all I needed, and I felt like I would (and could) sacrifice anything to keep it.

ALIGNING WITH OUR SELF-INTERESTS

It's a curious phenomenon—wholeheartedly believing in something and later feeling distant from it. This process is the unfolding of awareness. Remember, Zero creates life and experiences where we direct its power, whether we wield it consciously or unconsciously. This is why many people maintain unwavering faith and find solace and purpose in their beliefs. Zero will validate these beliefs, bringing about miracles within the framework of that faith. Such steadfast faith can lead to a good life filled with a sense of safety and security. For billions of individuals, their beliefs provide hope and the impetus to lead a purpose-driven life, and there's an undeniable beauty and peace in that.

However, some of us discover that the perfectly packaged set of beliefs bestowed upon us was never meant to be our sole destination. As our awareness grows, it illuminates aspects of inauthenticity within our core that might have once felt (T)rue.

Embracing awareness that revealed my authentic self prompted me to question everything. However, my beliefs didn't unravel overnight; it was a gradual process, unfolding layer by layer. There were still enough threads of my Human Story Code holding my testimony together. This created a yoyo effect, where if I ventured too far into the depths, I would inevitably bounce back to what felt safe.

I didn't understand why the temple and its masonic-like rites existed only for the elite and worthy to experience. I couldn't comprehend how the verity of what occurred behind those doors had been a closely guarded secret from me for nineteen years. I understand now that I innately was not ready for the fallout had I questioned it. There was too much at stake. So naturally, the lens of my Human Story Code filled in the blanks like a Mad Lib. I chalked it all up to another mystery of God—something that was just not of this world and something we weren't meant to question. I reasoned it must have been designed to keep those of us who were worthy bound to and protected by the church. Suddenly, it all just seemed to make sense.

I understood why no one ever talked about what happened in the temple. Whether the secrets were kept based on fear or based on love and learning didn't matter to me. Whether they really were cultish or not was of no concern, not anymore. All I wanted was to focus on the feeling I had experienced in my mother's arms. I knew then that there was indeed something genuinely sacred and magical in our embrace. For a moment— for *that* moment—I felt worthy, righteous, and happy.

We are all just navigating life, seeking one thing: happiness. Happiness for ourselves, happiness for those we love, and (hopefully) happiness for others. One lesson my grandfather lived by was that all human action is for improving one's condition or the condition of one's world. Receiving this lesson as a child was perhaps one of the greatest gifts I could have been given, and it still serves me well today.

The thing is, it can sometimes be challenging to admit that you are seeking happiness. Many of us are taught that self-interest is selfish. We are made to feel guilty when we act or respond in self-interest. This (t)ruth makes happiness a complicated affair.

Oftentimes, our self-interest agrees with others, creating connection, relationship, and collaborative results. It creates this positive response because the parties involved all act in concert toward a shared vision. This is a beautiful thing. It is the backbone of human connection, human ingenuity, and, in many ways, humanity itself. There is power here—beautiful power that can provide phenomenal resources and affect beautiful change. It was this power that allowed for my developed health and healing as a child.

Sometimes, however, our self-interest does not always agree with others (and vice versa), which can create conflict and even strife. This, too, is human nature. Everyone has different drivers based on their unique Human Story Code. We all have unique feelings, unique desires, and unique beliefs, and we all consider different factors when in pursuit of happiness for ourselves, our loved ones, and others.

Have you ever experienced unrequited love, not been selected for a job, or even argued about which restaurant to go to for dinner? You should be able to easily recognize how we are all, in one way or another, competing on behalf of our own interests. Sure, sometimes it's covert, but it's there.

Even when we're all wrapped up in negative behaviors, we act in self-interest. This is because we are seeking what we think will make us happy based on our coding—even if temporarily. When we steer off course from our (T)ruth and get ambushed by our (t)ruths, this can lead to a sense of disconnection, confusion, and existential unrest. This is how alcoholism, addiction, toxic relationships, and even envy and greed find their footing in our lives. There is great enjoyment in doing what feels good, even if it's not good for us. This is a slippery slope that we all know too well.

The knowledge of this slope and our innate human ability to find our way onto it inclines us to do one (or more) of three things: we either exert power as control, we relinquish our power and fall into victimhood, or we release our control to the powers that be. All along, we look at power as something that exists outside of ourselves or as something we exert outside ourselves. As humans, we tend to view power as something we can use to manhandle the world in which we live. Beyond this, much of our struggle with power and control is rooted in our hesitancy to define our happiness or carve our own paths. If we stumble into happiness from outside sources, it is so much easier to accept; we can even believe that we deserve it, so it becomes our answer.

If, rather, the idea is to intentionally define happiness *for* ourselves, things can get costly—something might have to give—and well, that circles back to feelings of guilt, discomfort, and fear.

So, what do we do? Rather than be different, rather than be uncomfortable, rather than step into the unknown, we cast away and surrender our power to the (t)ruths of our Human Story Code. We consign ourselves to the status quo and choose to keep walking the well-beaten path. We lower our heads and cast our eyes away from the heavens, and we negate the adventure that calls to us from the very Source of all Creation.

9

THE ROOTS OF SELF-CONTEMPT

Conformity is not an admirable trait. Conformity is a copout. It threatens self-awareness. It can lead groups to enforce rigid and arbitrary rules.

—Alexandra Robbins, *The Geeks Shall Inherit the Earth: Popularity, Quirk Theory, and Why Outsiders Thrive After High School* (2012)

There are over ten Missionary Training Centers (MTC) worldwide. These training centers prepare the missionaries for the mission field. The one in Provo, Utah, is the largest and became my training ground for the next three weeks. Missionary training involves memorizing extensive amounts of scriptures and expectations, teaching the structure and beliefs of Mormonism, and learning to build a relationship of trust with people.

Arriving at the training center felt like a mix of the first day of college and a bustling holiday airport, minus the delightfully sinful scent of coffee. With my entire family in tow, we snapped a quick photo outside before entering what felt like an alternate reality behind the glass lobby doors. The air was charged with infectious enthusiasm. Everywhere you turned, an individual with a radiant smile, dressed in their Sunday best, was ready to welcome and guide you.

The staff directed the luggage to be placed in one room and sorted the crowds of new missionaries into an orderly, organized line to check in at the main desk. I was amazed by the number of fresh-faced missionaries who looked just like me, as if we stepped off an assembly line with our crisp dark suits, shiny shoes, and *Leave It to Beaver* haircuts. I was just a single number among the fifty thousand Mormon missionaries serving worldwide.

As I reached the end of the line, a kindly older woman extended a warm welcome as she led me through the necessary paperwork procedures. When all was said and done, she flashed a reassuring smile as she presented me with a pristine, gleaming black name badge bearing the title "Elder Hardy" in bold white print. My hands, filled with excitement and apprehension, fumbled slightly as I attached the badge to my suit. You see, in the world of missionaries, we were to live by stringent rules of conduct, so much so that we had to bid farewell to our given names. At that moment, I embraced my new identity as Elder Hardy.

When I reunited with my family in the lobby, we quickly gathered in front of the iconic oversized world map on the wall. This was where every new missionary captured a moment, pointing to the place in the world where they were called to serve by God—a cherished tradition. For me, it was a breeze to extend my arm and proudly point to my home state of California.

Soon after, they escorted us into a spacious assembly hall, its rows of classroom-style seating reminiscent of a college lecture hall. My stomach turned into a flutter of anticipation and nervous energy as the speakers ignited a blazing fire of purpose within us. They emphasized we were all chosen to do the Lord's work. When the session concluded, we shared tearful goodbyes with our loved ones. The families headed left while the missionaries, including myself, went right to enter the MTC campus.

Inside, we were paired with a companion who we'd spend every moment with, including sleeping in the same dorm room. We were also assigned to a congregation known as a branch, further dividing into groups called zones, forming a smaller network of districts. Over the next three weeks, we would spend most of our time with the members of our district for classes and church meetings. During orientation, the staff passed out our daily schedules. My head kept spinning. It felt like diving into an intensive, advanced college course.

My first morning at the MTC, our district had a specific time to shower and get ready. As I entered the communal bathroom with all the missionaries from my dormitory, a disquieting sight greeted me—a shower area reminiscent of a prison with a smorgasbord of completely naked young men facing each other around the watering poles with all their bits out in the wide open.

A familiar fear washed over me as I surveyed my surroundings. In an instant, I was transported back to high school, haunted by the shame that had once clouded my conscience for having what I perceived as unnatural feelings toward other guys in the locker room—feelings I had sacrificed my virtue to suppress. I began to realize that I had willingly given up my identity to be here; beyond that was the jarring realization of losing the most intimate aspects of my privacy. Surrounded by a diverse assembly of nude young men, all raging with teenage hormones, the idea of disrobing weighed heavily on me. The possibility of getting aroused was a real and present fear. The man in the mirror would expose me as a fraud; the idea of that embarrassment shuddered the depths of my inner core. I had to man up.

As my heart beat outside my chest, I carefully peeled away each layer of my temple garments. My hands betrayed me with their nervous tremors. I stood, entirely exposed, clutching my towel like a lifeline amidst turbulent waters.

However, I understood that yielding to fear was not an option. I saw this as yet another trial, a chance to demonstrate to God that my repentance process had purged me of any lingering homosexual inclinations. To distract my thoughts from the overwhelming situation, I conjured up a mental mosaic of both heartbreakingly sad and uproariously funny thoughts, like dead puppies and peeing on an electric fence—anything to divert my attention and keep the man in the mirror and his cunning curiosity out of sight. With that, I cautiously stepped into the shower area, determined to avoid any eye contact amidst the sea of youthful, pristine male physiques surrounding me.

Upon reflection, that first morning was characterized by an overwhelming sense of shame, vulnerability, and fear. Alongside these emotions, I embraced my unwavering resolve to cling desperately to my Human Story Code, even as its core crumbled within me. The daily showers at the MTC remained an ongoing struggle. The shame I endured etched a more profound trauma into my code. They reinforced my belief that I didn't quite fit in with the other missionaries and that something was undeniably wrong with me.

SHAME

In retrospect, this experience caused me to reflect on all the shame in my life and the roots of my self-contempt. I've come to realize that many societies and most religions teach us that sex and most things associated with sex are bad. That being intimate in any way with people outside of the marital bed is bad. Masturbation: bad. Nudity: bad. The shame of being tricked into exposing myself to the neighbor girls was insurmountable.

When I'd first start to date someone and even look at someone else with interest or curiosity: shame. If I desired to date a few different people to figure out who I am or what I am looking for in a partner: shame. When I began to explore my own body: shame. Oftentimes, even intimacy, truthfulness, and vulnerability with a monogamous or marital partner can result in shame. There is so much shame prevalent in our society; you don't have to have a marginalized sexual identity, be sexually abused, or even be hypersexual to feel shame. Shame, after all, is a carefully crafted construct.

Since it was forbidden to date until sixteen, in my youth, I unintentionally suppressed any romantic feelings I had for girls and concealed them from my family. I was told that when you're dating, you're not supposed to do anything but a simple kiss. Do not even think about touching each other in any way that could be deemed inappropriate. These rules were extremely difficult for me because my sexuality was already blurred. I was confused by one set of thoughts and felt even more ashamed by the other. I already knew that being sexually attracted to guys was utterly unacceptable, but on top of that, I was told it was bad to have sexual feelings for girls.

My interactions with Madison had thoroughly confirmed this. In missionary training, they told us we weren't allowed to even hug a girl, we could only shake their hand. This left me in no-man's land. I couldn't prove the man in the mirror a charlatan without interaction with females, but those interactions were also interwoven with shame and disobedience. Nevertheless, the striking contradiction between the absence of modesty in a sacred setting like the MTC and the touching that went along with the washing and anointing in the temple, coupled with the pervasive shame instilled by the church from my earliest memories, left me profoundly bewildered.

After three grueling weeks of rigorous study, we were ready to depart the MTC and begin our journeys toward our assigned missions. Before our send-off, our district gathered for a "transfer meeting" to prepare us, which was presided over by one of our local branch leaders, Brother McKenzie. To put it bluntly, he embodied the stereotype of a retired army sergeant who seemed perpetually irate—grumpy old man was an understatement. He strictly adhered to the letter of the law, devoid of mercy.

His approach to tough love was unlike anything I had ever encountered, and it left us all trembling when he entered the room. He instilled the fear of God in us, warning that disobedience would lead to disgrace, a dishonorable return home, and embarrassment to our families. He reinforced his point with a quote from Marion G. Romney, a former member of the First Presidency of the Church. This quote, delivered during a General Conference from the pulpit, were words spoken to him by his father before leaving on his mission: "We would rather come to this station and take your body off the train in a casket than to have you come home unclean, having lost your virtue."[1]

On the way to the transfer meeting, I suddenly realized I had left my scriptures in my dorm. As my companion and I considered the time constraints, we knew returning to retrieve them would undoubtedly make us late. Tardiness was an unthinkable offense at Brother McKenzie's meeting. I would have preferred to miss the meeting altogether than arrive late and face his wrath. My companion and I decided to leave the scriptures behind, convinced the meeting would be just another pep talk akin to the first day's orientation, with no need for the scriptures.

Upon entering the meeting with our district, Brother McKenzie's wife was present—a typical, decently attractive, matronly Mormon woman. Her presence provided a sense of safety, almost as if her being there would encourage him to exhibit his best behavior, sparing us the need to endure the usual beratings.

Before we started, he instructed us to arrange our desks in a circle, facing each other. To our surprise, the entire meeting was spent taking turns reading scriptures out loud. There was no pep talk, just an uninspiring default to routine scripture reading. My stomach sank, a familiar feeling of impending trouble well within me. I knew he would chastise me once he realized I lacked my scriptures.

When it was my turn to read aloud, I casually glanced over at my companion's scriptures and began to read. As expected, I was abruptly interrupted by Brother McKenzie's scorn.

"Elder Hardy, where are your scriptures?" he barked in his gruff, unrelenting voice.

I began to explain my predicament, but he cut me off, launching into a tirade like none I had ever experienced, not even from my brother. His words were piercing and brutal. He proclaimed that I would be a terrible missionary, an embarrassment to the church, and suggested I should just go home. In an instant, I felt as vulnerable as I had in those showers, standing exposed with nothing but a towel to shield myself from the judgment of my peers. Shame washed over me as I fought back tears during his endless ranting.

My mind raced back to my former bishop's words, "There's something dark about you" and then to the transformation of peace and calm as I passed up the sacrament tray. And then to my mother. She had little tolerance for disrespect; her mother-bear instincts once led her to intervene in my sixth-grade bullying ordeal with my teacher, swiftly ending it, and subsequently ending her career.

When Brother McKenzie finally finished his harangue, I was surprisingly composed. I smiled at him and spoke my (T)ruth, channeling my mother's wisdom.

"Thank you," I said. "Thank you for bringing the spirit of contention into this room, which is of the devil."

I felt empowered by the (T)ruth of my words and the courage I had to say it. Brother McKenzie appeared utterly flummoxed, caught between a laugh and a cough. It seemed no one had ever stood up to him, not even his wife. For the remainder of the meeting, he deliberately skipped over me when it was my turn to read. At the end of the session, he shook hands with everyone except me, avoiding my gaze. His wife shook my hand, and I could see the pain in her eyes mingled with disgust.

As we exited the meeting, I was greeted with high-fives and expressions of admiration. "Elder Hardy, that was so awesome! Did you see the look on his face?" one of the missionaries exclaimed. Another chimed in, "Oh man, you're definitely getting sent home."

TOUGH LOVE?

Brother McKenzie personified a complex web of contradictions. On one side, he displayed a deep love for missionary work, willingly dedicating and volunteering his time to instruct us. Yet, on the other side, he harbored a seething anger and hostility toward us that starkly contrasted the very teachings we had spent three weeks absorbing. Contradictions from an authoritative figure, be it a parent, partner, employer, or, in this instance, a religious leader can be a breeding ground for shame. These incongruities can sometimes masquerade as a form of tough love.

Tough love, at its core, is a form of love itself. Driven by the desire to see another person thrive, its conditional support seeks to encourage that person to be better and do better through constructive criticism. It often involves establishing clear expectations and boundaries. Many of us have experienced this in some shape or form, especially as children.

While tough love can be a well-intentioned approach, it intersects with shame in frequently counterproductive ways. Shame itself is a paradoxical emotion. It arises from the need for social connection and conformity, yet it often isolates individuals by making them feel fundamentally flawed or unworthy. These feelings are often triggered by criticism, judgment, or rejection, resulting in sensations of guilt, humiliation, and self-doubt. When the bar is set impossibly high or unattainable, shame often follows suit as a relentless enforcer of self-doubt and discouragement.

Shame is also profoundly influenced by cultural and societal norms. We may grapple with shame when our personal values and beliefs contradict the expectations of our culture or community. As an example, an individual might experience shame because they desire to pursue a career path that diverges from the traditional expectations imposed by their family and community. Society often defines success in narrow terms, such as wealth, fame, or beauty. These societal definitions, amplified by social media, can create contradictions as we strive to align our personal aspirations and goals with these external standards, potentially leading to feelings of inadequacy and shame if we fall short.

I suspect that Brother McKenzie's version of "tough love," which produced a significant amount of shame and fear within us, might have been fueled by his own feelings of shame and fear. People who find themselves within a stressful prison of guilt and shame will often strive to bring others into that gloomy cell with them. They unwittingly project their inner turmoil onto others, perhaps as a way to divert attention from their own struggles. They may even justify their suffering by deeming it righteous, believing that sharing their burden is a form of care.

People who have been wounded tend to wound others. Perhaps my rebuttal to Brother McKenzie was so difficult for him because my few words held up a mirror to his Human Story Code of internal pain, insecurities, and shame. Looking back at this experience, I could easily wrestle in my mind as to what was *wrong* with him. But to have genuine empathy and to get to Zero with Brother McKenzie, I would first need to ask myself what happened *to* him. What happened in his life that shaped his code to be full of rage? Perhaps our short encounter might have nudged him toward a bit of self-reflection. But like many of us, we are too afraid of what we might find when we start digging into our own awareness of self—especially those with a Human Story Code firmly founded in (t)ruths.

In our pursuit of reaching Zero, self-awareness serves as the guiding light, enabling us to delve deep within ourselves, uncovering the concealed corners of our personal code where shame has firmly taken root. We must recognize the contradictions within ourselves and the external pressures that contribute to our shame. This emotion, often buried and left unexamined, can wield tremendous trauma. It serves as an unexpected catalyst for misalignment—disrupting the essence of divine alignment, creating a significant obstacle to unlocking our innate magic.

10

WHEN THE WORST LEADS TO ENLIGHTENMENT

Forgiveness is a strange thing. It can sometimes be easier to forgive our enemies than our friends. It can be hardest of all to forgive people we love.

—Fred Rogers, *The World According to Mr. Rogers: Important Things to Remember* (2019)

The day after my verbal altercation with Brother McKenzie, I arrived at my mission field as scheduled in the suburbs of Sacramento. There was no mention of the incident ever again. Like the missionary training center, I was assigned a companion, Elder Carter. We were told to remain within eyesight of each other at all times with the exception of the bathroom. Carter had the task of training me, as I was lovingly referred to as a "greenie." He was always so happy and friendly to everyone—an unbelievable kind of nice. He was a real-life rendition of South Park's stereotype of the happy, blissful Mormon. He delicately danced that fine line between authenticity and phoniness: no matter what he dished up, you wanted to have whatever he was having, regardless of sincerity.

Our schedule was highly regimented; every hour was accounted for on a little blue paper calendar that we turned in weekly to validate our work and productivity. We awoke at 6:30 a.m., dressed and studied scripture, then a half-hour of personal study before it was time to head out the door by 8:30 a.m. Off we went with our little paper calendars tucked neatly in our white shirt pockets.

We weren't allowed to return to the apartment until 9:30 p.m., and it was lights out by 10 p.m. We each had a bicycle to get around. Our days were filled with teaching lessons to potential converts, door-to-door proselytizing, service projects, church meetings, and, if lucky, free dinners with church members. Every month, there were transfers where we could be sent to a new area or be assigned a new companion. This was great if you didn't like your companion or your area, but bitter-sweet if you did.

We had just one day off a week, Preparation Day. This day was reserved for doing laundry and having time for activities like practicing piano, writing letters back home, or engaging with other missionaries. We weren't allowed to watch TV, listen to the radio, or read the papers, nor could we go swimming.[1] We were completely isolated from the real world and our families.

This type of isolation is next-level coding and, in my case, it took a toll on my emotional and physical well-being. You don't need to serve a mission to encounter a scenario in life where your autonomy and power are abruptly taken away. There are numerous occasions when we inadvertently surrender our control, such as in toxic relationships, employment, or even within our governments and political parties. As we navigate our lives, pursuing what seems right and adhering to the conventions of our code, an unforeseen tremor inevitably arrives—much like an airplane caught in abrupt turbulence, we experience a sudden and startling upheaval.

Trauma leaves its mark on our Human Story Code but can also disrupt its patterns, which are comforting and safe to us, and peel away the layers we've constructed. These moments act as revealers, creating a crack within the seams of the code itself.

These revelations are like lifting the curtain on a theater performance to reveal the backstage chaos. In the wake of such moments, the framework of our Human Story Code can feel like it is coming apart at the seams, leaving us with a sensation that our lives are spiraling out of control. Beyond the emotional turmoil, these experiences can also have physical repercussions.

When we earnestly seek Zero, and when it finds us, we must be prepared for the disruptive fallout. Once you allow the awareness entry point to fully open, wisdom will reveal the (T)ruth of You. What you once held as undeniable (T)ruths may be exposed as mere imposters, like a burglar triggering a stadium full of motion security lights. It's an unsettling experience, but hang in there! You *must* be brave and trust in this necessary step forward in distinguishing the difference between your personal (t)ruths and your universal (T)ruths. Once you are living your (T)ruth, harmony and balance just *are*. What once was lost is found in Zero.

THE JOURNAL

There's a New Testament saying that "the spirit is willing, but the flesh is weak" (Matthew 26:41, NIV). I could not have embodied that sentiment more. A year into my mission, I was met with exhaustion by the daily regime that oftentimes felt more like a prison sentence than God's service. I would lay in bed at night without anything left to give. *Was the "RM" badge really worth it?*

More than that, I started to see my missionary service more as a marketing and sales tactic than bringing people to Christ. We were constantly pressured to recruit new converts by way of baptism, and we had to report these numbers to our leaders on a weekly and monthly basis. If you didn't achieve a satisfactory number of baptisms, you would receive a visit from the mission president, who would deliver a harsh talking to, imprinting more shame. The pressure of this started chipping away at the testimony of my Human Story Code—brick by brick.

The stress from the fallout of my unraveling testimony appeared as daily tauntings from the man in the mirror. There he was, carefree and jubilant, gleefully flaunting how wonderful life was on the other side. I felt like the worst kind of fraud as I continued to write home every week about how everything was just great, living my best missionary life!

But, in reality, I was living my best missionary *lie*. Being completely isolated from my family and friends and having to keep this and *all* of my feelings secret began taking its toll. I journaled my struggles as a way to cope. I started getting sick, really sick. I would throw up every morning, accompanied by constant diarrhea. I had no idea what was causing my illness. Despite these new physical ailments, I kept enduring day after day, hemming the seams of my unraveling code. I had to believe the symptoms to be just another trial that my obedience and dedication would overcome.

I had been transferred to Oroville, a small mining town north of Sacramento, which, to most people, would be a foreign place on the planet. But to me, it was the home of my birth. Many of the church members there still remembered my parents, so our dinner calendar filled up fast. I felt like a celebrity. No one could believe I had returned to town as a missionary. I was four when my family moved away. My new companion, Elder Thomson, was a letter-of-the-law type of person, a mini-Brother McKenzie in the making. He didn't like the attention I was getting. He felt it was a distraction from "the work."

One late evening, Elder Thomson and I raced home on our bicycles to make curfew. He believed being out a minute past 9:30 p.m. would cause some sort of consequence, like a stripping of God's blessings. Needless to say, Elder Thomson and I didn't see things eye to eye. As we pulled up to our apartment, out of breath, we saw the mission president's shiny black luxury car parked in the alley. This was highly unusual. I checked my watch—9:28 p.m. Something was wrong.

We entered through the front door to find the mission president's two assistants sitting in the living room. One I knew very well was my trainer, Elder Carter. It was no surprise that he had climbed the ladder to the coveted position of assistant to the president. He was Mormon gold. But this time, he was not all smiles. Instead, his eyes were cold and his face was stern.

I tried to say hello, but my voice was caught in my throat. I stood there, frozen, like a deer in headlights. Carter looked as though he was about to deliver some very heavy news.

My mind started racing in a circle of panic as I found my voice: "Who died?"

"Elder Hardy, you need to pack all of your belongings and come with us," he instructed.

"Why, what is the matter?" I demanded to know.

"We don't know the details. We are just following orders from the president."

My mind painted countless scenarios as to why I was being sent packing by order of the man in charge. Elder Thomson started to pace back and forth nervously as if he knew something I didn't. I immediately began stuffing everything I owned into my two suitcases as quickly as possible. I felt a heavy pit in my stomach like I had never experienced before. I thought I might throw up.

As soon as my bags were packed, I was escorted to the alley, where the assistants lifted my luggage into the trunk of the car and positioned my bicycle onto the attached bike rack. While they were busy packing the car, a voice inside my mind spoke firmly telling me to throw away my journal. I didn't question the message. I opened my backpack and quickly tossed it in the dumpster in the alley. Carter opened the back passenger door for me, and I got in and we quickly drove away.

"Where are we going?" I asked quietly.

"To the Stake Center. The president is there waiting for you."

I went into full panic mode. *What happened? Is my family okay? What did I do wrong? Does the president know about the man in the mirror? Was my earlier repentance somehow no longer valid?*

The drive across town felt like it took hours. An eerie feeling reached me as I realized that we were heading to the very same church building that I had been blessed in as a baby. The irony of it all unnerved me.

Upon arrival, the assistants escorted me to the offices inside, where my mission president greeted me. He didn't smile or shake my hand. He simply beckoned me to sit down on the other side of the desk from him. "Elder Hardy, do you know why you are here?" he scoffed.

"No, I don't."

"Do not lie to me!" he said sternly, like a military commander.

I shrunk in my chair. "Did something happen to my family?"

His eyes softened for a moment. "No, they are fine."

He went on to tell me that my mission companion, Elder Thomson, had gone through my personal items and had read my journal. My heart sank to the soles of my worn-out shoes. After my incident with the bishop at Ricks College, I began journaling regularly. I had written about my struggles with being a missionary. Worse, I had written about my fears regarding homosexuality as well as all my previous transgressions. Not to mention, I had taken some photos of myself not wearing my temple garments using a timer on my camera. I was working on losing weight and wanted some before and after proof. They were tucked in the back of my journal. All my secrets were in there, now exposed in this room. I felt horribly violated.

"Do you have this journal?" he demanded. "I want to see it." He then grilled me about the photos and demanded to see them as well.

I explained to the mission president that I no longer had the pictures, which were personal for my eyes only, and the words in the journal were my intimate feelings and struggles. I assured him that every transgression in my journal had already been repented of. After I spoke my piece, he became somewhat apologetic. Not to mention, I felt utterly violated by my companion. I shared with the president about my health troubles and how I was struggling to get through each day. He told me he would call missionary headquarters in Salt Lake City the next morning to get counsel on what would become of me.

I spent the night in the mission home, where the President and his wife lived. It was a beautiful upscale home in the suburbs of Sacramento owned by the church. As I lay in bed in the immaculately decorated guest room, a deep sense of calm overcame me. I was grateful for that voice that told me to dump my journal. I felt so much relief that I wouldn't wake up to Elder Thomson and that daunting little blue calendar. I knew there was a possibility that I may be returned home to my parents with dishonor and the title of RM stripped from me. I thought about President Romney's impactful speech about how it would be better to return home in a casket than to come back unvirtuous. At that moment in time, I didn't care.

When we get to Zero with situations in our lives, it means we are completely neutral, indifferent toward the situation itself and its potential outcomes. This neutrality, particularly toward worst-case scenarios, calms the waters and liberates us from being tethered to specific outcomes. It diminishes the situation's power over us. In this state of Zero, we gain the ability to course-correct, directing our energies—like that metaphorical fire hose—toward the path that serves our best interests.

That evening in the mission home, I confronted the worst possible outcome. Worn by prolonged anxiety and illness, I had retreated to complete neutrality concerning whatever might be. After all, there were some Mormons who didn't serve as missionaries or complete their missionary work but were still committed members of the church. I settled my mind from spinning into the what-ifs and rested back into the peace that I'd just felt encompass my entire being. This calm, this peace, was what I needed more than anything else, and in that moment of deep comfort, it was all that mattered. Moments later, I drifted off to the most restful sleep I'd had in months.

RECOVERY AND REALIGNMENT

Amid this dynamic backdrop, I was unaware that an extraordinary miracle was taking shape within the core of my current adversity. Zero was at work for me as my awareness had exposed a gaping hole in my Human Story Code that literally sent me packing. I was too caught up in the specters of the unknown to imagine that divine treasures were concealed in plain sight, remaining in waiting, yearning to be uncovered. What I didn't know, and what Elder Thomson didn't know, is that his actions saved my life that night.

The following day, I was informed that I would indeed return home and undergo psychological and physical evaluations. I was given permission to call my parents to deliver the news. I admitted that all my letters home every week about how great everything was going and how happy I was were a lie.

Once home, the doctors discovered that I was much sicker than I thought. I was on the brink of kidney failure and needed immediate surgery. Apparently, I was indeed extremely ill. My body was trying to shut down due to the high levels of stress I was experiencing. Ignoring my symptoms for another few days in the mission field could have killed me.

After my surgery, I was put through a weekly psychological evaluation. The only thing I was told was that I'd passed. I was grateful for that. I was given three months to stay home post-op. Thankfully, I was not removed from the missionary program. After my stint of staying set apart at home, my health had improved enough for me to return to the mission field.

My parents were ecstatic that I was getting back on track from my little derailment. Rather than returning to Sacramento, I was routed to

Wellington, Utah. The city of Wellington was settled in 1878 by a band of thirteen Mormons and boasts a population of about fifteen hundred. Size-wise, the whole of Wellington is about five square miles. Living there was like something I'd never experienced.

I was assigned to a set of two missionaries. The three of us lived in a dilapidated single-wide trailer home smack next to railroad tracks. The rigid winds would whip through the walls so fiercely that we were constantly cold. Numerous times a day, the entire trailer felt like it was going to rock free from its unskirted foundation as the train would rattle by. I remember waking up shaking, unable to know whether it was from the train or the cold. Given I was a temporary missionary in this location, I knew I could receive a reassignment from the mission president at any moment. About three months in, the phone rang for me.

It was indeed the mission president. But instead of hearing that I was being moved to another location, I was told that the missionary committee brethren in Salt Lake City wanted to meet with me. To put this in perspective, this would be similar to a Catholic being called to the Vatican to meet with a cardinal. I was told that I would be picked up the following day. When I asked why, I was not given any further details except that my mother would meet me in transit.

When I arrived on the other side of the mountain, my mom and sister were there waiting for me. I was petrified. I could tell my mom was nervous as well. None of us knew what was going on. It baffled me to fathom that out of approximately fifty thousand missionaries currently serving around the world, I would be hand-selected to speak to the highest level of government in the church. As much as I was curious, I was equally dreading the possibility. What if the brethren wanted to talk about the things that were in my journal? I was terrified that my mom would have to hear this. I had told my family nothing about the entire reason I had been sent home.

We arrived at church headquarters and were greeted by the front lobby secretary. She told me the gentleman I was supposed to meet with was called into an emergency meeting and Elder Neuenschwander would meet with me instead. Elder Neuenschwander was one of the seventy quorum leaders who were below the twelve apostles, the two counselors, and the prophet.

My mother, sister and I entered the elevator to his office. His secretary greeted us outside his intimidatingly large ornate door. As the secretary signaled for us to come in, we stepped into an office that looked like a stateroom suite straight out of the Titanic, complete with lavish wood paneling and a roaring fireplace at its heart. Elder Neuenschwander was an extremely tall man in his late forties with a handsome, rugged face. He greeted us pleasantly and invited us to sit with him on the fancy sofas in front of the fireplace.

We chatted briefly, and I remember him asking my sister if she had any questions. She was only eleven and asked him where God lived. He chuckled and danced around the question. After that, he asked my mother and sister to wait out in the sitting room with his secretary as he invited me beyond another door to his office.

As I entered, I couldn't help but admire the office's exquisite, hand-crafted bookshelves, lined with a plethora of books reminiscent of a scene straight out of *Beauty and the Beast*. As Elder Neuenschwander closed the door behind him, he sat behind his ornate wood desk and curiously smiled at me. I could feel my heart racing. I still had no idea why I had been called to talk to one of the highest authorities in the church. I quickly realized that Elder Neuenschwander didn't know why I was there either. The only person who had any idea why I was there was the person who was called away to that emergency meeting. So, we sat in front of an enormous wall of books and began to visit.

He asked me how my mission was going. I explained to him that I'd been struggling with health issues. I didn't like some aspects of missionary life, and mostly, I felt I had little to no control over my life. I had essentially lost the identity I had been working so hard to find, resulting in extreme amounts of stress and anxiety. I told him that sometimes I felt fake, and it often seemed like everyone was just going around playing the role they'd been handed.

"Everything just feels phony, and that really bothers me."

He then asked about my relationships with my family. "Well, your mom and sister seem like really lovely people. It seems like you have a great relationship with them."

"Yeah, I do."

Next, he asked about my dad, and we discussed how he was always physically there as a provider but offered little to no emotional support or comfort.

"I don't think my dad knows how to be a father," I told him.

I confessed how it used to crush me to the core on Father's Day when the other kids would talk so highly of their dads because I felt like I didn't have one. I was so envious of them. I wanted to feel that kind of love from my dad.

"I can assure you that your father loves you. Perhaps the amount of love he was able to show you was only the amount of love he is capable of giving."

I started to choke up a bit from his empathetic words as he continued, "I challenge you to seek not so much to be understood but to understand and seek not so much to be loved but to love."

My jaw nearly hit the floor. He literally quoted a line from my patriarchal blessing. I couldn't believe it. How would he know this? He was like a prophet.

He then asked me if I had any other siblings besides my sister.

"Yeah, I have a brother."

"Well, how's your relationship with your brother?"

It was like he flipped a switch, and instantaneously, I just fell apart. I began sobbing uncontrollably to where I could hardly breathe. It was almost like an out-of-body experience. I had no idea I had all these pent-up emotions built around my relationship with my brother. Elder

Neuenschwander sat patiently and let me cry as I poured out tears like a hundred-year flood.

Once my sobs subdued, he began asking direct questions about my brother.

I told him everything from the bullying and blackmail to the rumors he would spread about me and many things in between.

When I'd gotten it all out, Elder Neuenschwander looked me square in the eye and said, "You need to forgive your brother or you're never going to progress."

I was stunned. I was stunned because it was true. I knew he was right. "But how do you do that?"

He replied, "You make a decision not to hold him accountable for any of it. Who is being most affected by these past experiences? You. What he did to you is affecting you, not him. You're the one who is in pain. You're the one who is suffering from it, not him. You need to release him of any accountability for it. Then you'll no longer blame him, and you can move on with your life and heal."

He suggested I write a letter to my brother, addressing all of the hurtful and painful things that he did to me throughout our childhood. He said I could choose whether to give it to him or not.

I took a moment to take in everything he said. I tried to comprehend all the imperfect dots that had to perfectly align for me to be sitting in this office on this day, receiving this message from a truly inspired man of God.

Then, my mind wandered to my journal. *Oh no. I am sure that is why I am really here.*

"Is there anything else you need to talk to me about?" I asked, hoping he would say no.

"Not unless there's something else you want to talk to me about," he replied with a smile on his face.

I shook my head no, more so in relief and disbelief of what just transpired. We stood together as I thanked him for his advice, and he walked me out the door to where my mother and sister were waiting with wide-eyed anticipation. I fought back tears while we rode the elevator down to the main lobby in silence. The minute we got outside, I burst into tears. My mother put her arm around me as I gathered my words.

"What did he tell you?"

With a massive lump in my throat, barely able to speak, I told her that I needed to forgive my brother or I'd never progress.

"That's all?" she asked with a look of disbelief on her face.

"That's all."

She hugged me tightly as tears of relief and gratitude streamed down both our faces. In that sacred moment, she whispered a (T)ruth which resonated deep within me—that all the twists of fate had conspired to bring me to Elder Neuenschwander. It was nothing short of a miracle, an inexplicable alignment of events.

It felt as though the very universe had orchestrated this meeting, pulling at the strings of destiny to bring us together in a moment of serendipity and purpose; to receive the profound wisdom of the third entry point to Zero: Take Ownership.

TAKE OWNERSHIP TO RELEASE TROUBLES

I mention in the introduction that there is one prerequisite to Zero: harnessing your will. Taking ownership of our trauma and forgiving those who have trespassed against us is one of the hardest things to do. It requires all of your willpower. If we do not take ownership of our traumas, they will take ownership of us, like a parasite.

Up to that point in my life, the trauma inflicted by my brother had infected the core of my Human Story Code. It was attached to every fiber of my identity. Elder Neuenschwander recognized this trauma and, thankfully, called me out on it. I cannot imagine where my life would be right now if he had not given me this profound gift of taking ownership.

Taking ownership of traumatic experiences is the only way to effectively release and banish them from your orbit. Similar to cleaning up that trash dumped on your lawn, when we take ownership of our trauma and raise it to the power of Zero, we seize control over what once controlled us and boldly reclaim our power. This enables us to take action and discard that trauma, just like bagging it up and tossing it away.

To become the Zero Hero of your life and rescue yourself with your newfound awareness of self and state (and your progress toward Zero), you must remove judgment from your perception of the people who have wounded you. One path to removing judgment is to consider the perspective that time has granted your situation and apply that perspective to the things that hurt you. This means that, as time passes, our understanding and feelings about a situation can change. By reflecting on how time has affected your perspective, you can try to see the things that caused you pain in a different light, possibly with more empathy or understanding.

Another approach is to harness the wisdom of self and others, remembering that to seek is part of the process. Knowledge is power. Seeking information and learning from various sources is a valuable process in removing judgment and finding a more balanced perspective. You must recognize that no one is entirely good or bad and that we are all each, in part, a product of our Human Story Codes and trauma timelines. Extending grace to the situation and/or person that wronged you (and/or yourself) provides ownership of the experience—this removes the power from a place of others and places it where it belongs, with *Self*. It is here that you can find peace and harmony within your being—it is here that the neutrality of Zero is possible and accessible.

Much like how awareness and alignment work hand in hand, taking ownership also works in tandem with the Release to Receive entry point. Just like Elder Neuenschwander explained to me, once you take ownership of your trauma, redirecting all the accountability to yourself, you grant yourself the authority to release it. This newfound control over your experiences empowers you to proactively receive positive change in return.

Embracing the Release to Receive entry point to Zero brings about a profound gift—forgiveness. I like to think of forgiveness as pure healing magic. Its power goes beyond mending broken bonds. It has the potential to deeply enrich our lives and free us from the shackles of trauma and pain.

Forgiveness offers us the precious gift of *release* from the heavy burdens we carry so we can *receive* the abundance and peace that's on the other side. It liberates us from the suffocating grip of anger, resentment, and thirst for revenge and retribution, allowing us to regain our lost momentum on the path to our fulfilled life. More than just seeking apologies or restitution from those who've wronged us, forgiveness grants us the chance to heal our own wounds.

The true depth of this gift lies in its ability to address the unchangeable past. Even when the individuals who inflicted harm upon us express remorse or make amends, they cannot erase what has already transpired. Our deepest desire is for them to have never caused us any harm in the first place. In those moments, the responsibility shifts to us, and here lies the magic. We have the power to release the pain that has haunted us, creating space for the boundless possibilities that Zero has in store.

Echoing the wisdom of Elder Neuenschwander, we come to understand that, without forgiveness, our journey remains stagnant, a halt in progression. In my personal journey, forgiving my brother for the suffering he inflicted upon me felt like removing a suffocating boot from my chest. It allowed me to breathe freely for the first time since childhood. This act of forgiveness was a gift, not just for him but profoundly for myself. It created space for endless possibilities in my future.

Being invited to church headquarters and the transformation that unfolded from that pivotal moment in my life were nothing short of miraculous events. It illuminated a clear path to healing and wholeness.

The true power of forgiveness is found in Zero, a gift that restores, rejuvenates, and reshapes our lives for the better.

I wrote the letter to my brother and mailed it to him. While he acknowledged receiving it, he never spoke of it again, nor did he ever apologize. Surprisingly, I didn't need an apology. I had forgiven him and released it all. Immediately, I began to see the transformative power of Zero working within me. The space within my Human Story Code, once occupied by years of trauma, had been emptied and was now being filled with daily doses of good news and miracles.

About a week later, I received a very unexpected phone call. Elder Thomson, my old mission companion, received permission from his mission president to call me. I was shocked to hear his voice on the other end of the phone. He sincerely told me how sorry he was for what he had done. I let him know that I forgave him and expressed gratitude for the ripple effect that followed. Despite the moments proceeding that fateful night seeming so scary at the time, everything ultimately aligned in the most perfect divine way. The miracles of healing I experienced, both physically and emotionally, perhaps would have never happened without being pushed headfirst into deep, unfamiliar waters.

Two weeks later, I heard the familiar voice of the mission president on the other end of the phone. It was January 1996, and I still had eight months to go on my mission. The president notified me that I was, yet again, getting reassigned, this time to sunny San Diego. It wasn't Florida, but I was ecstatic. Finally, my life was shaping up as the magic within me reignited. Forgiving my brother had changed everything. For the first time in my life, I felt in control of my future. I had touched the power of forgiveness, and as a result, I didn't just progress—I catapulted into Zero.

While in San Diego, my life completely changed. I began addressing my health concerns with proper diet and exercise, and it transformed how I looked and felt. My reflection in the mirror looked nothing like the man in the mirror and his reckless lifestyle. In fact, what I saw was more in alignment with me in my vision of heaven. I was popular and made friends quickly. At one point, I was asked by the mission president to sing for a very high-level missionary conference attended by another leader from the Quorum of the Seventy.

Later that fall, I returned to Ricks College with the dream of getting one of the spots in Showtime, a school-sponsored singing and dancing touring group. Being in this group made you an instant campus celebrity, performing at various school events and concerts, and it was the one thing I wanted most. I was even granted permission to leave my mission a couple of weeks early from my scheduled transfer date to attend the auditions. I had auditioned my freshman year and didn't even make callbacks, but this year would be different.

All the fear and uncertainty that had defined my freshman year was behind me. I felt like I had come through a fire and been reborn with a renewed sense of passion and drive to achieve my personal goals. I was internally aligning with what I wanted and setting my sights on the prize.

By connecting the dots backward, I know now that as I gained perspective and alignment with my (T)rue Self's goals, I accessed Zero by green-lighting each entry point. I not only gained awareness and alignment amid chaos, but through forgiving my brother, I took ownership of my story and began to release the pain that blocked my internal peace. And finally, I engaged my power and went after what I wanted with razor focus.

Remember my earlier statement that Zero is always at work, even when we do not realize it? What followed when I arrived back at college is a prime example of this (T)ruth. When my mother dropped me off at my apartment at Ricks, I was the last roommate to check in. I moved into the only available bedroom. My roommate wasn't there but had already unpacked his things and hung pictures up around the room. Upon inspection, I immediately recognized him in a group photo of other campus celebrities. He was in Showtime my freshman year and the performer

I envied the most. My heart sank. What were the chances? I could see myself blowing the audition like I had done before and then having to share a bunk bed with someone living my dream the entire school year.

Just then, my roommate walked into the room and introduced himself. "Hi, I'm Paul. Nice to meet you."

"I know, you were in Showtime. I am actually going to the auditions tomorrow. I'm Chad."

I felt so nervous and somewhat starstruck. Paul was bona fide Broadway material.

"No way, what a coincidence!" he exclaimed. "Well, I was just leaving to hang out with the director's daughter, Molly, at their house. If you want, you can come with me, and I can introduce you."

He didn't have to ask me twice. Moments later, I was in the home of the Showtime director, hanging out with him in his kitchen and sharing my dreams of being in the group. The next day, I nailed the audition and was invited in as one of the six coveted male positions. I had never felt happiness like this before. I couldn't help but feel like it was all thanks to my choice to exercise forgiveness. This experience was my first step in understanding the power and possibility that exists on the other side of forgiveness. That when we *release*, we *receive*.

After an amazing school year of performing and touring, I transferred to Brigham Young University in Provo, Utah, only to find that my Midas touch had decided to take an unscheduled vacation. I auditioned for the Young Ambassadors, the prestigious big brother to Showtime, still brimming with my eye-on-the-prize ambition, but like my freshman year, I didn't make it past the first cut. The competition was tough, and I felt defeated as the door to my performing dreams seemed to slam shut. I retreated to focus on my studies and tried to put my love of being on stage behind me.

But you can't escape the clutches of Zero when your intentions are in motion. As the old saying goes, when one door closes, another opens. One day, I saw an audition notice posted around campus for Disney. They were coming to BYU to cast singers, dancers, and face characters. Next to being in Showtime, another dream of mine was to perform at Disney—a lofty goal as I felt I was far from Disney material. But what did I have to lose?

I showed up to the audition to face off against many of the Young Ambassadors who beat me out of my chance to be one of them. One by one, the Disney casting directors cut them. It was narrowed down to two: a female dancer and me. The directors got up from their table and invited me into a small practice room with a piano. They had me sing my scales and belt some lines from a few Disney songs. Once the vocal interrogation was over, the director looked at me and told me that my vocal range was impressive. He said I could sing all the male tracks in every show at Disney World and play several of their Princes. He offered me a job on the spot. I was in shock. Me? A Disney Prince? But to accept the job, I would have to withdraw from school as rehearsals started in a week.

My excitement quickly turned to fear as the man in the mirror came into view, dressed as Prince Charming, almost mocking me as he twirled about. I couldn't drop out of school. This would steer me out of alignment with my promise that if I continued my education, I would be led to my mate, worthy to marry in the temple.

For a moment, I felt like Pinocchio battling my conscience. This dream was being offered up on a silver platter, staring me straight in the face. Florida. Disney. Being Prince Charming. All of the magical dots were connecting me right to this moment. Then, the fateful words fell out of my mouth.

"I can't."

I thanked them for the opportunity and left the practice room feeling the biggest pit of regret in my stomach that I had ever experienced. What did I do? Why had I just walked away from my dream, which had been handed to me with such ease?

I beat myself up over that decision for quite some time, to the point I really started to struggle and resent my decision to stay at BYU. Though it may seem trivial that I would be swimming in a sea of regret over not working for the mouse, at that time, everything in life felt so big and final. Every choice was life or death in my limited life experience at age twenty-two. And with all the good karma that was boundlessly offered me, I felt like I had turned my back on the magic. Even though I gave myself countless pep talks that I had made the right decision for my future, deep down inside, I knew I had sacrificed what I *really* wanted for what I *believed* I needed.

Regardless of whether I chose correctly or not, what I did know was that my choice caused me to be emotionally stuck in that practice room, even though I wanted to be at peace with it all. My solution was to leverage this newfound power in forgiveness and to work toward forgiving myself for slamming the door on a dream when it had effortlessly opened for me.

THE JOURNEY OF FORGIVENESS

Circling back to awareness, it is the first of many steps to acceptance and forgiveness, and it is often a long journey between these two states of being. What I was beginning to learn then, and what I do know now, is that the most powerful method I've found for managing negative feelings is forgiveness.

Many people think that forgiveness is merely the conclusion of a particular cause-and-effect interaction. We practice forgiving from the time we are toddlers. Child One smacks Child Two. Child One cries. Parent responds, "You can't do that, say you're sorry and give him a hug."

Child One, "But he took my toy."

Parent responds, "Then you both say sorry and give hugs."

"I'm sorry."

"I'm sorry."

Parent: *"Now forgive."*

Child One: *"I forgive you."*

Child Two: "I forgive *you*," *and they return the hug.*

Parent continues: *"You guys love each other. You need to act like it. Keep your hands to yourselves, share, and play nice."*

The simplicity of such a lesson makes it easy to adopt the idea that forgiveness is something you should simply do—because it's the "right" thing. But there is often (not always) far more to forgiveness than a word or a touch. It's an excellent place to start, sure, but forgiveness is rarely so clear-cut.

Forgiveness is not merely an automated response to a cause-and-effect event. More so, it is a conscious, deliberate decision made in the heart of a human to release feelings of resentment (or vengeance) toward a person or group that has harmed them—whether they know it or not and whether it was warranted or not.

In that context, forgiveness seems like an easy fix—but not so fast. Forgiveness is a process. It's a process very similar to the grief process. It is, more often than not, a long, difficult journey that requires awareness, alignment, ambition—and power—to fulfill. The beauty of forgiveness is found in the art of it.

Forgiveness is a state of being more than anything else. It is being resilient when things don't go your way, a process that allows a person to be at peace with the truth of their lived experiences. Forgiveness is finding harmony with the inherent pains and vulnerabilities of life.

Just like my miraculous experience with forgiveness, one of the most powerful aspects of it is that it can liberate a person from the past and grant them renewed focus and newfound access to the future. This is not something to be taken lightly. Neither are the powerful benefits of forgiveness. When we look at the physiological benefits of forgiveness, we learn that forgiveness enhances optimism, elevates mood, lowers the risk of high blood pressure and heart problems, and guards against the ramifications of anger, stress, and depression.

Yet, beyond all these evident mental and physical health benefits, forgiveness stands at the very core of the release to receive entry point on the path to Zero. Embracing forgiveness, both toward yourself and others, acts as a fast-track to Zero. However, this practice is a continual one to master. People, intentionally or unintentionally, will inevitably cause hurt, and you will likewise make choices that may cause you regret. Each such instance becomes an opportunity to reach within yourself for the courage to forgive and release.

In essence, the power to receive everything you've ever desired is in your control, waiting to be harnessed. To unlock this potential, you must create the space for it. The most direct route is through forgiveness, allowing yourself to release the past and receive a future filled with hope and miracles.

11

WE ARE ALL UNIQUELY MADE

*Love may have the longest arms, but it can
still fall short of an embrace.*

—Megan McCafferty, *Charmed Thirds*

I would love to say that, in that moment of time, I became highly capable of taking responsibility for my struggles and that I regularly set out to address, release, and heal all that encumbered me and my life—but that would be miles from the truth.

As life carried on, despite the remarkable progress I had made through self-awareness and forgiveness, I still struggled with staying true to my authentic self. This stemmed mainly from not fully understanding who my (T)rue Self really was. I constantly found myself tiptoeing on the tightrope between my Human Story Code programming and an insatiable curiosity to unmask and dance with the man in the mirror. He remained ever vigilant in his goal to lure me into his capricious world. Little did I realize that this tango propelled me two steps closer to my authentic path, only to take a gigantic leap back as I desperately worked to conform to the storybook I was handed at birth.

The reality is that true satisfaction and lasting happiness can only be found in a life that aligns with our (T)rue authentic self. When we give precedence to the (t)ruths of the Human Story Code, in other words, the expectations and "shoulds" imposed by external influences that contradict our (T)rue selves, we inadvertently construct a foundation for our lives riddled with fault lines. Any house built on such a shaky foundation will collapse over time. I know because I had carefully built my life upon a crumbling foundation for years.

When we stray from our core values, passions, and principles in pursuit of goals that do not resonate with our innermost desires, we are compromising our own well-being for the sake of other people's expectations. This misalignment creates a profound inner conflict that can lead to dissatisfaction, anxiety, and an overall sense of emptiness. In essence, attempting to live a life that contradicts your authentic self is like squeezing a swan into a flamboyance of flamingos—it may seem possible for a while, but eventually, the inherent mismatch will become glaringly apparent.

This misalignment fails because it becomes challenging to muster the necessary motivation and enthusiasm to excel in any pursuit. Success isn't just how much you have in your bank account or awards placed upon a shelf, but a life lived with a sense of purpose, passion, and dedication.

When you embrace your (T)rue Self, the path to Zero will become more apparent. You will experience a sense of purpose, inner peace, and higher self-confidence. This alignment leads to greater perseverance and resilience, as you're more motivated to overcome challenges and stay committed to your chosen path. Success, in this context, is the internal contentment and harmony that comes from living a life that is (T)rue to your authentic self. Once this is reached, Zero will bring the outer trappings of success to your door more freely than you can possibly imagine.

Though turning away from the Disney offer and choosing to prioritize my school career at BYU could arguably be a representation of a misalignment or a form of self-sabotage with my authentic self, I did continue to take steps toward alignment. They were smaller steps, but still steps in the right direction.

That summer, I took a job in Utah performing at Lagoon, a family-owned theme park, in a rock and roll western show. It was certainly not the Magic Kingdom, but I did what I loved, and it worked with my school schedule. As fate would have it, the gig connected the dots to another local job as a dancing server and roaming entertainer at a brand-new restaurant called The Mayan. The theme park-esque eatery was a passion project built by Larry Miller, owner of the Utah Jazz. It featured three stories of treehouse seating surrounding a thirty-foot waterfall with real-life cliff divers and animatronic tropical birds and iguanas that would sing. I would often spot Larry in the restaurant with his executives, observing me interacting with guests. He would always request that I be his server whenever he brought VIPs and celebrities to the restaurant.

Within months, I was promoted to entertainment director, not just for the restaurant but for the entire complex that housed it. The new job allowed me to put my passion for creativity and entertainment to the test. I was suddenly making a terrific salary for my age, drove my dream truck, and started construction on a quaint little home. My new house would be perched high on a cliff above the suburbs of Salt Lake City. All of this opportunity was handed to me before I even had the chance to walk across the stage and graduate from BYU. Everything from the outside looking in was picture-perfect.

But on the inside, I struggled with the juxtaposition of two identities: one that waltzed with the man in the mirror and entertained his occasional visits, and the other that was still working to achieve my patriarchal blessing.

Since my dad always taught that the first law of heaven is obedience, it was deeply ingrained in me that my luck, success, and all the dots connecting them were tied to my faithfulness to the church. After meeting Elder Neuenschwander and forgiving my brother, I truly saw that intervention as divine. I was invited to the Vatican of Mormonism and given a message that changed the course of my life forever.

Because of this, I developed a renewed respect for the ways of the church. Forgiveness was such a cornerstone of the teachings, and it worked for me. Therefore, I concluded that being obedient to the rest of the church's teachings would eventually lead me to all that was promised for me. I believed that my happiness and the wave of good fortune would remain steadfast if I stayed obedient and continued to manage my thoughts and feelings. Indeed, the fragments of these two paths would somehow weave together and work itself out in the end.

I held quite firm to this idea until just before Christmas. I was digging around in my parents' basement for holiday decorations when I came upon a familiar-looking antique wooden chest. For the life of me, I could not recall what was inside, but I faintly remembered the chest. My brother had popped open the latch with a butter knife when we were young.

I quickly found a screwdriver and went to work. When I lifted the lid to the chest, the scent of old cedar wood transported me back in time. Inside was a collection of Sunday School felt board stories with picture cut-outs, organized and labeled individually with their own oversized manila folder. As I sorted through them, warm memories flooded forward from the recesses of my mind. I used to play with these at great lengths as a child. I loved the way the pictures felt with the soft backside that attached to the felt board.

As I sifted through the stories, one caused me to pause. Laying on the floor before me was a shining bright sun, three lovely trees along a golden path, silver-glitter clouds, and the perfect-looking blonde family. This image was all drawn to the exact specifics of the celestial world I had long envisioned. Time stood still as tears billowed on the edges of my eyes. The unwelcoming sting of reality began to take root. I realized in that moment that my personal heaven was manufactured, cloned, and defined—not just for me, but for all the other kids in Sunday School.

What did this mean?

There, in that basement, I came face-to-face with the teachings of man, not a manifestation of my own inner (T)ruth. Like most children in the world, I was taught the traditional faith of my parents as absolute (T)ruth, laced with anecdotal evidence of where we come from and where we go after death. My church most certainly had an answer for everything, and when it didn't, my questions were reconstructed or reversed as a test of faith. Though I always had many questions and numerous doubts, I had spent a lifetime holding tightly to the only reality I knew.

If I could only step back into the comfort of blissful ignorance, back to before I found that felt-backed heaven, before cognitive dissonance became a constant state of being. I felt like I was watching my life from afar. All the careful constructs I'd held so adamantly in place began to crumble around me.

The seeds of discernment that were planted in my childhood—the same seeds that caused me to question unnecessary rules and the blind judgment of both my church and the society around me—began to sprout flowering buds within my soul. For years, I mistakenly believed that I needed to rip out what seemed like "evil" weeds within me, inadvertently stripping the seedlings of my authentic self and stunting my own growth. The more I became aware of my (T)ruths, the more I began to recognize the value of these seeds. I allowed them to take root and lay a firm foundation in the fertile soil of self-acceptance. Slowly but surely, I ceased to clip back every sprout and allowed the blooms to flourish.

FLIRTING A DANGEROUS LINE

Balancing between two identities became increasingly difficult to manage. I moved back in with my parents during the construction of my new home and attended church services with them. I was called by the bishop to be the primary chorister in Sunday School. The kids loved me.

And their parents loved me even more as I did a great job encouraging their children to sing their little hearts out. I did an even greater job keeping up with appearances.

After attempting to date a nice marriage-material girl at BYU, I got dumped via email. Her words were difficult to read through the tears: "Chad, you are absolutely beautiful and perfect. You are going to make someone so happy. But that someone is not me." It stung. She, like my high school crush Karla, knew I was not destined to have that hetero-life promise. My chest was filled with hurt and embarrassment—but mostly anger. It felt so unfair. I had to meet the man in the mirror face-to-face. I needed to know the truth.

I opened the browser on my laptop, and he gleefully took over my hands as I typed "www.gay.com." I joined a chat room and started chatting with the first guy who would engage in a conversation. The chat quickly went from "Hey, how are you?" to "Masc or fem?" to "What are you into?" I had no idea what this lingo meant. But I was a willing student and curious to find out. We agreed to meet up in Provo Canyon at a trailhead parking lot late that evening. As I drove up the windy road in the dark, my heart raced as sweat formed on my brow. "What was I doing?" I kept asking myself, wanting to turn around. But the man in the mirror was in complete control. He knew what he was doing, and he was loving every second of it.

As I waited anxiously in the parking lot, a set of headlights flashed across my review mirror as a car pulled up beside my truck. An attractive, young, dark-haired man got out and walked up to my window. I rolled it down.

"Hey," I said nervously.

"Hey, what's up?"

It was clear we were here for one thing. Without another word, I got out and joined him in the back bed of my truck. His hands quickly took action as he rubbed my chest on the outside of my shirt. My heart started beating in my throat. He took my hands and guided them up his shirt. I could feel the stubble from his shaved chest. I noticed he was wearing his sacred Mormon underwear. It felt so wrong, but there was a tantalizing allure to it as my mind flashed to the washing ceremony in the temple, wondering how far this would go. He removed his shirt and his garment top. When he unbuttoned his pants, I started shaking violently as if some sort of demon was thrashing to make its way out of me. Assuming I was cold, he climbed on top of me as he pulled his garments down to his knees. I had a naked Mormon man lying on top of me. He unzipped my pants and put his cold hands down my garments. As much as I wanted to enjoy it, I hated it. I felt dirty and scared. Guilt flushed over me. I rolled him off of me and let him pleasure himself until he finished, just to get it over with so he would leave.

I drove home feeling a sense of relief wash over me. That encounter was unsettling. The man in the mirror had it all wrong. I was definitely *not* gay. For a brief moment, I was back in high school, proving him a fool by losing my virginity to Madison. But that feeling was fleeting. Weeks passed, and the man in the mirror emerged again. This time, he was likened to an alluring red-light district madame, tempting me with rotating figures in a storefront. Each one presented a new male variety that might match my tastes. Maybe the guy in the canyon wasn't the right fit, but another could be.

It wasn't long before I was back in the chat room, this time meeting someone at Applebee's rather than a quick touch-and-go in the back of my truck. He was handsome like the other guy, but a bit older than me. It appeared he had his life together. He was successful, charming, and secure—and completely out of the church. He resembled the man in the mirror much more than I did. He had a way of being that didn't make "gay" feel sinful or dirty. However, sitting with him in the restaurant, I felt like I was in an alternate reality in the metaverse. I was in public on a date with a gay man. There was no hiding behind a chat room or secret encounters in the dark. It felt as if all eyes were on me with a whisper of judgment. This was the beginning of my new normal.

After our lunch at Applebee's, I never met that man again. It was clear we were in two different places in our lives. But I did allow the man in the mirror and his colorful world to have a permanent seat at my table, even though I resented him. I allowed myself to have connections with other men. I explored feelings I had buried for so long due to fear and shame.

Strangely, after that first encounter in the canyon, I didn't feel the same shame with men as I did with women. Perhaps this was because I kept my interactions innocent for the most part. When I was honest with myself, I realized that connecting with men felt good and right, even without sex being part of the equation. In this realization, I continued to pursue my patriarchal blessing. Perhaps I *could* have these feelings and still be obedient—even if my vision of heaven was a construct of a Sunday School lesson, perhaps it could still be real, could still be true. I wanted this proverbial white picket fence more than anything else I could imagine.

Living with my parents was a throwback to earlier times; I had less privacy and a sense of childhood accountability to parental authority no matter the age. With my brother having moved back in as well and my sister still in high school, our family found itself reunited under one roof. It was an odd reunion of sorts.

One evening as I came home from work, I encountered my dad's grave face at the door. He had that look, the kind you see in movies when the news is dire. "We need to talk," he said, a statement that never means anything good. In their bedroom, my mom was in tears. The air was thick with gloom. I knew it then—somehow, I was the tragedy.

"What's wrong?" I asked, tension knotting in my chest. My mom, choked by her sobs, struggled to find her voice. When she did, her words cut through the silence with the sharpness of shattered glass. My sister had borrowed my laptop, stumbled upon an open tab—gay.com. Then the question that hung in the air, heavy and foreboding, "Are you gay?"

I felt sucker-punched by the moment, utterly unprepared. My own understanding of myself was a jigsaw puzzle with half the pieces missing. And now I was being asked to label myself. I scrambled for words, managed to express my confusion, and told them I didn't think I was gay. That seemed to bring them some comfort. But for me, it was the sound of a door softly closing.

In that heavy, sorrow-laden air, I looked at my mother's tear-streaked face. In the reflection of her tears, I saw the shadow of sadness and shame that would fall over my family if I stepped out of the straight and narrow path they had drawn for me. Her tears were a silent testament to a life of conformity I felt pressured to lead. And I understood, with a sinking heart, that revealing my (T)rue Self might just be an act I couldn't afford—emotionally or otherwise. It was clear that coming out, if that was ever a reality I'd face, would be like dropping a bomb on the very foundations of my family. In that moment, I saw the silhouette of a future where my (T)ruth might never find the light.

COGNITIVE DISSONANCE

The law of Zero tells us we have access to a wellspring of power within our very being. Still, it's not going to work for us if we cannot get into alignment with it, and we cannot get into alignment with it if we are denying who we are or how we are uniquely made. This is why I struggled with the man in the mirror for so long. My greatest fear as a child, teen, and young man was that something was seriously wrong with me, that I was broken and thus unworthy of my promise and everything worth having in life. This fear was strengthened by the powers that be within my church, it was strengthened by my family, and by my confusion, guilt, shame, and actions.

Every time wisdom would appear to me and reveal my (T)ruth, I was cast back into the metaphorical fire of damnation. This was not because of the (T)ruth that was revealed, but rather what I was conditioned to believe of such a reality. The very idea that same-sex attraction could be a natural reality for me, or anyone else, was impossible as everything I had ever been told negated this.[1] More anger, more confusion, more guilt, more shame—more fear.

As I think back now to the trials I went through and all the trauma I endured in finding my way to accepting and loving myself just as Source made me to be, I can't help but think of all the people who live with equal measures of cognitive dissonance. The thing is that I never knew that gay, lesbian, and bisexual identities were present, identified, and even accepted to varying degrees in numerous cultures worldwide across time. As I've begun to look at the world through my own lens and done research that has grown my knowledge of the world outside of the constraints of the views, opinions, and beliefs of others, I have learned that I am not nor have I ever been broken or unworthy.

True freedom comes from the release of benign perspectives that hold you hostage per the ideals, beliefs, and understandings of others. These (t)ruths ensnare us, keeping us from reaching Zero. They chain us to a mirage rather than reality. I know it's a tall order, particularly when those nearest to us might not grasp or embrace our (T)rue selves, but it is essential to let go. We must unclench our fists and release the hold on what others think we're supposed to be in order to set free the (T)ruth of who we are. Zero's transformative power is stifled when we cling to an identity that doesn't mirror who Source created.

My parents grieved over my sexuality, holding onto doctrines and teachings that painted a life like mine as one devoid of eternal happiness. The only way to dismantle such deep-seated beliefs is to live in contradiction to them. Be a beacon of joy. Be the epitome of what it means to love and be loved. In doing so, your life becomes a testament, an unspoken invitation for others to comprehend and accept your (T)ruth. There's that age-old saying: you can lead a horse to water, but you can't make him drink. We can't force our (T)ruth on others. In time, through example, others may come to see the power of your authenticity. And from that recognition, they may find themselves drawn to partake in the profound understanding you offer, drinking deeply from the wellspring of acceptance and shared human connection.

To the twenty-five-year-old me and to anyone else wrestling with the journey of self-acceptance and love for the person Source has crafted you into: know that you are not alone on this path. The road to embracing your (T)rue Self, the one carved out by Source, can be winding and steep. It's filled with moments of doubt and shadows of societal or familial expectations. But remember, within you is Zero—an unparalleled strength, a unique essence that Source intended for you to share with the world.

In the moments when you find it hard to look in the mirror, when you grapple with (T)ruths that seem to defy the norms or challenge the beliefs of those around you, hold firm. These struggles, though fierce, are the forging ground of your authenticity. The love and acceptance you seek first must bloom within you, nurtured by the knowledge that you were created as you should be.

To my younger self: take heart. The journey is not about altering your essence to fit a mold; it's about breaking the mold and living unabashedly as you were meant to. And to anyone else in this struggle: step into the light of your being with courage and love. Source made no mistake in creating you just as you are.

Dispelling any suspense, I can affirm that, in time, my family grew to embrace the authentic, real me. They came to understand that the parts of me I once thought broken were, in truth, the very facets that make me whole and human. These pieces, seemingly fractured, have always been the best parts of me—where the light gets in, where growth happens, and where love finds its purest expression. In this journey of acceptance, we all learned that it's within our imperfections that our (T)rue beauty lies.

Indeed, the path to self-acceptance is rarely straightforward. Despite the beauty of our creation, we often cling to our Human Story Codes, those deeply ingrained narratives that have shaped our understanding of who we're supposed to be. Embracing who Source created us to be is not a linear path but a spiral. It moves upward, but with turns that sometimes loop back upon themselves. It's a complex waltz with our authentic selves, where the music of our own progress can sometimes falter, lose its beat, but then find its rhythm once again.

MY FUTURE WIFE

The progress the man in the mirror made—venturing into the depths of self-exploration and edging me toward acceptance of my (T)rue nature—spiraled backward dramatically the following summer. I was at work on an average Friday night when everything changed. The year was 2001, and all that I'd been waiting for, all that I'd been obedient for—for so very long—walked right in the front door of my job.

I was still working for Mr. Miller. I produced a song, dance, and entertainment show inside the children's theater of The Mayan. Another element of my job was to book live bands and entertainment for additional outdoor events. That night, I had to fill in for one of my entertainers who was out sick. I was all decked out in full costume and preparing to perform when I got a call from the theater manager stating that the band outside was too loud and disturbing the other performances. I still had about twenty minutes before going on, so I made a quick dash outside to rectify the volume.

After adjusting the sound equipment, I entered the band's audience to check the volume. I soon noticed a beautiful blonde woman with her young daughter smiling at me. I smiled back and had this weird, cosmic feeling like I already knew her. I glanced at her again, and she was still looking at me with the most beautiful smile. My heart began to race. This was strange. Very strange. *Why is my heart racing? Who is she?*

Suddenly, she approached me. I froze.

"Hi, do you know who books the bands here?"

I worked hard to act cool and collected. "Actually, I book the bands here."

"Really? Well, can I get your card?"

I didn't have a card on me, so I told her to hold on and sprinted to my office. As I returned to her, I got this sinking feeling in my stomach. *What if she was gone when I got back?*

I turned the corner into the crowd; there she was, still smiling that bright, beautiful smile that reached all the way to her eyes. While handing her the card, I realized I had to get back to my show; a glance at my watch confirmed it.

"Hey, my show's about to start. I have to get back . . . do you both want to come and watch? It starts in five minutes."

With an affirming nod of her head, I escorted them into the theater and slipped backstage to put on my headpiece. My female counterpart was freaking out at my absence,

"We're on in thirty seconds! I didn't think you were going to make it!"

If my grin didn't say it all, my mouth did. "I just met my future wife. And she's in the audience." And with that, I stepped onto the stage. I performed the best show of my life that night, looking right at the mystery woman and her child. After the show, I gave the woman and her daughter a quick tour backstage and walked them to the exit. As I watched her walk across the parking lot, it was as if I were in a dream. A strange, beautiful dream that made no sense in real life but felt natural and right in its very own way.

The entire next week seemed to crawl along. I couldn't stop thinking of this woman. I constantly checked my voicemail, waiting for a message, but there was nothing. Days of waiting turned into weeks. Eventually, I just kind of let it go. Then, one evening, I was heading home after a long shift and bumped into someone.

"I'm so, so sorry."

As I looked up, I couldn't believe my eyes. There she was, smiling back at me, looking just as surprised as I was. "Oh! It's you! I lost your card, and what's your name again?"

"My name is Chad," I said.

"My name is Jerri. I kept coming back, hoping to run into you again."

This time, I had a card on me, and I handed it to her. She called me the next day to set up her friend's band, and I just so happened to have a cancellation the very next Saturday.

I counted down the days like it was Christmas. Saturday came around, and I was there far too early, anxiously waiting for the band to arrive.

"Hey, so it was Jerri who set this up for you guys. Is she coming tonight?"

The band leader looked at me and said no. She was dating the guitar player, and they had just broken up today. He didn't think she would come. My heart sank. This was my only chance to see her.

As the band started playing their first set, I looked out across the way and saw her walking down the stairs from the parking lot. My eyes were fixated on her the whole time. She walked straight up to me with her big, beautiful grin.

She gave me a huge hug and said, "Hi, Chad. Thanks for setting this up. I really appreciate it."

"They told me you weren't going to come out tonight."

"Yeah, there's some drama. I wasn't going to come, but I really needed to. I really needed to see . . . you." I looked back at her, a quizzical expression on my face. She continued, "I don't want you to be freaked out or think this is weird, but I felt a cosmic connection with you the moment I met you. It's really been on my mind. I don't know what it is or why I feel connected to you, but I needed to come tonight and tell you."

My heart was racing as she spoke. I looked at her and said, "I feel the same way. I have not stopped thinking about you since that day we met." We looked at one another and hugged.

I said, "I don't even know you, and I love you."

"I love you too," she replied.

"What are you doing Monday?" I asked.

"Hanging out with you," she said.

That Monday, we met at Red Rock, my favorite restaurant and brewery in downtown Salt Lake City. We sat in the back corner for over four hours and just poured ourselves into one another.

Turns out that we had grown up forty-five minutes from each other in Southern California. She was recently divorced and had two kids: a seven-year-old daughter, whom I had met, and a four-year-old son. An instant family, just like I wanted. Everything was beyond perfect.

The only hiccup was, just about two weeks prior to meeting Jerri, I'd quietly come out to my close friend and old roommate David from Ricks College, who was full-blown out. He was the one person I knew I could trust, the one friend I knew would understand.

Haunted by the tear-stained memory of my parents' probing, their inquisition laced with worry, I moved cautiously. I struggled to not make the reality of my being gay "real" by saying it out loud. Sure, I'd been secretly meeting other men and exploring my sexuality. But until I came out to my friend, I had never planted the rainbow flag—and I had certainly not waved it. But there was no denying who I was, and I needed to speak my (T)ruth. I admitted to Jerri that I had recently come out and didn't understand the feelings I had toward her.

She smiled and said, "Chad, that just makes me love you more. You just be who God created you to be. I don't have a problem with it. I just love you."

Her words hung in the air, almost too extraordinary to grasp—a true miracle. After that, we were inseparable as our courtship brought us closer together with every sunrise. I got to know her kids through get-togethers; they called me Chaddy. Her ex-husband even liked me. Since he lived in the same area of town, I would bump into him often. He would ask me how I was and even tell me how much his kids loved me and talked about me all the time. I would take the kids on hikes and to theme parks, and they would have a blast.

I thought, *this is the answer to my prayers; this is the family I always wanted.* I knew I was gay, but I also knew I was attracted to Jerri. I was in love with her, and my sexuality didn't matter. I loved her. We connected in some otherworldly fashion. I would be driving along thinking about her, my phone would ring, and it would be her calling just because she was thinking about me.

At this time, the construction of my new house was just finishing, and I thought, *we are going to live in this house on the hill. This is it. This is why I was drawn to this family neighborhood and not living in the cool hipster part of town. It was because I was supposed to be here. We were supposed to be a family.*

The good, obedient Mormon boy in me had found an actual route to my patriarchal blessing. This was it! For the first time in my life, the words of love songs resonated, colors were brighter, sounds were lovelier, and when I was around her, my spirit felt wide awake. I knew beyond all certainty that this was love—full on, full stop. We were in beautiful sync with one another, dual flames.

Feeling what I felt for her did not undo everything I knew of myself. It did not change the fact that my lived feelings and experiences were true. What it did do was draw forward a different kind of longing. Her response when I told her that I was gay—but was still attracted to and enamored by her—was more than I could have ever hoped for.

I knew that my felt-board vision of heaven was manufactured, but despite this, it didn't change the fact that the longing for such a simple reality was always present within me. With Jerri at my side and in my life, I could maybe, finally, be righteous in the eyes of my family, the eyes of my church friends, and possibly even in the eyes of my religion.

I felt like a piece of my heart had been missing my entire life, and there it was. There she was. She was holding my missing piece. Our relationship was going to fix everything. She was precisely what I needed. It had to have been God who sent her to me.

And then, about three months into our relationship in early December, she called me and spoke those familiar four worst words in the English language: "We need to talk."

"Okay . . ."

She went on to tell me that she couldn't see me anymore; this wasn't going to work. She couldn't explain it, but she couldn't see me anymore. She then told me not to call her and hung up the phone.

I was devastated. I had no idea what was going on. *Why was this happening? What was wrong?* Everything had seemed so perfect. I felt like I was going mad. Nothing made any sense. I began driving by her house every day, sometimes multiple times a day, just hoping for a glimpse of her. I tried calling her to no avail. Eventually, I got a message that her phone line had been disconnected.

About two weeks after that fateful phone call, I mustered the courage to knock on her door. The freshly fallen snow on Christmas decorations placed purposefully around her home gave the illusion that everything was still that picture-perfect postcard dream I longed for. Despite my ambition to be brave, tears began to roll down my face.

"Why Jerri, why? Why did you leave me? Why did you do this?"

"I'm sorry, Chad. I'm so sorry. I can't. I just can't see you, and I can't talk to you." And she shut the door.

I was beyond devastated. My heart shattered into a million pieces.

THE TRAUMA OF INAUTHENTICITY

Jerri was the catalyst that truly set my discovery of self into motion. You see, the day I met her, I felt as though the heavens had opened themselves to me. She was here! Here she was! Despite having romantic connections with women throughout my life, this was the first woman to stir something deep within me—something beyond what I thought was possible. Being around her made me believe not that I *should* but that I *could* live a heterosexual life.

But here lies the dilemma: I yearned for that picture-perfect, white picket fence life, a felt-board cutout of a life that was never meant for me. While it's possible to activate the entry points to Zero and craft a magical fairytale life, that life, built on inauthenticity, is like constructing a sand castle. It will eventually crumble when Zero finds its way to your core through the entry point of awareness. Perhaps this is why we encounter countless tales of individuals who, despite living seemingly perfect lives, harbor their (T)rue selves in secret, only to emerge later, leaving behind a trail of heartbreak and trauma for their families to navigate.

I had been bewitched into a fantasy that painfully confused me, and this reality emanated from my being. The bottom line was this: Jerri was as close as a person would ever get to the partner I'd so long dreamed of. She was kind, loving, and beautiful, and I was in love with her—truly in love. Yet, Jerri knew then what we both know now. She knew why it wouldn't work— why it couldn't work. She could see my striking resemblance to the man in the mirror more clearly than I could at that time. She saw all the messy trauma I worked so hard to mask with a big silver bow. On some level, she knew that for us to build the kind of life I was trying so hard to create would be virtually impossible. Moving forward with me seemed like a safe route for both of us, but it wasn't what she needed—and it certainly wasn't what I ultimately needed either.

When there is extensive trauma in a person's life, it becomes an encumbrance of every relationship that comes along. Inauthenticity is a form of trauma in and of itself. Jerri could see the pain caused by this trauma of battling my authentic self with the promise of eternal happiness as I desperately tried squeezing a gay man into a straight man's shoes. She knew what this would do to us if we continued.

This doesn't take away from the fact that the essence of our relationship was true love—as I believe to this day that it was (and might even still be). It does speak to the simple fact that where there is significant trauma, there is a heavy, more eminent truth competing for the light. Until an active light is shone on this trauma, it has properly been dealt with or rectified in some manner—and no longer holds power over a person—nothing will outweigh it and nothing can supersede it. Not even love.

12

BLOW DOWN YOUR
HOUSE OF CARDS

*Man's ideal state is realized when he has fulfilled the
purpose for which he is born. And what is it that reason
demands of him? Something very easy—that he live
in accordance with his own nature.*

—Seneca, *Letters from a Stoic,*
"On the God Within Us"

With every visit from the man in the mirror, the promises of my obedience drifted further and further out of reach. I could see myself disappearing from the family photograph like Marty McFly in *Back to the Future*. I tried to salvage what was left of my promise by shoving the secret parts of me into the dark corners of my mind, heart, and life, so much so that they cast shadows on every kind and lovely thing I encountered. The dueling paths of my life etched a rift so profound into the mortar of my Human Story Code that they gradually suffocated my happiness.

I now know that where trauma is severe or pervasive, it also disrupts the formation of one's sense of self and perverts authenticity. This is what happened to me. The realization that I was something that goes against God's plan of salvation and the horrors of knowing that there were not enough prayers in the universe to fix it was traumatic. And when I tried to change who I was and failed, it was only exacerbated by more trauma. The entirety of my existence felt like a carefully constructed house of cards that could, at any moment, come tumbling down.

Despite forgiving my brother and basking in the momentum of multiple successes in my life, a lingering sense of emptiness persisted. I was in the midst of desperately trying to manage a massive leak in the Awareness entry point, which relentlessly unveiled overwhelming (T)ruths I felt ill-prepared to confront. Simultaneously, I diligently worked to heal what I felt were the broken parts of me by attending intensive self-help seminars and diving head-first into *The Secret*.[1]

Regardless of my efforts, my life spiraled into chaos, much like releasing that relentless fire hose at full throttle. No amount of "think and believe" and career success could silence the incessant check engine light from under the hood. I did not feel safe. I did not feel secure. I did not feel stable in any way. I no longer felt magic.

RADIO SILENCE

It all came to a precipice about nine months after Jerri broke up with me. I stood motionless in the kitchen of my new house on the hill. I stood there, fists clenched and lips trembling as tears streamed down my face.

Staring through the large panes of glass, I counted each breath as I observed the unobstructed view of the seemingly peaceful world below. Cars mechanically zoomed up and down the freeway in a single file line like an army of ants as big cotton clouds danced across the sky. I remember thinking, *this is the land of my ancestors, the land that they sacrificed everything to come to. This city was their utopia, their haven. So many people call this land Zion—but it is far from that for me.*

I had just returned from the funeral of a friend who had died in a tragic car accident. She was the same age as me. Though my heart ached for her and the loss her family was experiencing, the anguish I felt was not explicitly for her. My soul was being tormented and eaten alive by toxic, self-deprecating thoughts.

Something was definitely wrong, but I couldn't wrap my head around it. A grim darkness had overtaken me as visions of death constantly polluted my mind. I'd grown accustomed to the nightly ritual of tossing and turning, followed by ruminations and heartfelt pleas that God would just take me in my sleep. I pleaded with the heavens to put me out of my misery. I fantasized about how long it would take for someone to stumble upon my bedridden corpse in my lonely house on the hill. But God didn't take me. Instead, he took my friend. I was sad, angry, and lost.

Despite my "successes," I felt wholly unfulfilled and thoroughly disconnected. I struggled with depression stemming from heartbreak, lack of spiritual testimony, and my beaten-down self-esteem. I constantly felt exhausted and empty after attending church services. All my perfect-looking neighbors and their perfect little families poured salt on the wounds of my broken heart, as I knew I could never have that.

I searched for comfort, lying under the stars in my backyard, casting my frustrations toward the heavens as tears poured down my face. I wanted so badly to believe I was normal and that I mattered. I desperately wanted to feel loved, regardless of my brokenness. Most of all, I wanted to believe that all the beautiful promises of happiness and eternal life were mine. But the message I received back from the heavens was complete radio silence.

I had felt increasingly more like a phony as I strived for perfection. I struggled with imposter syndrome as I became an overachiever in my efforts to maintain the status quo.[2] I strove to prove my place in this world and, thus, my value. Success became the answer. Yet, in quiet moments, I was filled with fear, petrified by the possibility that my reality was merely a manufactured box full of felt storybook picture cutouts—and that love, real love, was only an illusion. The harder I forced myself to believe, the more miserable and frustrated I became with my unfulfilled state.

Each new blow of trauma continued to snuff out my belief in the internal magic and the personal power my grandfather had taught me, leaving me more helpless. My only antidote was a forced smile on my face, pretending everything was fine.

Fake it 'til you make it, right?

Everything is perfect. Focus on the good. Be grateful. Be happy.

To keep myself thinking positively, I would reflect on a simple lesson from a song called "Smiles" from the children's songbook of the Church of Jesus Christ of Latter-day Saints.

SMILES

If you chance to meet a frown, do not let it stay.
Quickly turn it upside down and smile that frown away.
No one likes a frowning face. Change it for a smile.
Make the world a better place by smiling all the while.[3]

Remember, the grand purpose of life was simply to be obedient and endure through hardship. There was this understanding that if something was "wrong" with you, you could will it away. If it didn't work, you could pray it away. If that didn't work, you were meant to endure it, give thanks, and smile, as it was a test of faith.

I was taught that life was a test—full of difficult trials and tribulations—and that I had selected the entire menu of hardships I would endure before I came to Earth. I intentionally chose the difficulties I faced as a testament to my faith and loyalty to God. The end-all goal was to work hard enough, be obedient—and righteous enough—to reap the golden reward of eternal happiness in heaven.

As I stood in my kitchen, my mind wandered back to memories of the previous summer when I had met my beautiful Jerri, who I could not have because of who I was. Then, my thoughts shifted to my more recent relationships, one with a woman named Michelle and another with a man named Mason.

Through another online chat room, I met Mason, a psychiatrist who was ten years my senior. We immediately sparked a friendship over our shared love for dogs and the outdoors. We often went on hikes in the mountains and had playdates with our pups in tow. It wasn't long before I developed romantic feelings for him, but my desires remained a lips-sealed secret. I could tell no one, not even Mason.

Even though I had come out to myself and my closest friends, I was not ready to identify as a gay man in a public way by having a bona fide boyfriend. Plus, being full-out gay meant a complete stop to the promises of my patriarchal blessing. That was a one-way ticket on a runaway train I was not prepared to ride.

As if Jerri's cautionary tale hadn't already weighed heavily on my fragile heart, I found myself once again adding more notches to my trauma timeline chasing the dragon to that white picket fence life. This time with a new romantic interest, Michelle. She lived on my street and welcomed me with open arms when I moved to the hill. We were the only two single people without kids in the neighborhood. I was still reeling from the breakup and was honest with her about the struggles I'd had with my sexuality. She, too, was a member of the LDS Church and, like my high school girlfriend, adamantly believed that I wasn't gay.

After I shared my heartbreak story about Jerri and how it made me lose hope of ever being "normal," her prescription was simple. I needed to have healthier relationships with heterosexual men. So, as we began spending more and more time together, she invited her straight male friends along as well.

She encouraged me that if I had faith in God, Jesus, and the promises given to me in the temple, I could overcome this "problem." We talked hypothetically about how, if we got married, her dad would basically take me in as his own son, which would help me overcome my struggles. We hypothesized that some of my struggles most likely stemmed from my relationship with my dad. It's not that he was a horrible and unloving person. He simply lacked the emotional ability to intimately connect with his children and others. He was a traditional workaholic. His rulebook for raising a family was to align with the church's teachings to the letter of the law.

I had shared with Michelle that when I was given a leading role in our high school's musical, my dad told me to turn it down because there was a matinee on Sunday—the Sabbath, which would go against one of the laws of obedience.[4] Thankfully, this was one of the few times my mother opposed him and supported me. Incidents like this drove a wedge between my dad and me, planting a seed of resentment toward him in my heart.

His compliance and obedience to the church seemed to consistently supersede us, our feelings and needs. I knew I had a gift to perform. It made no sense for me to reject opportunities to express this gift. Throughout my youth, singing was the one thing that made me truly happy. I felt that my dad's dedication to the letter of the law was an attempt to strip me of the one part of me that felt real and complete.

One day, when I was sick in bed, I asked Michelle to run down the hill to pick up some medicine. On her return, she let herself in and found me sprawled out on my bed, not wearing a shirt, unable to move. She stood there for a moment, staring at me before taking a seat at the edge of my bed, still clenching the items I requested in her hands. She proceeded to pitch the idea that we should get married. She was seven years older than me, but we were both adults. We got along so well. We loved many of the same things, like our taste in home decor.

She proposed that it was the perfect solution to both our needs. We could build my idealized white picket fence life. I am not sure if it was the fever talking, but as she spoke, I laid there in bed thinking, *yes, yes, absolutely yes. This could work!* Once I agreed with her plans, she gave me the bag from the pharmacy and left.

And so, we began officially dating, and one of her first initiatives was a thorough audit of my wardrobe. She decisively removed any item she deemed too gay, much to the dismay of the man in the mirror—who, incidentally, had a particular fondness for those lowrider flared jeans embellished with rhinestone buttons.

And then there was another potential problem—my friendship with my crush, Mason. Remember him? He remained in the closet with the man in the mirror as my dirty little secret. To complicate this sticky situation further, not long after Michelle's proposal, Mason made it known that he was very much into me and wanted to advance our relationship. In layman's terms, he practically wanted to put a ring on it too. Of course, my heart wanted this, but I didn't dare consider it a possibility. I was trying to balance my relationship with Michelle as a life preserver for my soul as my unsanctioned secret relationship with Mason bloomed. I was frightened, so I told Mason I wasn't ready. He was unsurprisingly quite hurt and expressed that we shouldn't see each other anymore.

As I walked down the steps of his front porch toward my truck, that familiar knot in my stomach churned inside me. I could feel how misaligned I had become by denying my (T)rue, authentic self. I realized that I had once again rejected what I knew deep in my core I wanted for what I believed was right. I chose the path my Human Story Code presented to me. The magic of Zero moved further away from me.

A few days prior, Michelle had invited me to meet her in Idaho, where she was visiting her parents. Her father was serving as mission president for the church in Boise. She was eager for me to meet him. The idea of this was overwhelming from every angle. I let her know that I didn't think I'd be able to go.

You see, the man she wanted to enlist to save me from myself was in the same position of power in the church as the man who had sent me packing in the middle of the night in California several years prior. That trauma had been carefully tucked away, and I wasn't ready to unpack any of that. However, after things broke off with Mason, I thought I needed to give Michelle 100 percent of me without any secrets. So, I called her, accepted her offer, and set off for the weekend trip to Idaho.

Meeting her parents was not as awkward an experience as I imagined. They were very welcoming and inquisitive. After a nice homemade meal, Michelle and I set out to see what nightlife in Boise had to offer. After a few recommendations from people on the street, we settled on the Balcony—unbeknownst to us, the local gay bar.

Moments later, we were tearing up the dance floor. It didn't take long for Michelle to notice the men were more interested in me than I was in her. Visibly upset, she stormed out and asked for the door cover back. I followed her, and we walked silently for a few blocks until we found ourselves in a circular plaza. We laid down side by side on the cool concrete gazing up at the stars. My mind raced through a hundred things I wanted to tell her, but my mouth wouldn't move.

She finally broke the silence with laughter. "I feel so stupid. How did I ever think this would work between us?"

Even though we both craved that Hallmark card nuclear family life, it was clear that I was not attracted to her, and no amount of role-playing would ever change that. As we lay under the stars, we both decided that this perfectly crafted fantasy was just that—a fantasy.

On my drive home, I waded through this sordid mess I now found myself in. It became crystal clear I needed to see Mason again—perhaps he would take me back. I decided being his boyfriend was exactly what I wanted and needed. So, upon my arrival in town, I went straight to his house. Well, I immediately found out that he'd already moved on rather quickly—as in, he had someone there when I knocked on the door.

"I'm sorry, Chad, I am dating someone else."

Was this a cruel joke? He had practically proposed to me on Thursday and had a new boyfriend on Sunday! I was crushed—again.

I was not just crushed because I was rejected. I was heartbroken because I was right back to square one, still stuck between who I needed to be and who I was. And not only this, but I also felt like I needed to clear my conscience and come clean with Michelle.

From Mason's house, I drove straight to her house, sobbing the entire way. I stood at Michelle's front door for a long time, trying to regain my composure and muster up the necessary courage. When she opened the door, I could see the hurt on her face; the weight of guilt pressed against my throat.

"I'm so sorry I hurt you."

I told her the truth about the secrets I had been keeping, how I felt about Mason, and what had just happened. I explained that I was more confused than ever, but one thing I knew was that our decision not to go through with the marriage idea was the right thing to do. I felt relieved that I told Michelle everything, but naturally, she was upset, so upset, in fact, that she called the bishop and told him I was gay.

BIG RISKS FOR BIG REWARDS

The very next week, I got a call from the church secretary explaining the bishop would like to meet with me in person. I reluctantly obliged. Once again, I was in the hot seat behind closed doors, sitting face-to-face with my ecclesiastical leader. When he questioned me, I was completely honest. He must have thought I would deny the allegations because once I spoke of the situation and the confusion I was experiencing, he said this was all beyond him and that I would get a call from a higher church leader. I anxiously awaited that call the same way one might wait for big test results. I felt consumed with anxiety, dread, and fear.

I lived in these emotions for the next several days through my friend's funeral. And still, all I could feel as I stood in my kitchen with my tear-streaked face looking out my windows at that beautiful view I was so proud to have was the overwhelming dread of religious repercussions.

Maybe it should have been me who died. Why would God take my friend's life when mine was such a disaster?

I'm not sure how much time lapsed in my kitchen as the sky turned to twilight, but eventually, I began to feel something else. A small spark of magic stirred deep inside my soul, much like the empowering feeling I had experienced sitting in my college chapel after passing up the communion. The spark ignited and turned to flame as a burning desire to no longer feel this angst came over me. My friend had died, but I wanted to live. I didn't want to wait for death to experience happiness. I wanted it now, in this life.

I quickly cleared everything off my small kitchen table and shoved all four chairs to the side. I stood there, prepared to test my faith and the faith of my ancestors. I conjured up a simple experiment in my mind. If it were true that my happiness and abundance of blessings were strictly tied to my obedience to the church like I was taught, what would happen if I removed myself from it? What if I stopped attending church and quit paying my tithe as well as a number of other heavy-weighted commandments and promises that I swore by my life to obey? According to what was explained to me in the temple ceremony, turning my back on these covenants would cause the Holy Spirit to withdraw itself from me. My life and finances would crumble to pieces, and I would fall prey to the power of the destroyer.

As frightening as it seemed, I was ready to take the risk and remove my armor, allowing the man in the mirror to take me as a prisoner of war. I was willing to find out if the warnings and fears firmly constructed into my Human Story Code held any merit. The way I saw it, the greater the risk meant the greater reward, and the only way out was up. I couldn't go on living the way I was if I genuinely wanted to live a happy life.

Harkening back to my grandfather's teachings and understanding the mind as a powerful visual manifester, I drafted a visual clean slate. Then, one by one, I visualized each memory that spiritually connected me to my ancestors, every belief that was programmed into my DNA, each fear and every ounce of hope, all my Sunday School lessons, my parent's teachings, every insecurity, every heartbreak—literally every building block in my Human Story Code that made me who I was striving so hard to be. I placed each of these on imaginary playing cards and stacked them in a deck that I held firmly in my hands.

I stood there for what felt like hours, gripping my metaphorical deck, unable to let go. My heart pounded, and my hands trembled for what I was about to do. A battle was at work within me. Was it good and evil? Was it past and future? Was it pain and promise?

Without warning, a bolt of energy knocked me into a meditative trance. I transitioned into what seemed like another dimension: a place outside my body but deep within my being. I was no longer standing alone in my house on the hill. An overwhelming feeling of love encompassed me. The room seemed to fill with angelic beings who only had my best interest in mind. Though I saw no physical forms, I felt like a child surrounded by family and friends on their birthday; love, peace, and safety enveloped me. Just as I felt myself relax into the energy I was encircled by, once again, I heard that familiar, soft, gentle female voice. She whispered, "Let go."

I had utterly forgotten that voice. Suddenly, I was eight years old again and sprawled under the stars between the olive trees. I remembered how loved I felt when she first spoke to me. With complete ease, my hands released. I watched as my imaginary deck of cards fell to the table and multiplied to cover the entire surface. Suspended in time, I looked down to observe my life showcased through colorful movie-like scenes that played their role in forming my core memories and personal identity. Each of them now like fleeting dreams from someone else's life.

Then the voice spoke again, "These no longer serve you." And just like that, a gust of wind picked up the very real yet ultimately metaphysical cards, carrying them through and out the window of my beautiful home.

Down the cliff, they tumbled toward the city lights of Salt Lake and eventually out of sight.

As quickly as it came, the trance departed, and I stepped back into the present reality. My tears had dried, and I stood before my table somewhat dumbfounded. A strange sense of peace radiated through my soul. Suddenly, great joy danced through my entire body as though my heart were singing a song I had always known the words to but could never quite hear. Visions of endless possibilities opened before my mind's eye. The same voice that had spoken to me at eight years old was right. I would achieve great and wondrous things in my life—in many ways, I already had. And I was indeed loved beyond measure. I didn't have a name for it then, but I was at complete Zero at that moment. I had found Zero. Or better yet, Zero found me.

The next day, I received the scheduling call to meet with the local stake president and instinctively waited for the familiar dread to encompass me. But this time, I felt different. No dread or fear-induced nausea. I felt at peace; what was to come was meant to be. The state of Zero was still with me. I had raised everything in my life to the power of Zero. I was completely neutral.

When I walked into my meeting with the stake president, the environment was familiar, but not the treatment. This kindly man expressed empathy and understanding, the opposite of everything I expected. I repeated what I'd told the bishop and then elaborated in greater detail. He looked me square in the eye and said, "Chad, you need to be who God created you to be. The church needs people like you, but most importantly you need to be happy. If you want therapy, we will pay for therapy. If you want to take a step back from the church, I understand. You just need to be authentic and do what is best for you to be happy."

I could hardly fathom what I heard. This unforgettable experience and this meeting—just as the one with Elder Neuenschwander—changed the course of my life. I had yearned to hear these words of acceptance and support my entire life, and here they were, coming from the mouth of my church leader.

As soon as I got in the car, I called Jerri. We had started talking again when I was dating Michelle, deciding that having each other in our lives, even in a limited fashion—as friends—was better than nothing.

"Listen to what he said, Jerri; he said that I need to be happy, that I need to be who God created me to be—the stake president said that. Can you believe it?"

"I'm so happy for you, Chad. Please know that I love you no matter what. I just love you."

"I love you too, Jerri, and you know what, I'm going to do it. I'm going to be who God created me to be, and I'm going to be happy—no matter what."

It was decided. I'd said my intention out loud. I'd spoken my (T)ruth into existence, and I meant it with every fiber of my being. I could no longer live life with a broken heart. I could no longer live with the scrutiny of being a broken man. I wanted happiness. I wanted acceptance. I wanted love. And I deserved all of these realities despite my obedience, despite my performance, and despite any worldly view of "success."

It didn't take long to see that my deck of cards experiment had worked. Ironically, I felt more connected to spirit than ever before. By removing the structure and expectation that governed my life up to that point, I could finally feel the vast reality of a God indescribable and uncontainable by any religion—or, for that matter, any human understanding.

For the first time, I could intimately understand the depth of verses that spoke of the peace of God. I was reveling in my first authentic understanding of the unconditional love of God. Rather than feeling guilt or fear when I thought of God, I felt only love.

I began to understand that this concept of God couldn't be encompassed by any one religion. The ways and attributes of this universal power far exceeded *any* human's capacity to understand even remotely. Humility washed over me like a flood of living water as I meditated on God's depths of wisdom and capacity.

I clung to the (T)ruths that rang through and tossed everything else out the window. I began to call God a new name—Source, which felt like the most exacting of all possible names. Immediately, I hungered for knowledge like a curious child. I wanted to understand all the laws of the universe. I wanted to know where I fit—just as I was—into everything that was, and is, and will come to be.

An incomprehensible reality beckoned to me. I finally deciphered the first message that was trying to reach my young mind lying under the starry sky—I could hear her voice loud and clear: "You are the light of the world."

Awareness cleared the storm clouds of judgment from my eyes. I could see clearly. The light within me was perfectly divine in all my imperfections. I found myself meeting wise teachers in the most curious forms and the most colorful of places. It seemed that everywhere I turned, I would encounter the most amazing humans, who were eager, open, and willing to share stories of their understandings, truths, and awakenings.

One thing above all else was made clear, releasing the stories, beliefs, and judgments that were constructed to keep me small—to keep me obedient and in fear—had changed me. It was like the shedding of an old skin, or perhaps more so, a metamorphosis—as everything had changed.

Everything was made new. This is the power of Zero at work.

CATEGORIZATION VERSUS INDIVIDUALITY

Once I stepped outside the constructs of my upbringing, I learned that people (all people) have various ways of naturally loving and connecting with Source. This was an amazing epiphany, something certainly not embraced or encouraged in the environment I was accustomed to—a place wherein the (seemingly) only warranted ways to exist are in service, tradition, and asceticism.

I've found that celebrating all the other modes of connection has become a beautiful experience. I believe that there is no singular, correct way to commune with Source; there is no one specific mode or methodology. Likewise, there is no carved pathway to Zero. Instead, there are a multitude of practices that fund the Source–Self relationship. There is praise and there is prayer. There is song and there is silence. There is messaging, magic, miracles, and even great, undoubted sacrifice. None of this is to be questioned. What is to be questioned, however, is the very human idea that we can in any way know the unsearchable, insurmountable ways of Source.

Humility is the most important posture of all when it comes to looking at the world around us. We live in a world that just loves to judge and categorize. We judge others for their behaviors, how they look, and even the vehicle they drive. Interestingly, this judgment is as much about categorizing ourselves as it is about anything else. We categorize behaviors, ideas, objects, and people according to how we see ourselves. Categorization is an innate ability that establishes itself naturally in early childhood. If you've any children in your life, it is not difficult to witness how they are inherently able to categorize concrete objects through physical play or how they categorize abstract ideas through imaginative play. They are even quite capable of categorizing people according to subjective or objective criteria at a very young age.

It is the activity of sorting people that illuminates not just commonalities but also differences—and it is what we think about these differences and what we do about these differences that matter most. Rather than celebrating the vast diversity among people, humans have the tendency to develop prejudice and stereotypes as well as social hierarchical structures that often lead to systems of power such as control, discrimination, and violence. If history tells us anything, this capacity is (unfortunately) highly innate to the human condition.

There are some social categories that carry immense baggage with them due to centuries of hierarchical and divisive societal structure. Some handy examples include the caste system, religiocentrism, and racial relations. Interestingly, even among these examples, there is vast categorization. The idea of race is probably the most clear-cut example of broad social categorization wherein various races are distilled into broad descriptive categories such as Black, White, Asian, and Native. These descriptors dilute a multitude of distinct and unique ethnicities and nationalities down to very base people groups that are governed by skin color alone. Various sectors of religion are managed similarly, as are socioeconomic sectors within society. This becomes increasingly pertinent as one recognizes the intricacies of their unique Human Story Code.

To best understand your Human Story Code, you must first step away from the idea of categorization and into the idea of individuality. Your individuality entails your personality, preferences, emotions, feelings, thoughts, behaviors, and will—all the (T)ruths of your personal orientation. This includes your gifts, talents, and possibilities that dwell within who you uniquely are. This also encompasses your way of being, which manifests from the (T)ruth of who you are, whether you or anyone else likes it or not.

My experience with Zero has taught me that shedding confining labels and categories that do not serve our authentic selves involves much more than mere wishing. Adopting a positive mindset without accompanying it with tangible actions is essentially a form of avoidance. Realizing your dream life requires active work, especially for those whose Human Story Codes are entangled with trauma, baggage, and mental blocks. Before we can fully harness the power of Zero, we must start on the complicated and challenging task of addressing these underlying issues. It's about digging deep to the very core of these complexities, understanding them, and then working through them, paving the way for Zero to truly transform our lives.

RELEASE WHAT IS NOT YOU

That singular practice of releasing the cards and everything they represented made me feel more excited about life than I'd ever been. As I moved through my new life, the possibilities I received felt endless.

New opportunities that I previously thought were impossible to achieve without my church's firm direction seemed to manifest themselves. Instead of going to sleep at night begging God to take my life, I would doze off with feelings of immense gratitude. I would wake up in the morning excited for the good news of the day. I reveled in the guiding light that radiated through me and couldn't wait to see what magic and miracles would find their way to me—and I to them.

While one might argue that the miracles I experienced after forgiving my brother were in complete alignment with my religion and its teachings, it was indeed the case for that specific phase in my life. Through the miracle of forgiveness, I did manifest great success and experiences. However, as time passed and the Awareness entry point swung wide open, the light of wisdom revealed an uncomfortable (T)ruth: I was not entirely aligned with my authentic self, and this misalignment eventually caught up with me.

Letting go of the formative teachings of my youth served a great purpose in my life, but it was not without consequences. The regular encounters of shame for thoughts or feelings I was having despite my understanding that being who I was—who Source made me to be—was nothing to be ashamed of. These feelings were, of course, present long before the deck of cards. I had never wholly addressed them because I feared what I might find.

If there's nothing else to be learned here, there's this: you cannot heal from something you cannot release, and you cannot release something you are unwilling or unable to address. It took me a long time to realize that if a person wants to embrace another human to the highest degree, they must first embrace an awareness of their (T)rue being without shame, fear, or limitation. The felt board discovery in my parent's basement kicked off the chain of events that sent me on my unexpected journey, not just to envision my happiness but to find and live it.

For so long, I had yearned for the kind of happiness not determined by communal expectations, archaic standards, or societal judgments. I wanted little more than genuine love, true acceptance, and deep understanding. I now know that to find such a thing, one must first express it for themselves. The first step to truly loving, accepting, and understanding others is first to love yourself, accept yourself (just as you are), and seek understanding of yourself through the power of Zero.

13

THE HIGHER THE CLIMB . . .

"Two roads diverged in a wood, and I—I took the one less traveled by, and that has made all the difference."

—Robert Frost, "The Road Not Taken"

Not long after the deck of cards experience, Larry Miller invited me to his office to tell me I could have a job working for his company for as long as I wanted. He expressed gratitude for everything I had done to bring the fun and magic to his restaurant. The next day, his vice president stopped by my office unannounced. He handed me tickets for Larry's dinner table and seats for the upcoming Utah Jazz game. He said Larry wanted me to have them. I felt touched by the gesture and recognition of my talents and efforts.

However, a long-term career with Mr. Miller couldn't offer me what my heart desired. After tasting a real grown-up job sitting in weekly profit and loss meetings, what I really wanted was freedom. I didn't want someone else to determine my financial worth. Through producing events at my work, I became friends with an English entrepreneur and manager for Utah Jazz alumni, Thurl Bailey. He encouraged me to venture out independently. He helped me to realize that my talents were too extensive to be kept in the box of my current employment.

I listened to the advice given to me, along with the brave voice inside myself, and I took a leap of faith. Just like I released the deck of cards that held the constructs of my life, I quit my awesome job without any real plan. I knew I needed to journey into the unknown on my own terms. The experience of releasing the limiting factors in my life and reclaiming my personal power reignited the magic within me. I knew that the greater the risk, the greater the reward, and no matter what, I would land on my feet. The road less traveled was the path I wanted to take; it was my destiny. I was determined to follow a dream solely of my own creation.

MY BIG BREAKS

I started an event planning business, producing everything from corporate events to weddings. About a year after starting my business, the "big break" opportunity arrived. I got a call from a land development company in Salt Lake. They were seeking a party planner to produce their grand opening for a new housing development called Daybreak on the west side of Salt Lake County. During the introduction interview with the marketing director, she described the community as a nod to the classic California Craftsman and Spanish Revival homes in San Diego. Since I had spent time there as a missionary, I could perfectly envision the look they were going for.

Holding back nothing, I let inspiration flow through me and described to her the kind of event I would want to attend. It would be a quintessential all-American neighborhood party with a children's carnival, petting zoo, pinewood derby racing, a chili cook-off, roaming entertainment, and a main stage featuring live musical performances—oh, and while we were at it, we'd get a member of NSYNC there for a meet and greet. After all, they needed kids there to sell those family homes.

After I made up everything I could do for them—literally, I made it up as I went along—the marketing director asked if I wouldn't mind waiting for a moment and excused herself from the room. Moments later, she returned with several middle-aged men in suits. She introduced me to them as their event planner who would be producing the grand opening party. I was dumbfounded. She then asked me to repeat what I had just told her. They were salivating at my words.

"You can make all of this happen?" one of the men in suits asked.

"Yes, absolutely," I said confidently, even though I was asking myself the same question.

"We want the biggest party that Salt Lake City has seen since the Olympics!" another exclaimed.

I had no idea how I would do this, but *YES* had become my motto. I would find a way. We shook on the deal, and the next two months were a whirlwind of planning, organizing, and executing. Taking on the responsibility of producing an event of this magnitude in such a short time with limited resources was a monumental undertaking. But in the end, I delivered exactly what I had promised—a quintessential all-American neighborhood party—and yes, Lance Bass from NSYNC attended the meet and greet. The event was a massive success, and it even earned recognition with a Golden Spike Award for the best event in Utah.

My next big break came in early 2005, thanks to my dear friend Quinn, who encouraged me to write this book. He informed me that the Queer Lounge at the Sundance Film Festival in Park City was in search of a local event planner. They needed someone to help produce the release party for David LaChapelle's movie *Rize*. Now, I had no idea who David LaChapelle was, and the film was completely unfamiliar to me. Nonetheless, I jumped on the opportunity as a chance for networking, and Quinn connected me with the organizer, who hired me.

My task was to create the red carpet media wall and the VIP lounge. With a budget of just $3,000, I had to get creative. The party's theme was "urban hideout" to match the film's vibe, so I scavenged a junkyard for materials. I crafted tables from large wooden copper spools, chairs from egg crates, and decorated the walls with Christmas lights, tinfoil, car parts, graffiti-tagged traffic signs, and *Rize* movie posters. The graffiti artist would only communicate via payphone and required cash up front. The artist conjured up an impressive media wall on large plywood sheets, complemented by sections of red carpet I attached to the floor with duct tape and caution tape strung between blinking a-frame barricades, replacing the traditional velvet rope.

Once everything was in place, the lounge organizers arrived to inspect my work. A man named Trevor, a big-shot event planner from New York City, accompanied them. He was impressed with my creation and eagerly approached me, asking numerous questions. It turned out that he had been hired to design the disco in the adjacent room, and his production was on a much grander scale. He produced events for A-list celebrities and major corporate brands.

He made me an enticing offer: "What are you doing in Utah? You're too big for this place. You need to come work for me in New York City."

I shrugged off his offer, thinking it was merely a compliment. I excused myself to change for the party, but as I was leaving, one of the organizers reminded me that we needed wristbands for the VIPs, which I had left in my truck.

With the small budget allocated to me, I assumed the VIP lounge was destined for a gathering of B-list actors. I didn't give much priority to the wristbands; they were merely tokens for access, or so I thought. Little did I know that these unassuming wristbands would become gold.

When I returned that evening, the event had transformed beyond my expectations. Paparazzi were swarming the venue, and a parade of big-name celebrities lined up for photos in front of the media wall I had spray-painted just hours earlier. It became clear to me that David LaChapelle and his movie *Rize* were a big deal.

As I entered, Trevor spotted me and ushered me into the VIP lounge. "I want to introduce you to some people," he said.

Inside, I found myself face-to-face with Paris Hilton and her sister Nicky, Kevin Richardson from the Backstreet Boys, Jenny McCarthy, Taryn Manning, and Jamie Bell, among others. No big deal, right? Pamela Anderson was sitting with Stephen Dorff on the egg crate chairs I had zip-tied together. I couldn't believe my eyes.

Trevor proudly introduced me to many of the celebrities and boasted about my design of the lounge and media wall. Paris even told me it was "hot." It felt like I had indeed made it, and my leap into the unknown had paid off. This was my moment, and I intended to savor every drop of it.

A week later, I found myself on a one-way flight from Salt Lake City to the bustling heart of New York City, ready to embark on a new adventure working for Trevor. From the moment I landed, there was no time to spare. We hit the ground running in the city that never sleeps, working tirelessly from sunup to sundown. My home base was Trevor's loft apartment in Chinatown, where I bunked with some of his other team members. Trevor's vision was for me to learn every aspect of the event planning world from him and eventually open an office in Los Angeles.

The first morning in the Big Apple, I was roused early, still battling jet lag, for a staff meeting where we discussed the upcoming events for the next few weeks. The schedule was packed to the brim with back-to-back events, but one in particular caught my attention—the release party for 50 Cent's *Valentine Massacre* album, set to take place in Mike Tyson's former Connecticut residence, which 50 Cent had recently acquired.

Reality hit hard once we dove into the work. Our days were non-stop, with no time for respite. Trevor expected me to accompany him to dinners each evening, followed by visits to the local Turkish spas for massages and pool dips. While it may sound glamorous, the novelty quickly wore off. I felt like a prisoner with no say. If I dared to suggest meeting other friends in the city for dinner, he'd dangle the California opportunity above my head as a reminder: "You want to understand what it's like to be me, then you've got to walk in my shoes."

The allure of being part of these A-list events began to sour as my freedom was gradually stripped away, one moment at a time. It felt eerily reminiscent of my missionary days when my life followed a rigid schedule I couldn't control. I grew weary, day by day. Trevor's verbal and emotional abuse escalated. He expected me to anticipate his every need, and any lapse would lead to him screaming at the top of his lungs, berating me for perceived stupidity.

The breaking point came while working on 50 Cent's party. The MTV production crew was present, capturing the setup, and a fellow event planner, who made Trevor seem mild-mannered, was the star of the show. She went around barking orders and being overtly rude for the sake of tantalizing TV. Amidst the chaos, I realized that this glamorous Hollywood world had a darker side, one I no longer wanted to be a part of.

I approached Trevor's assistant, quietly pleading for a flight back to Salt Lake City. He empathized with my plight and managed to book a flight for me, set for the next evening after our return to New York. After Trevor had gone to bed, I quietly packed my bags, trying not to make a sound. When the taxi arrived, I made my way down the stairs as stealthily as possible, careful not to wake him. Despite my efforts, Trevor heard me leaving. He charged down the stairs in a fit of rage, demanding to know where I was going.

When I opened the cab's door, I glanced back to see him flailing his arms and screaming, warning me that I'd never work in his town again. My heart raced, unsure if his anger would turn violent, but I found my voice for a final message: "My bark may be weak, but my bite is strong."

"What does that mean?" he screamed, desperate for an answer.

I shut the door, and the cab sped away. I took a deep breath, exhaling a sigh of immense relief. I had escaped without pay, but I didn't care. Freedom, as I soon realized, was priceless.

DÉJÀ VU

The next day, I woke up in Salt Lake City to my phone ringing. On the line was a personal assistant representing a high-profile Beverly Hills family searching for an event planner for their daughter's Bat Mitzvah. It turned out that a contact from the Sundance party had referred me for the job. The assistant asked if I could attend an interview the following day at none other than the iconic Beverly Wilshire Hotel, made famous by *Pretty Woman*. Despite my exhaustion from my intense New York experience, I agreed to make the ten-hour drive to Los Angeles to meet a woman named Christine.

When I arrived at the opulent Beverly Wilshire, I felt like a hopeful contestant on a high-stakes reality show competition. Inside the grand ballroom where the event was to be held, I finally met Christine. She was the epitome of the kind of person who'd spare no expense, dropping $250,000 on her little girl's birthday celebration. She was beautiful, blonde, and exuded an over-the-top personality reminiscent of the Real Housewives.

I was the last event planner she was interviewing, and she quickly rattled off the names of A-list event planners she had considered, including Oprah's own event coordinator. She posed the pivotal question: Why should she hire me, an unknown from Utah?

I could feel the pressure building as I listed my limited experience, striving to project confidence, fully aware that in the world of event planning, perception is paramount. Abruptly, Christine interrupted me mid-sentence to inquire about my birthday.

"August second," I replied, somewhat unsure.

To my surprise, she gasped in astonishment. "I can't believe it! I'm August first! I knew there was a connection between us, my fellow Leo."

Astrology held a special significance in her world, and I'd later discover that many of her life decisions were influenced by some sort of belief in magic. She often looked to shamans and psychics for guidance, venturing off to the four corners of the earth for spiritual retreats.

A contemplative pause followed, during which Christine rummaged through her notepad. She peered at me, her gaze seemingly penetrating into my soul. "I want my daughter's Bat Mitzvah to be a fairytale," she mused, still studying me. "There's something about you, though I can't quite put my finger on it. I'm a risk-taker by nature, and for some reason, I'm willing to take a chance on you. Be at my house at five p.m. this Sunday, ready to present your vision to me and my family and show us how we can transform this space into a magical fairytale kingdom."

She jotted down her address, tore the sheet from her notepad, and handed it to me. I was left in stunned silence. I couldn't fully grasp what had just transpired, but one thing was certain: I owed a debt of gratitude to my mother for carrying me for those ten months, ensuring I became a Leo.

On that Sunday evening, I arrived at Christine's residence promptly at 5 p.m. Her husband, sister, and mother welcomed me, with the little princess in tow. As we sat down for dinner, I observed the dynamics of their family. To my surprise, they appeared remarkably down-to-earth and hospitable. They made me feel genuinely welcomed.

Following the meal, Christine stood up and delicately chimed her knife against her wine glass's rim like a bell. "I now pass the floor to Chad, who has prepared a vision and overview of our Bat Mitzvah."

I stood at my seat and retrieved a neatly folded paper from my jacket pocket, where I had detailed my concept for the event's design and flow. I cleared the gulp in my throat and read it aloud to the entire family. While I read my vision, I could see a sparkle in Christine's eyes. As I concluded, she enthusiastically clapped her hands and dramatically exclaimed, "Bravo!"

That was it—I had the job.

Following that initial proposal dinner, everything kicked into high gear. Christine insisted that I move into her house to plan the event. Not only would we be planning this event together, but she had started an event planning business and wanted me to be her partner. Our days began early and extended into the evening. Any attempt to make plans with friends outside of work was met with suspicion and guilt trips. I often found myself sneaking out after Christine had retired to her wing of the house, feeling a bit like a rebellious teenager.

Déjà vu?

Her true motives became crystal clear during a lunchtime outing. She revealed to me a grand scheme that involved me helping her leave her husband. Together, we would build Los Angeles's most prominent event company with her husband's money. Her Hollywood connections would lead to a reality show about us, culminating in her divorce. Everything began to feel like a grim shadow of the situation I had just escaped from in New York City.

However, this time, I didn't flee in the dead of night—at least, not yet. I was determined to see the event through to its success. When it concluded, Christine and her husband sat me down and presented a life-altering proposal: for me to relocate to Los Angeles. They would give me a salary, provide an office, and help me get an apartment. All I needed to do was say yes.

Instantly, I was transported back to that practice room at BYU, confronted once again with a dream presented to me on a silver platter. Still, I couldn't bring myself to accept. I was acutely aware that such a choice would shackle my freedom. I'd become a pawn in Christine's grand plan to sabotage her husband, a path I was adamantly unwilling to take. With heartfelt appreciation for the opportunity, I collected my paycheck and began the journey back to Utah with my freedom and integrity intact.

ALIGNING WITH PURPOSE

As we navigate through life, striving to align our path with our dreams, we often find ourselves at crossroads where choices can redefine the course of our future. It's only when we look back that we realize some decisions were influenced by self-sabotage, stemming from our reluctance to let go of (t)ruths that keep us bound to familiar patterns. I, too, succumbed to such self-sabotage when I turned away from my dream of performing at Disney in pursuit of fulfilling the promise of my patriarchal blessing. That choice left me with years of regret.

With an expanded perspective, driven by self-awareness, we may recognize that certain choices were, in fact, the right ones. Reflecting on my experiences at Sundance, New York, and Los Angeles, I can confidently affirm that walking away from those people and those opportunities proved to be the correct path. They did not serve my higher purpose, nor did they honor my authentic self. Again, this insight only emerged in retrospect.

Given that we lack a crystal ball to glimpse the future, how do we, when standing at a crossroads, distinguish whether choices arise from self-sabotage fueled by fear or from the divine paths rooted in our authentic selves? To answer this question, we must return to the entry point of self-awareness, shedding all preconceived judgments. We must ask ourselves, "What do I genuinely desire? Is this aligned with my life's purpose? Am I making this choice for myself, or does it merely appease the desires of others?"

Eventually, we must align ourselves with our chosen path, whatever it may be, assume full ownership of our decisions, and release any hindrances obstructing our way, thereby clearing a path to our intended destination. From there, you must engage your power and take a leap of faith, much like the day I decided to quit my job and jump with confidence into the unknown.

When living a life that authentically aligns with our purpose, we possess an innate ability to discern the right choice in the present moment. If we are still unsure, once we make a choice and set our path in motion, it is crucial to extend grace to ourselves. Often, it is the road less traveled that offers the wisdom to ultimately reveal our (T)rue life purpose, guiding us toward our divine destination. Even unforeseen detours lead to where we are meant to be when guided by Zero.

After I returned to Salt Lake City from Los Angeles, I took some time off to recharge and refocus my energy by returning to music. I had been so busy chasing dreams that were ultimately not my dreams that I had abandoned this part of my life, forgetting how much it made me feel alive. I started writing with a couple of local musicians and put my heartache from the breakup with Jerri into written word and song. Through the process, I composed a song I was genuinely proud of, one that encapsulated themes of loss and liberation.

Around the same time, I shifted my focus to building my events company, seeking growth opportunities. I envisioned leveraging my event expertise for street fairs with artisans and live music, like the one I experienced in Palm Springs while growing up. St. George, Utah, stood out as the ideal location, strategically located between Las Vegas and Zion National Park. After presenting my idea to the city and gaining their enthusiastic approval, I relocated to Southern Utah to produce the weekly events on Main Street downtown.

What made this experience truly special for me was not only being a part of something to bring the community together but also the opportunity to immerse myself in the city's music scene. Local artists and bands wanted to perform at the fair, and this network eventually led me to a recording studio to record the song I had written. With the help of my friend Quinn, who came up from Los Angeles to assist with production, we created a professional studio single. I decided to submit my song to various contests on platforms like Myspace.

I came across a competition for the film *John Tucker Must Die*, where they were looking for original songs for the film soundtrack. While my song was not selected for the film, they did make me their #1 top friend on the movie's Myspace page, which quickly grew my fanbase. Shortly afterward, my song received a nomination for an LA Music Award, and

I was invited to perform it live in Malibu. Naturally, I was thrilled by the positive response to my song and eagerly accepted the invitation.

Out of the blue, I received a call from a woman who introduced herself as Carla Ondrasik. She had obtained my number during a massage at one of the spas and resorts in St. George. It turns out a good friend of mine was her massage therapist and during their session, she mentioned her work in music publishing. My friend conveniently had my demo and passed it on to her. Carla called me on her way back to Los Angeles, expressing her love for my song and her desire to help me with publishing. She revealed that she was John Ondrasik's wife, the artist *Five for Fighting*, and mentioned she had discovered him before marrying him. She gave me her email to keep in touch and asked me to compose three more songs.

I couldn't believe how quickly everything was unfolding. It felt as though a shooting star of fame was hurtling toward me. I made my way to Malibu, ready to perform my song live. But as I stepped onto the stage, a sudden wave of anxiety and resistance welled up within me. I no longer wanted to be there. Despite performing on stage throughout my college years and dreaming of moments like this, all I wanted to do was run.

I pushed past the panic and dread that churned within me and delivered my song. As soon as it was over, I wanted to throw up. Once offstage, people approached me, telling me how much they loved the song and how well I performed. I didn't care. Their compliments did not matter to me. All I could think of was a swift exit. That day, I left the stage, never to write another song.

Just like before, I walked away, or perhaps more accurately, ran away from my dream. Once again, I invested my energy into what I believed I wanted, and Zero began to create what I call a "baby universe." Everything within this realm aligned with my efforts, propelling me toward success.

But why did I turn my back on this opportunity? Why did I abandon the baby universe of being a singer-songwriter that I had brought to life? I could have had a career on stage, rubbing shoulders with celebrities. Or perhaps hosting my own trashy TV show, screaming orders at people like that woman at 50 Cent's house party. Was I not strong enough to swim with the sharks? Did my emotional sensitivity render me incapable of success, or was I simply too afraid to engage my power?

No. I shoved a proverbial cork in that baby universe because I would not be controlled by anyone, nor did I want to be in a situation in which I was not in control. There it was, the final entry point to Zero. I was Engaging Power—my power. I had the ability and courage to walk away from a dream not meant for me. I engaged my personal power to say "no" for all the right reasons. Not out of fear. I knew I had made the right decision, and my gut—my natural *knowing*—verified that for me. When you engage your power, you will feel a certainty with your choices, a confidence that emits from deep within you. Choices made when you are coming from a place of Zero are in perfect alignment with your authentic self. There is unlimited power when you allow the beauty of Source to flow through you. When you no longer resist who you are created to be, you act from a place of self-acceptance and self-love.

And here lies the elegance of Zero. We may set out on a path only to discover it's not leading where we genuinely wish to go. That is okay. Exploration and discovery are essential parts of life and Zero. When you access Zero, you will be presented with every opportunity you set your sights on, and some won't be what you expected or wanted. This is when you must fully engage your power and listen to your authentic self—wisdom will light the way.

The power of Zero allows us to swiftly course-correct without the burden of shame or the fear of repercussions. It's not about what you are walking away from; it's what you are walking toward that you cannot always see. As the adage goes, it's not the destination that truly matters but the journey itself. Keeping with this perspective, there is no such thing as failure; there are only the endless possibilities of what lies ahead.

What holds us in the past ceases to exist when it's raised to the power of Zero. This includes our regrets, missed opportunities, or old narratives—they all lose their hold over us. This process is not about erasing our stories or denying or invalidating our experiences. Instead, we're changing our relationship with them and how they influence us. By applying Zero, what has held us back loses its negative charge and becomes neutral, opening up a landscape where we are defined not by what has been, but by what can be.

14

IT'S IN YOUR GENES

Negativity is the enemy of creativity.

—David Lynch, Interview with Marianne Schnall,
Huffington Post (2014)

It's been said that "hurt people, hurt people."

Well, few truer words were ever spoken. That's the difficulty of being human; we collect our trauma and carry it with us. Not only this, but we also acquire new trauma as we go. Even more striking is that we often pass on these unresolved issues from one generation to the next, sometimes without even realizing it. It's like a hidden legacy, as parents unwittingly hand down their trauma to their children, and the cycle goes on. I had a firsthand experience with the profound impact of intergenerational trauma during my time in St. George.

With my savings and some seed money given to me by the city of St. George to advertise and get things rolling, I successfully opened the street fair. From its first night, it was a hit, and it only improved from there. Every week, the event gained more and more momentum. The towns-people were excited that someone had come into their community to do something new to bring people together. I was being approached and thanked every time I turned around.

As the fair grew in popularity, a small group of local business owners who were part of the Retailer's Association of Downtown (RAD) began to make a fuss. As with all such scenarios, there was a ringleader, a woman named Annabelle. She was a member of a Mormon family that had been in St. George for five generations. Annabelle and her group did not like this "outsider" and his vendors coming in and taking over the downtown retail space. As a result, the city council approached me and asked me to work with RAD moving forward. No problem. Revitalizing downtown could only be improved by partnering with an organization dedicated to the good of the community, right?

Far too quickly, it was apparent that Annabelle and her supporters were not interested in a partnership. They would nitpick every aspect of the street fair, block any semblance of progress, and attempt to sabotage everything I tried to do. It didn't take long before I got additional push-back from the city. My street fair had been in place for about six months the day I received a phone call from the city manager. He informed me I should attend the city council meeting that evening but didn't go into any specifics. Despite being short notice, I cleared my schedule, arrived at the town hall, sat in the back of the room, and was surprised to see my street fair was first on the agenda.

As the meeting commenced, the RAD group, led by Annabelle, stood up and took the podium together. One RAD member was carrying a giant poster board with photos pasted to it. I felt the blood rush to my face. The images were personal photos of me and blocks of text from my Myspace page—all of which were to claim that my personal lifestyle did not represent "good Mormon character." They proposed that I was not who I represented myself to be and not a good representation of the community.

The police chief took the mic to say my street fair brought numerous weekly arrests, vandalism, trash, and many "unsavory characters, the type

St. George does not want in our community or our streets." I was flabbergasted by how fast this witch trial had turned into a kangaroo court.[1] My entire identity and livelihood were being burned at the stake. The meeting adjourned with the city council voting to revoke my license and close the street fair.

I later discovered RAD appealed to the council for their own street fair license in the following meeting. Naturally, they received it, and they opened their own fair not long after. Given that I had been working with them for the past several weeks, they had access to all my systems, processes, and vendor contact information. And that was it; Annabelle had won. In one fell swoop, I'd lost all the money I'd invested and was out of business.

I had let it be known to members of RAD that I was working with the city of Henderson, Nevada, to create a similar street fair event. This was a fatal mistake on my part. When I called my contact in Henderson, they had already received a phone call from Anabelle in St. George and were no longer interested.

I was embarrassed and devastated, not to mention spitfire angry. I had very little left in savings. All I could think about was how unfair it was. I got no due process or opportunity to defend myself. I had learned firsthand what it was to be "hometowned." Before I moved to the town, I had heard of St. George's reputation for being exclusionary to outsiders. I thought the rumors to be a false remnant of the Mountain Meadow Massacre, but after what had happened to me, they felt strangely eerie.[2]

In case you have never heard of this tragedy, allow me to give you a brief overview of this dark chapter in US history. This bloody incident occurred on September 11th, 1857, in Mountain Meadows, a valley thirty miles north of St. George that emigrants used as a resting area along the Mormon trail to California. At that time, there was extreme tension between the Mormon leader Brigham Young and the US government. Young was the governor of Utah, but conflicts between his theocratic rule and non-Mormon federal officials led to accusations of intimidation and document destruction. This situation escalated to the point that President James Buchanan declared Utah in "rebellion" against the United States, which brought federal troops into the picture.

Fearful of past violence against Mormons, Young's followers prepared for war. Declaring defiance against the government, Young was quoted as saying, "I will fight them, and I will fight all hell." Brigham Young had a strategy to avoid fighting the federal army directly. Instead, he targeted their supply lines and blocked the trails that emigrants used to pass through Utah on their way to California. This included stopping Mormons from selling supplies to emigrants and allowing Native American tribes friendly with the Mormons to harass the wagon trains.

Amid this turmoil, a group of emigrants known as the Baker-Fancher party crossed paths with the Mormons in Utah. The wagon train consisted of a majority of families from Arkansas en route to California. Upon reaching Salt Lake City, the party was refused stocks and continued their journey southward along the Mormon trail, eventually stopping to rest at Mountain Meadows. During their trek, rumors and conspiracies began to circulate about the party's behavior toward Mormon settlers, which added tensions as the climate of war hysteria toward outsiders prevailed.

On September 7th, the Baker-Fancher party was attacked by local Mormon militia disguised as Native Americans with the help of some Native American Paiutes. The emigrants did their best to withstand the onslaught, much to the frustration of the militia. The siege continued for five days, during which the families had limited access to water, food, and dwindling ammunition. Eventually, concerns arose among the Mormon militia leadership that some emigrants had seen white men, leading to an order to kill all the emigrants, except for small children under the age of seven, to prevent survivors from testifying that Mormons had been involved in the attack.

On September 11th, two militiamen initially approached the Baker-Fancher party with a white flag, followed by militia officer John D. Lee. He claimed to have negotiated a truce with the Paiute Native Americans under Mormon protection and offered to safely escort the emigrants back to Cedar City in exchange for their supplies and livestock. The emigrants accepted, exiting their camp and being separated by gender. Upon a signal, the militia turned and shot the men while hidden militia members in nearby areas ambushed and killed the women. The massacre was kept secret.

Lee and his men murdered nearly one hundred and twenty civilians that day. They stole their supplies and livestock, and they adopted the surviving children out to local families. The Mormon militia struck a vow of silence, and a place was devised to falsely attribute the massacre solely to the Paiutes. A cover-up began throughout the church hierarchy, with the sole goal of protecting the church's image.

While the Mormon war ended in 1858, the stain of the Mountain Meadows Massacre persisted. John Lee, a fugitive, eventually went on trial for murder in 1876, and Brigham Young ensured that the trial would focus solely on Lee's guilt, sparing the LDS Church's involvement. Lee was convicted and executed in 1877, marking the tragic end of this dark chapter in Mormon history.

Of course, I am not comparing my experience and that of the massacre in any real way. However, I am saying that entitlement, judgment, and fear of the unknown are often the root of wrongdoing, which stems from trauma embedded into our Human Story Code.

INTERGENERATIONAL TRAUMA

Our codes are built initially by the stories our parents, teachers, and society teach us. These stories create building blocks from which our Human Story Code is constructed. More than this, there is the context of our genetic codes and ancestral lineage. As it pertains to trauma, this includes what is called intergenerational trauma.

Intergenerational trauma, also termed historical trauma, multigenerational trauma, and secondary traumatization, is passed down from a person who directly experiences a traumatic incident to subsequent generations.[3] Interestingly, according to the American Psychology Association, parental communication about the event and the nature of family functioning appear particularly important in trauma transmission.[4] Initial research on intergenerational trauma concentrated on the children, grandchildren, and great-grandchildren of survivors of the Holocaust and Japanese-American internment camps, but it has now broadened to include American Indian tribes and the families of Vietnam War veterans, among others.

An individual's life experiences are as unique as their fingerprints, including the traumas they've endured in their lifespan and those that have been passed on to them. When it comes to our individual human development, this is the most overlooked and underappreciated truth known to man.

A developed understanding of the interrelated and independent nature of human needs is critical for individual growth and development. It helps to understand human nature and the integrated effects of human *nurture*, as we discussed in Chapter 6. Studying psychology and sociology allows for a deeper understanding of both of these perspectives. Interestingly enough, the study of biology, particularly epigenetics, tells us even more about how they are verifiably interrelated.

Epigenetics studies the actual mechanisms that switch genes on and off. Genes work within DNA sequencing to provide the body with instructions on making complex molecules that trigger various biological actions that carry out life functions. Because of this, we can understand how epigenetics control genes through *nature*. It's why a skin cell looks different from a blood or hair cell. All these cells contain the same DNA but are expressed differently. Epigenetics also control genes through environmental stimuli—supporting *nurture*. It is due to the different combinations of the turning on and off of genes via both nature and nurture that make each human utterly unique.

To make things even more interesting, current research indicates that some epigenetics can be inherited. This aligns with the premise of the Human Story Code as it conveys that we are made not only from what has happened or is happening within and to our bodies genetically but also that which occurred in or to our ancestral DNA.

There was a study in 2015 that found children of Holocaust survivors had epigenetic changes to a particular gene that links to cortisol levels (a hormone involved in stress response). Rachel Yehuda, director of the Traumatic Stress Studies Division at the Mount Sinai School of Medicine, was excited by these findings, stating, "The idea of a signal, an epigenetic finding that is in offspring of trauma survivors, can mean many things." She says, "Where we are with epigenetics today feels like how it was when we first researched PTSD. It was a controversial diagnosis. Not everyone believed there could be long-term effects of trauma."[5]

This discussion of intergenerational trauma and epigenetics provides an interesting perspective of my experience in the city of St. George. The fear of outsiders was still prevalent among the city's residents. Many of the descendants of the Mormons who helped perpetrate and conceal the Mountain Meadows Massacre still resided within the St. George community. One of those was Anabelle. A close friend of mine who worked for the church, with access to family records, traced her lineage to a member of the Mormon militia involved in the massacre. And she was not the only one. Almost every person who stood up in that city council meeting to speak out against my character were also direct descendants of those responsible for the heinous murders of over one hundred innocent people in cold blood thirty miles north of city hall one hundred and fifty years prior.

The result of this intergenerational trauma was that my character had been assassinated by these people who, in the end, were simply afraid of me. Their fear ultimately destroyed my business and reputation because I was an outsider perceived as a disruptor of their established status quo. The RAD group, and many others in positions of power within the city, viewed me as a threat that needed to be removed.

I was justifiably angry at the treatment I had received, and every instinct in me demanded justice. I had to do something, so I hired a private investigator and started first by going to the police station to request the public records of the arrests at my event. To my astonishment, there were none, and there were no police reports of vandalism. When I approached the police chief about this, he got aggressively angry and accused me of calling him a liar. It became evident they had all conspired against me. Next, I found an attorney who helped me file a notice of claim, indicating my intention to sue the city for their actions. My investigator spoke to many of the retailers undercover and got a repeated response, "We don't need his kind in our town." They also said that if I'd just gone to an LDS Church, I would better understand their culture and would have produced an event that was more aligned with their values. It was clear they hadn't conducted any actual research on me.

I allowed this experience to completely consume my life. I couldn't talk to anyone without going into all the nitty-gritty details of what happened to me. I repeatedly shared the same story to anyone who'd lend an ear in the hope of gaining some sympathy. This turned my life into a cyclone of negativity like a never-ending tabloid drama. It felt as though the entire world was aligned against me, to the extent that I was getting pulled over by the police almost every month; my driver's license even got suspended.

By May, the year following the incident, I was categorically miserable. I burned through the money in my bank account and spent the previous months entirely consumed by anger. My thirst for revenge powered my efforts to assemble the documentation to pursue the lawsuit. The local news covered my story, where I bitterly confessed how the city and RAD had wronged me.

However, playing the victim didn't satisfy the gnawing hole of emptiness that had grown inside of me. I was depressed and pained by what felt like a never-ending cyclone of suffering and frustration. In the end, I believed I was defeated with no hope. I had no idea what to do. I'd spent the first half of 2006 lying in bed, wallowing in self-pity. I had taken a second mortgage on my house to help fund the street fair, and my payment due date was looming. I didn't even have enough money to put gas in my car. What little food I had left in my pantry dwindled by the day.

One morning, I was in bed thinking about what a waste of time and energy this all had been. I'd accomplished nothing over the past six months. The small leverage I did have was the lawsuit, which even worked against me by sucking up what money I had left. I was depressed, isolated, and lonely.

I thought back to the lessons of my grandfather. The beliefs and understandings I'd once held so dear. I knew how manifestation works. I knew I could attract the reality I sought into my life. I had successfully employed these principles before, so I knew it was within my capacity to do so again. I possessed the necessary tools. The trouble was, I'd been engulfed in a cyclone of toxicity for the past six months, inadvertently fueling it, granting it more and more power until it had escalated into a Category 5 storm. And that's precisely where I found myself, utterly immobilized within the eye of this tempest with no apparent escape.

As I've said before, Zero is the creator of everything. Looking back, if I had harnessed the power of Zero to clear space and align with the successes that brought me to St. George, then I had also used Zero to create all of the drama when the St. George mob came for me. I allowed a cyclone of victimhood to form, instead of remaining true to my principles and directing my power toward maintaining emotional control.

We can't control every situation life throws at us, but we can control how we react to them. It's like facing a real-life cyclone—you can't just grab that fire hose and try to push it back. Despite feeling powerful and invincible, some basic laws of physics are still in play, and the cyclone will come out on top. So when we find ourselves in the path of a negative energy cyclone, what do we do?

We seek shelter. We don't feed into the negativity or let it consume us. Instead, we let it pass and then carry on with our lives. It all boils down to choice, which begins in the mind. Our minds are powerful tools, and how we engage with life's storms starts right there.

At that moment, I became aware of what I'd done. I'd created a pit to wallow in. I couldn't see a way out because I had buried myself with my own pain. I knew that even the simplest thoughts can tremendously impact your emotions and behaviors. I'd allowed the toxic experience of St. George to mingle with the other traumas of my life, producing a perfect storm of ruminating thoughts. My mind had begun to narrate a mantra of self-doubt, pity, and despair: *I'm not worthy of success and happiness because of who I am. Life is not fair and especially cruel to me. Those who hurt me need to pay for what they've done.*

I'd allowed these thoughts to materialize into my entire reality. I suddenly realized that this is what rock bottom looked like. The only way out was up. I needed to switch into a completely different lane and build myself a ladder out of this pit I had dug for myself.

BE OPEN TO RECEIVING

So, I decided to take the first step toward the light. I would get out of bed and walk in the canyon I had grown to love. The house I then lived in backed up to Snow Canyon State Park.[6] It had been far too long since I'd ventured into that canyon. I knew if anything could help me find my way, it would be in the nature of the canyon. I needed to let go. I had to pour out all this negativity and release it to the canyon walls.

As soon as I parked my car at the trailhead, the gravity of everything I'd been through engulfed me. I began to sob uncontrollably. I struggled to the trailhead, where I let out a tremendous scream, empowered by the unstoppable flow of tears. I roared all the emotions that had kept me in bed for the past six months into the canyon. I released my feelings of how cruel life had been to me. I howled into the ether that I deserved what was mine.

The first half of my walk was a conversation with the canyon's walls. The red sandstone cliffs shot straight up from the ground, towering over me like ancient elders. One formation looked like a gigantic heart, which I had nicknamed the heart of the canyon. I stopped before the heart and focused my words and energy on it.

Strangely, it felt like the rocks were listening to me, absorbing the heaviness of my heart. That is when I could feel things start to shift. Intention was underway. I felt the tension in my shoulders begin to release. I noticed my breath traveling in and out of my lungs; they felt like the first real breaths I'd taken in so very long. I was present in my body. I began to feel alive—truly alive—and with this, I continued pouring my heart out to the canyon as I climbed.

When I reached the top canyon ledge, I looked out across the vista and saw so much more than the canyon. I saw the sky, the clouds, the trees, and the shrubs. I saw the intricate placement of precarious rocks and boulders that were lodged in the nooks and crannies of the great red walls. And I saw myself, standing there amidst all of it without a single other human in sight. I remember looking at my hands and knowing I, too, am part of this creation. And with that awareness, I raised up my hands, saying out loud, "I choose to receive."

I began to list all the things that I wanted to receive.

"*I choose to receive financial stability.*"

"I choose to receive *lasting happiness.*"

"I choose to receive *unconditional love.*"

"I choose to receive *a business that will create joy and happiness for others.*"

As I spoke, I conjured up an image in my mind's eye of power, resource, goodness, and abundance flowing into my body. I experienced a euphoric high like I had never experienced before.[7] I felt contentment and acceptance flow through my being as I marveled at the powerful beauty of it all. How could a person one minute be so far away from the magic and then, in a shift of spirit, be right smack amidst it? Recalling this experience, I now understand I was overcome with the majesty of Zero. I successfully opened all five entry points and set my intentions into motion. I felt my entire body lighten as I made my way to the trail in order to return home.

As I danced down the canyon, I could feel empowerment beaming through my entire body and soul. I felt magnetic. Unstoppable. With all this excitement flowing through me, not an ounce of fear remained. Convinced everything I'd just said aloud was on its way to me at warp speed, I was reborn.

Sooner than I could have imagined, the magic of Zero would prove fruitful yet again. When I returned to my house, I opened my laptop to find a new email from my past client, Daybreak. Fortunately, they needed my services again as they were moving into phase two of the development. I couldn't believe it. The email came in while I had hiked in the canyon. Here it was, my first step back to financial stability, my first sign that Zero was at work within me again.

I called the client directly, and we quickly negotiated a deal. I would immediately move back to Salt Lake City to produce all their events over the summer. They wired me an advance overnight to get started. I was far from where I needed to be emotionally as I nursed my wounds, but I had taken my next right step. My words in the canyon and the intention behind them had found their way, and that was enough—just enough.

TIME TO TAKE OWNERSHIP

Although I had found my touchpoint with Zero in the canyon, I still had a long healing journey ahead of me. I needed to release the trauma

I had experienced with the people of St. George, not to mention how it compounded my previous traumatic experiences that made me feel unworthy and unloved.

I still felt disabled by my pain. Even though I moved forward with my new career opportunity, in many ways, I was entrenched in what had happened to me. Their words "We don't need his kind in our town" replayed in my mind over and over. For a fair amount of time, I had developed a habit of identifying as a victim and ruminating over my traumas—one that I wasn't even aware of.

This is a difficult practice to break, especially when it becomes embedded deep into our Human Story Code. Even after I moved on from St. George, if I ever encountered a listening ear, I would tell them my story without sparing any of the theatrics, especially the part about the people being descendants of mass murderers. As a result, I put far too much energy into believing that any misery I experienced was caused by others—most recently, those people in St. George. I projected the responsibility of my happiness onto outside forces rather than focusing on the internal ownership of my life.

Thinking back, I am again so grateful for my grandfather's teachings. His life example inspired me when I was lying in my bed of utter misery. His lessons were the beacon of light I needed in that dark time. I'd hate to imagine my life if I did not have such a resource. The optimist in me wants to believe that every life has access to a sliver of hope. That sliver of hope is different for each person, but whatever that sliver needs to be will find its way into the dark during their greatest moment of need.

That said, if my grandfather's lessons had not pulled me out of the muck of my mind, it would have been something else that brought me to a place of awareness. I don't know. But I do know that, without awareness, it is impossible to break free from victimhood, to find new footing in not just the current reality but the one that is to be.

My own life experiences have taught me that two primary issues arise when we find ourselves facing adversity. First, getting stuck in the rut of negativity (or victimhood) is easy. Second, it's just as easy to forget that we have a restless creative power that consistently seeks to be released into the world. Ignoring these truths during adversity can wreak serious havoc on a person's health and well-being. Instability born here can quickly manifest into helplessness—and thus, powerlessness. As negativity is the enemy of creativity, losing personal power is the enemy of success.

When you've lost your way, it's crucial to assess the conditions and create an objective that will disrupt the status quo—if even just a small one. One right step in the right direction can do wonders for a person. Before venturing to the canyon, my negative feelings encompassed me. I lacked the perspective to see how powerful and capable I was. Thankfully, I found that sliver of hope that allowed me to identify the negative feelings I was experiencing and recognize them as something within my control. In my grandfather's wisdom, I was able to acknowledge that difficult situations and feelings are temporary. Just *how* temporary is dependent upon action, or the lack thereof.

It helps to remember first that all feelings are part of the human experience; life is indeed full of uncertainty, and change is inevitable. Whenever I feel the need to put the law of Zero into practice, I am reminded of what it is to be human. It is natural for us to be ravaged by fear, anger, grief, sadness, and even complacency when traversing a problematic time or contending with a particular affliction.

Understanding Zero does not take away the challenges and difficulties in life—it merely makes them easier to manage. Our feelings are important. They are warning signs and precursors to change. This is good news.

Negative feelings are valid; they exist to let a person know that change is present or imminent. As John Maxwell put it, "Change is inevitable, growth is optional."[8] So here's the deal: negativity is a sign that something needs to be managed. Negative feelings are often the result of trauma, stress, or anxiety. They are very real, and they have very real implications and very real consequences if left unmanaged. Unmanaged negativity creates stagnation or digression, while managed negative feelings allow growth and perspective.

Everyone experiences negative feelings both consciously and unconsciously; these are universal aspects of the human condition and nothing to be ashamed of. Many people fail to realize they are not powerless while contending with such emotions. The truth is just the opposite. People are truly powerful—*always*. They just need to find alignment to see it.

15

CLARITY COMES IN
MYSTERIOUS WAYS

You don't drown by falling in the water;
you drown by staying there.

—Edwin Louis Cole,
Profiles in Courageous Manhood (1998)

That summer of 2006, a month shy of my thirtieth birthday, my sister Cherylyn was preparing to leave for her eighteen-month mission in Illinois. She and I decided that a day together on Utah Lake would make for an ideal sendoff. We planned to borrow our mom's Ford Explorer and rent a couple of Jet Skis for the day. As luck would have it, the outfitters let us pick up the machines the afternoon before our scheduled day rental, which meant bonus time out on the lake before sunset.

At the last minute, I started making phone call invitations to friends to meet us at the lake. One of those calls was to our second cousin, Simon. He was excited by the invitation for time out on the lake. He and I had grown close since he'd moved to Utah to attend Brigham Young University. He had been facing some difficulties both socially and emotionally, as well as struggling with some personal demons. I guess he'd found a rare, confirming connection in me. On my end of things, it felt good to provide some support to him during such a difficult stage of life.

At any rate, my sister and I packed our life jackets and the safety whistle I had received as a Christmas gift and set out on what would be the eve of our last adventure together for a very long time. My friends and Simon were to meet us at the lake where we would run out as much gas as possible on the Jet Skis, one single and one double.

As we arrived at the lake, the conditions were picturesque. Mount Timpanogos, still capped with streaks of winter snow, towered over the calm blue waters with its majestic rocky formations. The sound of motorboats roared in the distant background as the sun peeked through the white summer clouds in the sky. I looked over at my sister, who grinned ear to ear as she, too, became enveloped in the beautiful embrace of nature. At that moment, I felt so happy and grateful.

My friends had yet to arrive, but Simon was there and ready. We wasted no time getting the Jet Skis in the water. Since sunset was fast approaching and we were only going to be out for a short time, I wasn't initially going to wear a life vest, but my gut instinct told me otherwise. I went back to the Explorer and grabbed vests for myself, my sister, and Simon.

Once on the water, we quickly realized that the single machine was much faster than the double, and with a bit of maneuvering, we could squeeze two people on it and amp up the fun. It soon became the machine of choice for everyone, and Simon, my sister, and I began to take turns with two people riding on the single and the third scooting around on the double.

As my sister and Simon were zipping along on the single, I stopped for a moment to call my friends to let them know where to meet me when they arrived. I opened the seat compartment and retrieved my cell phone. As I sat there, a small boat approached me and began to circle my watercraft. "Is everything okay? Do you need a tow?" the man on the boat asked. I told him I was just making a quick call and thanked him for the kind gesture.

As he drove off, I could hear laughter over the lawn mower–sounding engine as Cherylyn and Simon spun donuts around me. They were really having a great time. Simon motioned for me to swap machines with Cherylyn and join him on the single. "Hop on." he said, "I'll take ya for a spin."

I jumped on and firmly linked my knuckles around his rib cage before he took off full throttle. Next, he started cutting really hard back and forth. Just as I was about to ask him to slow down, he said, "I have some built-up anger toward you." And then, he gunned it and turned sharply at full speed, crashing us both hard into the water as the Jet Ski flipped over entirely.

I didn't know which end was up and struggled to get to the surface. By the time I'd gathered my wits, I was pissed. I had no idea what Simon was talking about, but it was obvious that the crash was intentional. Without exchanging words, I grabbed the key off his wrist and went about the effort of turning the jet-ski back over. From across the way, Cherylyn had seen our high-speed crash and rushed over immediately to make sure we were okay. She jumped off the double to help me get the machine squared back up.

We struggled to get the engine to fire, and it was soon very clear that the motor was flooded. It wasn't going to start. "We'll tow it. It'll be fine." She offered the sentence as more of a question than a solution.

"Yeah, okay," I agreed. "Let's get the rope from the other jet ski, and we'll just take it back."

We turned our attention to Simon to gesture to him to bring the working jet ski over. But it was like he'd never been with us at all. Simon and the other machine, with my cell phone and whistle, were gone, vanished without a trace. Caught up in the frustration of our failed joint efforts to get the engine to turn over, we didn't even realize he'd left. "He must have gone for help. We'll just wait," I reassured Cherylyn.

As we waited, I noticed the water becoming still as glass. It stretched out empty before us as far as I could see. The lake suddenly felt much more vast than it had just minutes before, and anxiety began to creep in.

Suddenly, about fifty yards away, a boat came into sight. Cherylyn and I stood up in unison on the Jet Ski and began flailing our arms, calling out for help. It looked like it could be the same boater who prematurely came to my rescue a short time before. But like a plot straight out of a movie, our hope sunk as we watched the boat cruise out of sight. The sky was darkening, and it was evident that all the boats had left the lake.

Was this really happening?

As time passed, I continued to reassure Cherylyn that Simon would come back for us, but all I kept thinking about was what he had said just before the crash. His words kept echoing through me, "I have some built-up anger toward you." I had this eerie feeling he was not coming back. It felt both certain and impossible.

Soon, we realized that we had bigger problems than a flooded engine. As we were sitting on the Jet Ski, we noticed it was sinking more and more beneath our weight. With some inspection, we discovered a crack in the hull, and it was slowly taking on water. Cherylyn started to panic and cry while I masked my fear in an effort to remain calm. I had to be the protective big brother that I always had been. She was my baby sister, and she needed me to be strong. There was no way I would let anything bad happen to her.

We decided to pray.

HOLDING ONTO THE FUTURE FOR DEAR LIFE

There are all kinds of prayers. There are prayers of gratitude, praise, celebration, intercession, and supplication. There are quiet prayers, loud prayers, prayers born of anguish and suffering, and prayers of desperation.

This was the latter, a prayer of deep desperation. My sister and I were in desperate need with no clear way out.

We pieced together a prayer that somebody—anybody would find us. Almost immediately after we stopped praying, I felt a clear answer. Nobody was going to find us. Surviving this was on us. We were the only people who could save us, and if we were going to survive, it was going to take everything we had. We had to be smart, we had to keep moving, and we had to work together.

Quickly, my sister and I formulated a plan. The seat served as a flotation device and was easily removed. We abandoned the Jet Ski and used the seat as a paddleboard to swim toward the direction we'd launched from. Together, side by side, we held onto the seat and kicked constantly for several minutes. It didn't take long for us to realize that we were making little to no headway as the winds began to pick up, pushing us in the opposite direction. We were never going to make it anywhere like this. Just then, we looked at each other and knew we felt the same answer, clear as day. We needed to set our sights on the opposite shore, the one behind us. There was nothing but desert on that side of the lake, but at least in that direction, the wind would work with us and not against us.

As we made our way backward, the sun dipped behind the mountains on the horizon, and my fear became a reality. The wind was picking up speed, making the waves an army against us. We could see the Jet Ski in the distance and decided we should swim back to it to ride out the waves.

As soon as we reached the watercraft, we were met with four to six-foot swells crashing over us, one after another. We reattached the seat and used all the strength we had to pull ourselves back on top. Not long after getting back up, the jet ski could no longer carry our body weight. The hull had filled with water and kept bobbing under the surface. We had no choice but to jump back into the water. Together, we desperately clung to the side of the sinking machine as the waves tossed us like rags in a washer.

Cherylyn cried steadily, and I started to feel truly panicked. I began to see the real possibility that we might not make it out of that water, that we might actually drown felt like a probability. Even though we both had our life vests on, the force of the waves was tremendous. Water continued to crash over us, with each swell we were pushed beneath the surface. Every time we'd come up for air, we'd try to climb on top of the machine, but nothing was working. All we could do was catch our breath, hold on for dear life, and prepare for the next wave.

As we continued to battle the waves, we realized only the seat was keeping the machine afloat, so we grabbed it and the rope in the under compartment. The craft sank ominously—nose up and out of sight, just like the Titanic.

I knew that the winds usually die down after sunset, so our only job was to stay calm and keep our heads above water. Without having the jet ski to hold on to, I feared we would get separated from the thrashing waves. I tied the rope to my life vest and tied the other side to my sister's. We stayed focused on the task at hand and held tightly to the seat while we rode the waves together. We kept giving each other pep talks, reassuring each other that we would make it. We had to believe that we would. It was all we could do to survive.

The wind and waves kept pushing us farther toward the opposite side of the lake. I knew from my Boy Scout training and occasionally watching the Discovery Channel that in our situation (given we had a flotation device), drowning was a second concern to hypothermia. The water was below seventy degrees already and would only get colder as the night progressed.[1]

As the winds started to settle down, we formulated our next plan. We needed to continue to swim for the shore, and we couldn't stop. I knew the shoreline was still an extreme distance away, but we really had no other choice. We were two small bobbing heads in a massive ocean of water. Waiting for rescue was not an option. We had to keep our bodies moving to fight off hypothermia; our continued survival depended upon it.

After about an hour of kicking in our new direction, we stopped to take a break and decided that the seat wasn't helping us much. If we abandoned it, we could shift to our backs and put our entire bodies into the effort. So, although it was scary to let go of the one item of stability we had, we did it. We surrendered it to the lake, just as I had surrendered the deck of cards in my house on the hill. Now, all we had between us was a rope and the faith that we'd made the right decision. We both shifted to our backs and began to do the elementary backstroke.

As darkness set in, the waters were once again calm. In fact, it wasn't long before the term pitch-black took on its true meaning. There was no moon; darkness simply was. The only light illuminating came from the cityscape along the foothills of the shoreline behind us, but it offered no guidance. I couldn't even see my hand in front of my face. I tried not to think about the depth of the water and continued to pray that we were swimming in the right direction.

Out of the darkness, a single light on the shore appeared off in the distance. It was a true beacon of hope in every sense of the word. We swam toward this light, and soon, it appeared we were making some headway. We kept our conversations flowing, talking about our hopes and dreams to keep our spirits high and to make sure we were staying alert. I confessed to Cherylyn that if we made it out of the water alive, I would move to Las Vegas and start my team-building company. I had dreamed of this company and had been talking about it for a long time but had spent too much of my energy in St. George playing the victim. I kept thinking that if I were never able to put action behind this dream, if my life were to end that night, I would be genuinely regretful.

This was the first time in my life I fully understood that a dream, if not put into action, is just that—a dream—nothing more, nothing less. Cherylyn shared her dreams of someday finding her life companion and having a family of her own. Her biggest goal in life was to be a mom. As we swam, our conversation grew quiet. The occasional tug of the rope we'd drawn between us was our best source of comfort. A reminder that we were in this together and were both still alive.

As hours passed, we each became deathly tired, extremely cold, and ravenously hungry. I wanted to rest, but each time we stopped, even for a second, I would feel the bones in my body turn to ice. As I glanced back at the city lights far behind us that once felt so tangible, all I could think of was eating a Wendy's junior bacon cheeseburger. Something so readily available was now so far from reach, and it became the one thing I wanted the most.

After over eight hours of swimming nonstop, we were within solid reach of our shoreline. Seeing land stretched out before us renewed our spirits and gave us a jolt of adrenaline to reach the finish line. Although we certainly weren't out of the dark, we still had our beacon. As we got closer to shore, we could see in the far distance a helicopter and boat lights in the opposite direction. Ironically, we didn't even want to be rescued at that point. It was like we felt we had accomplished this incredible feat of swimming across the lake and fighting hypothermia. As our minds fell into the idea that we were going to live, we had a renewed fervor for life—not just our present lives—but for our future selves.

Our triumph soon turned to horror as the boat lights we thought were in the distance were closer than we thought. A boat was coming toward us head-on, full speed! I began to scream and flail my arms in panic to grab the attention of the driver, but it was a futile effort. The boat showed no signs of slowing down or changing course. Just as we embraced for impact, I realized it was only my mind. And not just mine; my sister saw it as well. We were delirious and hallucinating . . . How wild, how strange, how absolutely frightening that realization was. This brush with blurring lines of reality kicked us into high gear with a legitimate warning of the very real trouble we were in.

When we finally reached what we thought was the shore, we found ourselves in a veritable swamp. A solid wall of ten-foot-tall blades of grass guarded the shoreline. Our new task was to push our way through a quarter mile of mud, muck, and sharp grass without shoes and without being able to see through the thickness of the vegetation. With every step we took, we would sink up to our calves in the muck, and it would take all our strength to retrieve that foot and step again. I remember being extremely thirsty at this point, remembering the rule of threes, and being grateful for all I'd learned from the show *I Shouldn't Be Alive*. I knew a person could survive for three minutes without air, three days without water, and three weeks without food. Suddenly, that cheeseburger was no longer at the top of my desires.

Once we were clear of the swamp, we were overcome with joy as we finally stood on solid ground. All at once, our legs felt weak, and we both began to shake uncontrollably as we went into shock. We were absurdly cold. And again, I don't know if it was delirium and we'd lost all ability to keep track of time, but it felt like just moments later, we were completely dry. I asked Cherylyn, "Is your swimsuit dry?"

She said, "Yes!" And we were both no longer shivering; in fact, more than that, we were warm, and we could see that the light we'd been chasing illuminated a cabin up on a bluff. Initially, we thought we should hike up to it, but just like we had the feeling after our prayer and again on changing directions while swimming, we felt adamant that we should go toward the highway instead.

The highway was about another quarter-mile uphill, and the terrain was primarily wild grass with cacti, rocks, stickers, and stones. Given this, we took off our life jackets, tore them at the seams, and made ourselves terrible sets of shoes. They were better than nothing. We stepped our way across the stretch in pitch darkness in what felt like record time. All the while we were in high spirits, we felt extremely fortunate—blessed even. But once again, that joy was cut short with a shrill scream from Cherylyn. A stick had punctured through her life vest and jammed into the bottom of her foot. From what I could see, the cut was deep. Thankfully, we were yards from the highway and together hobbled our way to the asphalt.

I remember pulling off my makeshift shoes just as we reached the road. The pavement felt like a wonderful gift in and of itself. So warm and secure—so sure of itself. It was as though we could draw strength directly from its very state of existence.

Right away, Cherylyn looked off in the distance and said, "We're definitely going to be on the news." Yes, this was certain. From where we stood, we could see the full efforts of the Utah County Search and Rescue team at work, helicopters and rescue boats scouring the far side of the lake for us. We began to walk along the lonely highway toward the closest town, which was about ten miles away. We were unsure that anyone would come along this late, but we didn't care. We were happy to be alive, and we had renewed strength. We would walk all the way to town if necessary. Eventually, headlights did approach. Instantly, we began waving our arms wildly in the air like we had done before—as if this time there was any way they could possibly miss the two of us muddied up to our thighs, walking down the middle of the highway in nothing but our bathing suits.

The car pulled over, and the window rolled down. Inside the car was a man and woman who'd decided to go stargazing in the moonless night. The time was 2 a.m., and they said they'd just decided to venture out on a whim. Again, gratitude rose up in us. We explained our situation and pointed out the search and rescue operation on the lake below. The man immediately called 911 and informed the authorities of our survival. They then let us call our mom. The relief in her voice is something I'll never forget. She said there was talk of calling off the search and returning in the morning in a recovery effort. We learned later the Sheriff successfully got a warrant for my phone carrier to unlock the GPS on my phone, which led them to the watercraft back on the shore—the one Simon had taken. At that point, my mom had been contending with the same idea that I'd had back in the frigid water when the waves were tossing us about. This might actually be the end; the two of us might not ever leave that water. Gratitude again filled our hearts.

The couple insisted we wait in their car until the police arrived. They turned on the heat to keep us warm. As we chatted, the couple mentioned they had met online and were on their first date. The man had driven up from Las Vegas to meet the woman. I remember thinking, what are the odds that this guy from Las Vegas had chosen this night and had driven up this road on a whim? What were the chances that we were all here at this moment discussing the very city I'd vowed to move to if we survived?[2]

It felt like the concluding line in a painstaking adventure book, like a gift of grace—like true confirmation. For me, it was a message that even in the worst of circumstances, even in the deepest of dark, there is always a beacon of light.

THE UNIVERSALITY OF JUSTICE

Every time I've shared the lake story, the discussion that follows is rarely about survival, or gratitude. It's not often about whether everything happens for a reason, or even if there's such a thing as coincidence. The immediate discussion is always about Simon. People want to know the rest of *that* story. Why did Simon leave us out there? Why was he so angry with me? Was he regretful? Did he get in trouble for what he did to us?

I never got the answers to these questions. When asked, he denied being angry and said he'd gone for help and that by the time he went back to look for us, we were nowhere to be found. I know this isn't true, because I followed up on his story. He didn't actually seek help directly.

I don't know if he felt regretful. I hope that on some level he did. I suffered with severe PTSD and wrestled for years with a longing for some sort of karma or justice for putting not just me but my sister in such grave danger. Eventually, I came to terms with this incident and dealt with the trauma and anxiety this experience had created. I had to learn so much about myself, about justice, and about the world in which we live to find my way out of my desire for this particular wrong to be righted—at least in the traditional sense.

At some point, I realized that Simon's actions that day were not truly directed at me but a reaction to his own trauma. He was lashing out from a deep-seated disdain for himself and the lack of control he felt within the world. I also needed to own the role I had played in my relationship with him. I must have done something that made him feel so much anger toward me. Maybe I was an insensitive jerk, maybe I wasn't. Even though I never received the answers, I still needed to own it.

The desire for justice or justification is not just present with this story. This desire is present in nearly every story. In fact, the desire for justice is a thread that weaves itself through the story of humanity.

Justice is prominent in all forms of law and order. It is embedded in all the great religions and is made evident in nearly every social construct. As proven by the questions that inevitably follow the lake story, this desire is not just a strong fundamental element found within interpersonal relationships, it is also a cultural universal.

The question I returned to for quite some time was how very unfair life can be. But the reality is, life is simply not fair. When I hear, or think the words, "Life's not fair," I'm always tempted to add the words "Is it?" in my best Scar (from *The Lion King*) voice. If you've seen the Disney classic, you're sure to remember the memorable scene.[3] Scar has entered deep apathy and expresses the root of his disdain for his brother.

Scar built his life around the resentment he had for his brother Mufasa, the alpha male and heir to the throne. Interestingly, he's a fantastic character for the study of the victim mentality. Research studies have shown that our brains automatically evaluate fairness—particularly when it comes to value distribution. The desire for fairness is a human instinct, and it is part of the human condition to respond with happiness and contentment when we are treated fairly and, likewise, to protest or to exhibit anger or disgust when we're treated unfairly. And this is where justice, and the innate desire for it, finds its place in the picture.

Now, the human condition is perhaps the most beautifully complicated notion of all. The term itself refers to the unique experience of human life. It encompasses growth, experience, emotionality, conflict, connection, and so much more. As mentioned, so much of the human experience follows cultural patterns worldwide. Human wounding and human trauma are both a part of this. As is the desire for justice.

For simplicity's sake, it is helpful to look at cultural universals as belonging to one of two categories: the laws of man and the laws of nature. Both sets of laws are warranted and valuable for humanity to survive and to thrive.

When it comes to the laws of man, the focus is on maintaining control, avoiding chaos, and enabling a justly structured society. The laws of man vary from culture to culture and (thankfully) amend as humanity evolves. An example of this can be identified in the well-known concept of demanding "an eye for an eye." Although the laws of man change over time and across cultures, there is a constant that remains within our societies and within ourselves: the desire for justice.

Justice and fairness exist because humans desire a balancing of the scales. We believe that finding justification, or enacting justice will, in turn, alleviate the pain, hurt, and suffering caused by one person to another. This is natural. We want to find harmony and equilibrium—to find balance—not just within our societies, but within our minds, and within our hearts.

The most difficult part in all of this is that, oftentimes, the want for justice gets muddled with the desire for revenge and retribution. It can even get mired by acts of vengeance. This is where darkness ensues and trauma is not just embedded but perpetuated.

Another difficulty is that when we finally do get some form of justice, it often doesn't work. It doesn't clear the slate. We are still left to feel the pain, hurt, and suffering that was caused not just by the initial incident, and the circumstances surrounding it, but also by our revengeful response. And when we don't get any justice at all? That too can be problematic as harboring resentment can be traumatizing.

But here's the deal: The *need* for justice derives not from a response to the wrong action, but from a great human desire for harmony *in the context* of that action.

As humans, we need ways to manage the wars in our society. We need ways to manage the warring parts of people—and the warring parts within ourselves if we have ambition to not just survive but to thrive in this world in which we live. Perhaps Simon tried to do this in his own confused fashion. He was striking out against his very own pain and anguish, not realizing how such actions were creating new traumatic threads not just in our lives but in his own as well.

I eventually got to Zero with what happened at the lake, but it wasn't easy. The compounding pain from the persecution by the people of St. George, my deeply-rooted religious trauma, and this betrayal from Simon left wounds that would take years to heal. When I did relinquish the urge for revenge and justice, I found my peace with Simon. My return to Zero and consistent development of my understanding of the sacred power that dwells there has become a saving grace for me in many situations. Zero has become my way to manage both the wars within society and those within myself.

16

ENTERING THE BATTLE GROUND

The safest road to hell is the gradual one—the gentle slope, soft underfoot, without sudden turnings, without milestones, without signposts.

—C. S. Lewis, *The Screwtape Letters*

Just a few months after the catastrophe at Utah Lake, I started my team-building company, having vowed to do so on the lake. I also relocated to Las Vegas. I had overcome insurmountable odds of survival, physically and financially, and I relished it all. Things were off to a decent start. In the process of building a business plan, I had networked with the local event industry.

I purposefully lived far beyond my means as I set my intentions to "think and grow rich." This kept me motivated to get out of bed every morning and to keep working hard. I secured a quintessential rat-pack bungalow in a gated neighborhood surrounded by large adobe walls. My house was protected by two enormous white plaster lions that made me feel safe and successful.

I quickly became an expert at manifesting career opportunities and material things. But on the flip side, spiritually and emotionally, I was nowhere near the harmony that Zero avails. At the core of it, I was living hurt, and Vegas was doing a great job of keeping me distracted from my pain while I built a life that was innately designed to blissfully keep me protected from my past traumas.

Although I was unaware of it then, I was pulsing with a desire for justice and retribution. I remained deeply resentful of the unfair treatment I had experienced from the LDS people in St. George, who had not only driven me out of business but also stole it from me. And Simon! That experience on the lake served as a sort of lynchpin. It was beautiful because it was the catalyst I needed to step out into my own life and to pursue the dream that had taken such a stronghold in my mind and heart, but it also did something else; it added to a great desire for justice. Somehow, some way, I would someday get even for all the hurt that I'd endured.

It is part of the human condition to respond with happiness and contentment when we are treated fairly and likewise to protest, exhibit anger, or express disgust when we are mistreated. In this instinctual human desire for fairness, the ambition and innate hunger for justice wove its wily way to me. Rather than dwelling on the goodness that did exist in members of my family, my church, and the people of St. George, I kept drawing back to the discrimination, the pain, and the suffering—the unfairness of it all. In retrospect, it is easy to see that I was angry, disgusted, and reactionary, and it was this energy, this great desire for retribution, that fueled me.

I knew two things: I wanted to be seen for who I was; no apologies. And I wanted to be wealthy—after all, the best revenge is success, right? I was digging into all the research that existed around the law of attraction and the power of intention. I even built a meditation room in my house in Vegas and worked daily to hone my intentions and desires to stay in tune and draw upon the sacred power that Source avails. The problem was that my need for revenge was an undercurrent that never subsided. Instead, it pulsed beneath the surface of my every action and eventually found its way into the world, manifesting precisely as I'd desired.

I would regularly drive back to Snow Canyon and stake claim to the power that pulsed in my great craving to be heard and seen just as I was. My friend Lisa and I would take regular "affirmation walks" up the canyon. We did these often as a testament to my first experience there, which had served to catapult me out of my depression and back into a life I could recognize.

We would start our walks with deep discussion and heartfelt connection. As we approached the top of the petrified sand dunes that overlooked the stunning red and orange canyon below, we would take turns casting our arms toward the sky, speaking our intentions out loud.

"I choose to create a project where my voice is heard around the world!" I shouted the words off the sandstone cliffs. I don't know where that idea came from, but I said it in the moment, and I meant it.

"Yes, Chad, and so it is!" Lisa responded as we hugged and giggled together.

It was as if the earth itself took heed of the words that came out of my mouth. You know that old saying, be careful what you wish for? Well, that's worth heeding because about six months later, my voice was indeed heard around the world.

MY SECOND MISSION

Shams-i Tabrīzī once said that the real dirt is not outside but inside, in our hearts. We can wash all stains with water. The only one we can't remove is the grudge and the bad intentions sticking to our hearts.[1] Often, when we hear the word intention, we think of positive things. The reality is intention doesn't always work its way to good. Our intentions go where our energy flows, and if the energy beneath something isn't pure, then you can bet there will be repercussions for the ill intentions that do exist somewhere along the line. Intention itself has two working functions. First, it's driven by an envisioned outcome; second, it's guided by specific feelings and actions.

It was a beautiful morning in March 2007, and I flipped the television on to keep myself company while straightening up the house. The channel was ABC, and *Good Morning America* was on. The cover model for a Marine beefcake calendar was being interviewed, and I became engrossed in the story. I remember thinking, this guy is not all that—but the innocence of him having been roped into this fundraising project was making the female interviewer flush a noticeable shade of red. I began to wonder *why are people so drawn to men in uniforms?* And that's when it happened.

What if? I thought, *what if someone produced a calendar of sexy Mormon missionaries?*

I laughed a little at the idea of it, but then I began to seriously think about it. This guy was getting national media attention, and he was just an average Marine and the New York Firefighter calendar always sold well and got great press. Surely, if a group of Mormon missionaries took their shirts off, *Good Morning America* would come calling. I remembered in my mission days hearing that Playboy had ranked Mormon Missionaries as one of the sexiest men in uniform next to UPS drivers. I had no idea if this rumor was true, but I remember it making me feel a little better about wearing that stifling white shirt, tie, and name badge that read "Elder Hardy" across the top of it for two solid years. After a minute of fantasizing about the possibilities, I brushed off the idea and went about my day.

Yet, later that night, I grabbed my laptop and went to GoDaddy. I clicked on the "register a domain" tab and typed in *mormonsexposed*.

As I stared at the words on the screen, I couldn't unsee it. I laughed out loud and shouted to my friends, who were over for dinner, "The words spell Mormon-Sex-Posed!"

How naughty. I couldn't believe I was actually looking to see if this domain was available. Besides, even if it was, what was I going to do? Would I actually go through with producing something like this? The consequences didn't even register—I was living in the moment.

The request came back affirmative.

"www.mormonsexposed.com is available. Would you like to purchase?"[2]

And then it happened. I spun my credit card like a six-shooter and entered the appropriate information. Just like that, I became the owner of a slice of pop culture for the bargain price of $7.99.

The next day, I had forgotten about my impulsive purchase while running errands in the beautiful Las Vegas spring weather. Soon, I found myself driving down Arville through the industrial area of Vegas. I was fairly new to the city, having only lived there for six months. Yet, I had made a few friends and several connections due to being in the event industry. One such friend was Dani, the owner of Vegas Props, a full-service event and decor company. We had met through a mutual friend and hit it off instantly. Well, it just so happens that Vegas Props was located on Arville, so I decided to stop in.

My creative energy began to buzz as soon as I got out of my truck and entered the wacky world Dani had created as her workspace. It was like the Willy Wonka of prop houses touting classic Hollywood sophistication, glittered with lawn ornament flair. Dani looked quite like the singer P!NK, boasting her refined form of punk with short, spiky blonde hair, pristine makeup, and some legit black leather.

"Hi, sugar butt!" she exclaimed as I peeked my head in the door. "What the heck brings you here?"

She continued to work on a proposal while she was talking to me. I realized then I didn't have a reason for being there. I had no idea why I had stopped by—I just did. "I was just in the neighborhood and thought I would swing by."

I tried to devise a reason why I was there—and that's when my mouth started to move involuntarily. "Well, I'm thinking of doing something kind of crazy."

She stopped typing and gave me her full attention. "You know I like crazy!"

"So, you've seen the firefighter calendars, right?"

"Of course, they're HOT!"

"Well . . ." I took a deep breath. "I want to produce a calendar of Mormon missionaries, and I want to call it . . . Men on a Mission." The name just came to mind. It fell out of my mouth like a heavy ball of wet clay and splat on the ground. Dani stared at me briefly as she registered what I'd said.

"Oh, my God!" she screamed. "That is hysterical! I dated a Mormon in high school. Mormon guys are SO HOT!"

Dani and I began to snicker like thirteen-year-old schoolgirls in hysterics as her husband walked in.

"What is going on in here? I can hear you cackling across the entire building!"

I told him my idea. To my surprise, he actually liked it. Not just liked it, LOVED it.

"Dude, that's genius." He then said, "This is a media magnet!"

"Haha, really?" I joked, "Want to invest?"

"Absolutely! How much?"

"Uh, what? Are you serious?"

"Dead serious. How much?"

"Uh . . . fifty thousand probably?"

"Done. I'm in."

He extended his hand to shake mine, and that was it. In just over twenty-four hours of conceiving the idea, I had the project fully funded with a business partner. I couldn't help but ponder the irony of me going bare-chested in a photograph during my mission, which had set off a series of misfortunate and fortunate events, now coming full circle.

A week later, I woke up from a nightmare. My heart was racing; my body was covered in sweat. I had dreamt that I was called to serve as a missionary again. In my dream, I had to give up my career, my house, my car, my dog, and welcome back the white shirt, tie, and black name badge. Just before waking, I was reading through the mountainous list of obligations

I would have to follow. Thankfully, my eyes shot open as I read from the missionary rule book that I can't ever be alone except to go to the bathroom. As the ceiling fan spun above me, it reoriented me to reality. I expressed a tremendous sigh of relief. I was still in Vegas. I was in my house, and my life was still intact.

As I began my devious little project, I realized I was late in the game to produce a calendar for 2008 as it was already April of 2007. This meant I needed to have the calendar shot by the first of July so it could be designed and ready to print by August for a September launch, and I still needed models. I put my head down and went to work. I began placing ads, hired a publicist, a photographer, and scheduled a test shoot with Jaymes Vaughan, a local non-Mormon Chippendale's model for press materials, who looked more Mormon than me.[3]

Things were moving at supersonic speed. Working with the publicist challenged me to search deep within myself to understand why I was doing this. I had to come up with the project's message so they could develop the angle for the press kit. Though I didn't fully recognize it at the time, my deepest, truest desire was to get retribution for all the hurt, shame, and broken promises I had experienced in the church and through its members. The coping mechanism I had used throughout my life to manage my traumas was certainly humor.

So, my desire evolved from doing something revengeful and shocking to doing something meaningful and funny. I had already decided and discussed with my business partner that it needed a positive spin if I were to move forward with the project. The calendar needed a deeper meaning than just eye candy and tongue-in-cheek humor to get my message across in the most passive-aggressive way possible.

In our development meetings, we determined that the only way to give the project validity was to have authentic Mormons in the calendar—men who had served full-time missions for the church; no more Chippendale models. We also decided that a portion of the calendar sales would go to the charity of the man's choice in the area where they served their missions.

We landed on a forward-thinking message with the calendar playfully titled *Men on a Mission*, which featured twelve handsome former Mormon missionaries who dared to pose bare-chested. The Mormons Exposed brand was predicated on the message of religious and cultural tolerance, ambitioning to reshape perceptions, heighten awareness, and push the envelope toward acceptance of both human and religious diversity.

Our calculated plan began to develop and materialize like particles of radio waves entering a receiver and turning out a solid message loud and clear. For a moment, I saw into my future; I saw the man in the mirror as a fearless vigilante, proudly holding a rainbow victory flag over the church as a symbol of justice for the island of misfits. I knew this would be my demise, but I continued forward like a moth to a flame, preparing for the burn.

PANIC UPON PANIC

As anticipated, the calendar started attracting attention as the talent search kicked off. Auditions took place in downtown Salt Lake City. Jerri joined me in conducting candidate interviews. The local radio station got wind of our casting call and sent their DJ to interview us. Initially, he showed strong support for our project, only to later criticize it on air, inviting callers to join a primarily negative debate. Shortly after, my business partner forwarded me a story from an online news outlet criticizing our project. He found it amusing that we were already generating significant buzz even though we hadn't sent out a press release. While he laughed, I felt a sense of anxiety wash over me. I realized then that this calendar was no longer just a funny idea. It was on the verge of becoming something very real and much larger than I had initially envisioned. I started to get cold feet. But I was in too deep and couldn't turn back.

Weeks before the launch, the long overdue reckoning arrived as all of the tangled bits of the project dramatically converged at a single, colossal clash at the intersection of my life. I was heading northbound on I-15 in Las Vegas, en route to approve the print proof for sending the calendar into production when my heart began to race at what felt like a million beats per minute. My eyes blurred, and I began to breathe rapidly and erratically as sweat covered my entire body. Was I having a heart attack? I quickly made it to the off-ramp, slipped through two red lights, and found my way to the back parking lot of Mandalay Bay. I put the gear in park just as my body collapsed flat across the bench seat of my truck. I was experiencing a full-blown panic attack, something I had never experienced at this level of intensity before, not even while being stranded in the middle of Utah Lake. When I felt capable, I took my phone and called for help.

For two weeks, I stayed in bed most of the day and could not get behind the wheel of a car. Every cell in my body was giving me a five-alarm warning sign that I was deeply out of alignment, but I chose to ignore it and used medication and meditation as dual band-aids to manage and calm my nerves.

This practice held me together through the launch of the calendar, and with the drop of a single press release, the story went viral. Within hours, I received an invitation for a satellite interview on MSNBC the next morning. Car service was arranged for a ride to the local NBC affiliate station as I was still unable to drive. I was a nervous wreck, and looking back on that interview, you can see the anxiety on my face.

The calendar created quite the international media frenzy as the reaction was truly polarizing within both the LDS community and the secular world at large—particularly because this all occurred in the political climate of 2007–2008.[4] Everywhere from *TMZ*, *Rolling Stone* magazine, the *Washington Post*, and the *New York Daily News* to the *Sydney Morning Herald*, BBC, and *Politico* covered the story. Calendar Club, the company responsible for the calendar kiosks in malls across North America, called with a large order just in time for the holiday season.

While the *Men on a Mission* calendar was humorous, daring, and sexy, it really did represent something beyond *just* this. It took on a life of its own and became a catalyst to get people to look at, express, and discuss their own prejudices and stereotypical views of both religion and gender norms and expectations. As anticipated, the calendars revealed the reality that there is not just room for exploratory discussions, but also that there's far too much fear, hatred, anger, and spite created within (and against) the entity of religion—in this case, the LDS Church.

We received over a thousand letters and messages that ranged from congratulating us for thinking outside the box and enabling Mormons to be seen as free-thinking and free-functioning individuals to those threatening physical harm or condemning us to eternal damnation. Additionally, we received absurd amounts of gay-bashing hate mail, which really bolstered the ambition of these calendars to give a nod to individuals who honestly had no real voice or accepted place within the LDS Church due to their sexual orientations.

At the height of it all, I got an unexpected knock at my door. There stood my brother, anxiously fidgeting, struggling to make eye contact.

"Hey, Chad," he said, with a nervous edge to his voice. "Do you mind if I crash at your place for a few weeks?"

I glanced past him at his car, crammed with all his stuff, sandwiched between the windows. All I could think was *this can't be happening*. The last thing I needed right then was my brother barging into my personal space, stirring up memories of past traumas while I was knee-deep in a media storm. While I'd forgiven him, I hadn't forgotten how he'd treated me. Our relationship had always been distant, more of a formality during the occasional family get-together. For him to show up unannounced asking for help, he must have hit rock bottom. I welcomed him and relinquished my cherished meditation room to provide him with a place to stay.

BURN IT ALL DOWN

There's an African Proverb that says: "The child who is not embraced by the village will burn it down to feel its warmth." To understand what put me in perfect alignment with producing the calendar in the first place, and how it became successful in giving me the warmth of revenge, we first must understand the emotions that motivated it.

To start, the primary emotion that the situation in St. George evoked in me was anger. And I wasn't just angry. I was burn-the-village-down-and-take-no-prisoners angry. I was livid that I had been treated so unfairly. I was furious I had been embarrassed publicly, and I was enraged I had spent so much of my life being judged and discriminated against. Reflecting on the dealings that I'd had with the church where I was made to feel flawed and powerless, an all-encompassing anger would well up in me that blacked out all the good the church and its teachings had done for me. This included the broken promises of my patriarchal blessing, which directed immense anger not only at the church but at God. I reached a tipping point where I was sick and tired of people in positions of power enacting their control on my life and the lives of so many others. I was ready to burn it all down.

Looking back I can clearly see that I had confined myself within a prison of anger, its walls thickened and compounded by the various traumas I had endured. I was utterly oblivious to the chains that bound me. Being angry felt so normal, an ever-present yet unrecognized shackle. Despite experiencing several significant moments of self-awareness that helped me get back on track with my authentic self, a substantial amount of work remained to be done. It felt like the slightest trigger had the power to throw me right back into the tangled thicket of anger and despair.

Unchecked traumas buried deep within our Human Story Codes can be silent killers, much like an undetected cancer. These traumas play mind games with us, often leading to unexplained paradoxes. One moment, you could be on top of the world, riding high on life's magic, and the next, you're left feeling like a worthless, uninspired impostor. It's an internal cyclone like none other.

The rollercoaster of these emotions led me to the point where, instead of looking back at my life as filled with miracles and abundance, my memories were clouded with all the bad stuff. All I could recall was being constantly sick and unceasingly bullied. I was often scared and, more often, ashamed. My bishop blamed me and treated me terribly for something I had no control over. My dad consistently chose church doctrine and the law of obedience over his family. My mother consistently walked the careful line of keeping up all appearances—a skill she undoubtedly learned from my grandparents. My companion ratted me out. My mission was a mess—and then, just when things were beginning to pan out, I turned my back on a dream opportunity to pacify my patriarchal blessing. Then I lost Jerri because the man in the mirror couldn't leave me the hell alone—or at least, that's how it felt.

Next, the people of St. George came after me with pitchforks. And to top it off, I was literally left for dead on a lake—as if my life was of no importance, as if I had no inherent value in this world. I now know that the bedwetting I endured for my entire childhood, adolescent, and early teen years was a regressive symptom in response to the extreme stress I experienced.

Nothing felt honest. Nothing felt real. In my cyclone of agitation and feelings of powerlessness, I'd allowed all the anger within me to morph into victimhood—and I allowed the victim in me to seek revenge.

All thoughts eventually turn into things, and that's precisely what happened with the calendars. I wanted to create something real, and I wanted to pay back the people who hurt me—directly, if possible, but even indirectly would satisfy me. I felt deep resentment for so many systems of power that existed in my life, and I allowed it all to culminate and direct itself at the people of St. George and the entity that granted them their perceived power, the LDS Church.

Even though I decided not to pursue any legal action against the city as it was expensive, time-consuming, and exhausting, I still couldn't get over how the St. George City Council and the members of RAD had gotten away with stealing my livelihood and my dreams out from under me. I would consistently catch myself dwelling on their words, "We don't need his kind in our town."

Well, if "unsavory" is what they claim me to be, then unsavory is what they'll get—only they'll get it cut from their very own cloth. As hard as it is to admit, this is how I felt despite my desperate efforts to find peace in my meditation room and among the canyon walls.

I kept trying to let go of the pain and the anguish. I tried SO hard. But I struggled to make any real progress. This is because I was working from a place of lack. I had no idea how to contend with the effects of the trauma, both large and small. I knew forgiveness had great value, but I didn't quite know how to forgive *for good*.

And so, I built a business around the idea that open minds are what the world needs more of. (In all honesty, open hearts are what I should have been seeking, but my own heart just wasn't in a place to understand such work, let alone do it.) I couldn't handle that so many people within the LDS Church could not see or understand the plight of those who are not exactly like them. I had spent my formative years neck deep in a system that claimed to be built on love and acceptance. Yet, it pushed away anything (and anyone) that did not fit the mold—all masked by the will of God. I spent my entire life aching for an honest appraisal of reality, and all I got in return was pretense. It was maddening.

At the time of the calendars, I was viewing all the trauma in my life linearly, seeing each traumatic event through a very simplistic A to B lens. This created in me a victim mentality. As such, the calendars became my victim impact statement—and not just mine, but a statement made for anyone who felt controlled, dismissed, or unseen by the powers that be within the walls of the LDS Church.[5]

There's a part of me that wants to claim this isn't true, but it is. Sure, I'd learned how to *let go* with the deck of cards, but since I never completely dealt with all the trauma in my life, the repercussions of said trauma would consistently creep back in and affect my equilibrium and, thus, my alignment. I eventually learned that, without truly facing my traumas and finding forgiveness for myself, for others, and for the situations in which the traumas occurred, I would never be truly free of them. Once I learned this to be a (T)ruth, much of the pain and suffering I'd endured began to make sense.

You see, (T)ruth takes hold in the depths of our beings just like large-T trauma does. The all-encompassing (T)ruth is the one thing we as humans cannot negate. Sure, we can run from it, hide from it, and try with all our might to deny and dismiss it—believe me, I know. The very last thing I thought I wanted was to be gay. From a very young age, I knew what such a reality meant in my culture. So what did I do? I ran from it. I hid from it. I tried to fix it with my fantasy girlfriends. I did this with all the strength and will I could muster. And when that didn't work, I surrendered to the man in the mirror with shame and disgust in myself.

But the truth remained. This (T)ruth was inborn. It was knit into my very being by the Source of all creation, and there was nothing the church, the bishop, my dad, my mother, my brother, my girlfriends—there was nothing the whole of all creation could do about it to make it any less true, any less real. There was and is no changing this facet of the way of me.

It is also true that the calendar project had a real message within it. It was a message to people in the church and those outside it. Sure, it was a message that tried to encourage personal analysis of policy and doctrine. Still, mostly, it was a message crafted of the hurt and anguish of being different and feeling unloved and unacceptable. It is also true that I was cheeky about the whole thing—and should I ever get to thinking otherwise, I've merely to look at the covers of the 2009 and 2010 *Men on a Mission* calendars that blatantly mock prominent LDS artwork. One glance at either of these covers reveals an immediate truth: my heart was not open, and my intentions were indeed awry. Despite my claims, this venture was less about the message to my fellow outcasts and more about revenge and retribution.

Further validation of this is found in my direct actions after my brazen project erupted an international media spitfire. I had sent the St. George city council, and the antagonistic members of RAD signed copies of the calendar, with a letter thanking them for the inadvertent inspiration.

I had won in a massive way. I had gotten all the press attention I could handle. The calendars were on racks in every shopping mall across the country.

Revenge was great . . . or so I thought.

17

... THE LONGER THE FALL

"It is the reformer who is anxious for the reform, and not society, from which he should expect nothing better than opposition, abhorrence and even mortal persecution."

—Mahatma Gandhi, *Young India* (ed. 1927)

A s you can see from my journey thus far, I didn't just wake up on a random day and decide to be a religious anarchist on a quest to shine light on the recipe for piety and punishment. Looking back at it all, I can't even pinpoint which specific experience made me want to shred that plastic-wrapped, Pulitzer prize-winning, pre-written storybook of life that merely had my name carbon copied and pasted on the "insert your name here" line. It was a gradual awakening. At some point, the large numbers of people liking and doing the exact same things in the exact same ways to validate their claimed position of righteousness just became too much, too blatant, and too difficult not to see.

Prior to that, I had merely taken what I had been taught at face value without questioning too much. I had only embraced what was given to me through the constraints of the system in which I was born. However, this profound awakening had set in motion the birth of a tenacious rebel within me, and I was about to break free and challenge the world.

CONDUCT UNBECOMING

"Hey, Chad, are you at your computer? Check out Fox News. You're famous."

I chuckled as I held the phone to one ear and typed the web address with one hand, wondering what silly scheme my friend Mark had up his sleeve. Suddenly, I felt the air escape my lungs. He wasn't joking.

It was true. I was famous—temporarily, at least. There I was on Fox News, grinning ear to ear as I held the inaugural *Men on a Mission* calendar with the caption "CONDUCT UNBECOMING" photoshopped to it in oversized font as if it had historical significance. The headline below firmly read: "Man Who Created Calendar of Shirtless Mormon Missionaries Is Facing Excommunication."

In a way, the whole situation was funny—hilarious actually—that in a grand effort to silence me, the LDS Church had just made me famous. On the outside, I was laughing hysterically. On the inside, I was melting like the Wicked Witch of the West after being doused with water.

"Oh, dear God! The whole world knows I'm going to be excommunicated!"

The countless phone calls from curious reporters around the world hungry for a juicy sensational story left my voice hoarse. As I made every effort to field the calls in a way that might somehow make this all easier on my family, I knew there was little to no hope of that.

Three months prior, I had been contacted by the church's regional stake president. He asked if we could meet, and I agreed. The next day, he and one of his counselors showed up at my door. They must have expected me to be aggressive or defiant as their energy felt like they had boxing gloves on and were ready to fight.

They relaxed when they realized I was just trying to prove a point and create dialog. They asked if I would stop the calendar production, but I said I couldn't do that because I had a business partner with a financial interest in the project. I told them that if I turned the project over to my business partner, I would have no control over the content. The meeting ended pleasantly enough, and although we didn't agree on anything, I felt they understood the project better for it.

At the same time, I was finishing up my last religion class, Church History, through BYU independent studies. After I completed my coursework in 2002, my advisor informed me that I was short two religion classes. Because of this, I was short of the requirements needed to graduate. There was no way around it: religion classes are mandatory to graduate from BYU. Jumping into entrepreneurship had put completing my degree on the back burner. When the media spotlighted me, it also put a bullseye on my back. I felt I needed to fast-track and finish my classes remotely, fearing fallout from the calendars. Completing these courses would allow me to officially graduate from BYU. I would finally have the communications degree I had worked and paid for.

Not long after our initial meeting, I got another call from the stake president. He asked me again to shut down the production of the calendar, and when I echoed my same reply, he said that it was brought to his attention that I had been living with a woman out of wedlock.

At the time, I had one employee working with me at my company. Her name was Heather, and she would come over daily and work from my home office. Given that I was living in a gated community, she was listed as one of the residents. This allowed her to get through the gate daily without checking in with the guard.

I laughed out loud. Once I composed myself, I responded that no, she didn't live with me. The woman in question worked for me and was listed as a resident at the front gate, so she could come and go without needing to be signed in.

He replied, "That is not what I have heard. There are other members of the church that are in the neighborhood who have reported that she lives there."

Then, I realized they were trying to find any avenue to strong-arm me into pulling the calendar. If they couldn't do anything about the calendar, they would punish me by leveraging church law. Living with the opposite sex outside of marriage was a violation of temple covenants and cause for disciplinary action.

I replied that I felt they were grasping at straws, and I didn't want him to contact me ever again. As soon as I hung up the phone, I called the front gate to figure out how they knew my employee was listed as a resident.

"Hi, this is Chad Hardy on Cherry Orchard Street. Can you tell me who lives next door to me?"

"I'm sorry, Mr. Hardy, that information is confidential. We are not allowed to share that with anybody."

The following Friday, I got a hand-delivered letter from the stake president. It stated that I was being called in for disciplinary council two days later, on the upcoming Sunday. The short notice meant I had no time to gather my family for support. Since only church members were allowed in the meeting, I was essentially on my own.

It was my turn to strike back. I faxed the letter to *TMZ* and the Associated Press as both had been continually reaching out to see if the church had a statement regarding the calendars. In a matter of three hours, a photographer showed up at my door, and I received that phone call about Fox News running the story. I sat there in awe as I searched numerous news sites. The picture I had just taken in my living room holding the calendar with a Cheshire grin was everywhere.

As I approached the church that Sunday to attend my hearing, there were local reporters and a camera crew from *Inside Edition* all gathered at the front doors. Everyone was anxiously waiting to report the juice. The doors opened directly upon my arrival, and a guard efficiently escorted me to a back room. At the same time, my friends who came along for support were instructed to wait in the lobby.

I had never stepped foot in that particular southwest-style church before. Yet, the room felt strangely familiar, like the ones from my youth with its rust-colored carpet and burgundy sofas. I surveyed the paintings of Jesus propped on the scratchy burlap walls and felt like I had been there a hundred times before. While I stared at the solid wood door that separated me from my fate, memories began to push against the barriers I had formed against them. I held my cold and clammy hands tightly together as I waited anxiously to be interrogated by my church leaders in what is the granddaddy of all personal worthiness interviews. Part of me wanted to make a dash for it like my first experience in the temple, but stubbornness and just enough morbid curiosity kept me in my seat.

Beyond the looming door in front of me was the stake high council, twelve men who were gathered as their non-paid clergy duty for the disciplinary council held on my behalf for "conduct unbecoming a member of the church." I had heard about "courts of love," proceedings reserved for those who committed a dishonorable sin like adultery, fornication, homosexuality, fraud—and in my case, apostasy.

As I waited, my mind raced through the memories that formed my Mormon identity. I had flashes of an eight-year-old version of me at my baptism, frightened my sins would now be counted; me receiving the honorary priesthood at age twelve and feeling unworthy to receive it; me going through the secretive temple ceremony for the first time to receive my sacred underwear; me unprepared to make the promises asked of me. There I was, my nineteen-year-old self, struggling as a new missionary with a shaky testimony of the gospel. I saw myself, the me promising my mother that "no matter what, I will never leave the church;" me attending BYU and never fitting in; me being rejected by every good Mormon girl I tried to date.

The memories all felt like fleeting dreams from someone else's life.

Multiple sermons about my pre-earth righteousness earning me a golden ticket to be born into a Mormon family clanged in my head like crashing pots and pans. I came to realize that, despite working so hard to be the model Mormon all that time, I'd always had the deck stacked against me.

I snapped back to reality as the door swung wide open. A man with a friendly face came into the waiting area to inform me that they were ready for me to enter. As I followed him into the room, the dozen old white men in dark suits circling a large brown conference table stood in unison—a solemn ritual to show respect for the person whose soul was about to be cast out of God's Kingdom.

I quickly took my seat, and the men followed suit. The stake president was there and introduced me to the brethren by my full name "Brother Chad Michael Hardy," for whom the disciplinary council was being held. It was at this moment that I thought my parents must be wondering where they might have gone wrong. How could their good son make such a drastic series of choices that catapulted him from being on God's A-list into a room full of men with suits for the heaviest, most extreme of all church punishments?

I blame my sweet mother. She always told me to pray for the gift of discernment. Little did I know that gift would be the very thing that would clear the path to throw me out of God's Kingdom.

After an opening prayer was offered, the stake president followed with the accusations.

JUDGMENT OF SOULS

"The reason for this council is that you are reported to have published a calendar project that negatively reflects the image of the church and have repeatedly refused to stop publication of it, which is in deliberate opposition to the church and its leaders. It has also been reported that you have broken temple covenants by living with a member of the opposite sex outside of marriage, have not paid your tithes, and have not been attending church and priesthood meetings."

I was asked to state for the record that I was not wearing any recording devices before he turned the floor over to me to tell my entire story from the very beginning, dating back to my earliest memories in the church, so they could make a fair judgment of my soul. It's interesting now to think about the fact that they were concerned about being recorded. You would think that recording such a proceeding would be encouraged for transparency's sake, like any court of law. That's obviously not how things work. Despite not having any recording devices on my person that day, it is a day that is recorded as a core memory in my mind. One I'll never forget.

I took a deep breath as I stared at the strangers in front of me. There sat the stake president, the counselor I'd met before, and twelve additional council members. Some of them looked back with warm smiles; others stared at their hands; others looked bored and agitated. I had a strange feeling that the final decision as to what my future standing in the church would be had already been made by the executive offices in Salt Lake City. These men were simply going through the motions to fulfill their duty to their God.

I filtered no details of my life story from my happiest memories, including how Elder Neuenschwander showed me the miracle of forgiveness, to thoughts of suicide, and the broken promises from my patriarchal blessing, forcing me on a path outside the church in search of happiness. I knew my words would not affect the outcome of my fate, but I had to speak my (T)ruth.

I shared that despite living my life within the church, I never felt accepted. I never felt like I was a part of them, and that pretense and hypocrisy ran rampant. I shared how badly I had always wanted to belong and be included—that the promise of my "inheritance" was six generations deep and that I had pride in this. However, neither the church nor my inheritance could answer for the truth. I didn't just feel rejected—I *was* rejected. This was made all the more evident as I consistently struggled with my sexuality.

It was a heartfelt conversation I had with these men. I cleared up the fact about not living with a woman. Though they never once asked me if I had sexual relations with a man, they did ask if I had sexual relations outside of marriage with a woman.

They asked again if I would stop the calendar production, but I replied again that I couldn't and wasn't in it alone, having a funding partner in the project. I thought they would leave it there and be understanding. They agreed we weren't on the same page, but they appreciated what I had to say.

One man, with tears in his eyes, spoke up. He said, "I am so sorry that this is the experience you had with the church." Yet, despite this, they still chose to excommunicate me.

I remember walking out of the boardroom, down the hall, and into the waiting room, where my friends sat nervously on my behalf. I didn't have to tell them what had transpired because the energy radiating off me as I called the Associated Press revealed the outcome. We walked outside to face the media members, who were waiting for their own turn to receive the "news." I told them the truth. I had been excommunicated for "conduct unbecoming of the church."

It was finished. On July 13, 2008, at the age of thirty-one, I was excommunicated from The Church of Jesus Christ of Latter-day Saints, and the very next day, it was a leading story across the country.

Inside Edition was teasing it all day, "Mormon Calendar Creator Excommunicated!" My phone rang nonstop as the news began to make global headlines, much more than when the calendar was released. *Newsweek*, *TMZ*, *In Touch*, and every major news organization wanted an interview. I fielded satellite interviews from Australia and the United Kingdom. It was wild. And I suppose the old adage is true, any publicity is good publicity. We were selling so many calendars that I had to bring in somebody full-time to ship the orders daily.

LOSING MORE THAN MY RELIGION

The following month, I traveled to BYU to attend my graduation ceremony and walk across the stage with my fellow graduates. Before the ceremony, we were informed that the physical paper diploma would be mailed to us. Over a month later, when I still hadn't received my diploma in the mail, I called the University's advising center to find out when I might expect it. The advising center informed me that the degree had not been posted, said they could not explain why, and told me to speak to my advisor. I immediately called the Honor Code Office and the Financial Aid Office. Both verified there were no holds of any kind on my record. They could see nothing on my records that might prevent my degree from being posted.

I then spoke with my advisor, Brenda Butterfield, one of the few non-Mormon faculty at BYU. We always had a great relationship. I had the utmost respect for her. She told me she had investigated the situation and was told to inform me that a non-academic hold had been placed on my record. She said I needed to speak with Norman Finlinson, the executive director of Student Academic and Advisement Services. I called Mr. Finlinson, who apologized for not speaking with me sooner and said that he had meant to send me a letter. He said this letter would explain the reasons for the non-academic hold and would be mailed shortly. He would not discuss the matter nor give any explanation over the phone.

Deep down, I feared that my excommunication had something to do with it, but I thought *surely not*, seeing as I had finished my required coursework before my excommunication.

Well, the letter came alongside proof that the gut feeling was right. My name had been deleted from the August 2008 graduation list. I would not be awarded a degree from Brigham Young University because a non-academic hold was placed on my record prior to the posting of my degree. The letter further stated that BYU became aware that I was not in good honor code standing to graduate because I had been excommunicated from The Church of Jesus Christ of Latter-Day Saints, the affiliated sponsor of BYU. Additionally, it said that if I wish to be eligible for my degree in the future, I would need to be reinstated as a member of the church in good standing. At that point, I could be invited to contact the executive director of Student Academic and Advisement Services regarding my possible eligibility for the awarding of the degree.

To come back into "full fellowship" is an arduous process. I would need to repent, be rebaptized, pay my tithing, attend services, fulfill the laws and order of the church, and be deemed in good standing. Until this happened, my transcripts would be frozen, and I would lose the degree I'd worked so hard to get and pay for—a degree I was still paying for in more ways than one.

RELEASE THE IDEAL IMAGE

After I received the letter from BYU, I called Mr. Finlinson to discuss it. He provided no additional information and did not offer any options. He did not mention that I had a right to appeal the decision. I was told BYU would stand by its decision and that it was within its rights to refuse to award my degree.

I learned that BYU did not abide by its own honor code in withholding my degree. Before disciplinary action is taken, BYU must give the student notice in writing of the alleged violations of the honor code, provide procedural instructions, and allow the student to respond. I then called Vernon Heperi, the dean of students. When I asked him how I could appeal the decision, he said he would also be standing behind the letter. I hung up the phone, devastated.

The Associated Press picked up the story, and soon it was international news. Newspapers in every English-speaking country in the world carried the story, from small, local papers to large national and international ones. Utah radio stations, blogs, and other media discussed the incident, with readers and listeners invited to "weigh in" on the controversy.

As the story continued to grow legs, attorneys started coming out of the woodwork. I was getting approached left and right by other people who knew or had heard of someone else who had also had their education documents withheld from them. People from all over began contributing to my legal fund as a rally of support. With the pressure of my attorney and the press, BYU granted me an honor code hearing six months after disciplinary action was taken against me. I was allowed one person to attend the hearing with me—and it could not be a member of the Associated Press as I requested.

The last person I thought would show up for me in this circumstance was my dad. At first, he thought the calendars were fun and cheeky until the church took action, then he quickly changed his mind about it and stood behind the opinion of the church leaders.

I was shocked. My dad wanted to attend the hearing with me. He thought what BYU did was out of alignment with gospel principles. His being willing to voice his frustrations against the institution he had sworn allegiance to his entire life meant the world to me. He felt that I had earned my diploma and that the school (the church) had no right to withhold it from me. In my memory, this was the first and only time he showed up and went to bat for me.

Through my journey to Zero, I came to understand that just as the words of wisdom spoken by Elder Neuenschwander, my dad truly loved me, even though it may not have been apparent during my upbringing with his strict, rule-based approach to parenting. I realized that he showed love by protecting me from the destroyer through rules and obedience. I can only imagine the weight he carried, feeling like he had failed as a father, especially in terms of keeping me safe within the teachings of our faith.

With Zero, I have since adjusted my perspective and set my expectations aside. I released the image of the ideal father I had carried for so long and embraced him with all his imperfections and inabilities. I chose to see him perfect in his own design. Only then could I receive the love he offered in the way he knew how to express it.

Through this change in perspective, I started to see that his beautiful, imperfect heart was so fragile and broken that he had built an impermeable wall of protection around it. He endured a lifetime of bullying and prejudices because of his handicap and stutter. His parents made him hide his hand behind his back for photos. It took stepping into forgiveness and getting to Zero for me to truly see the depth of his wounds. From this place of Zero, I could wholeheartedly embrace the love he gave me in the small, unconventional doses he was equipped to give rather than rejecting it altogether because it didn't come packaged as I'd desired.

THE MATTER IS CLOSED . . . OR IS IT?

The hearing with the dean of students seemed a bit like a kangaroo court as Mr. Heperi dug his heels deeper into the sand on the already-made decision. Once the lawyers who had sought me out did a bit of digging, their eagerness began to dissipate, and one by one, they began to shy away. They'd come to realize that to take my case, they wouldn't just be taking on an academic institution but the powerful and wealthy LDS Church as well. The reality was that the church could and would swallow me financially in legal fees. Come to find out, the rules for private schools, even though accredited, are somehow protected by a maze of loopholes that serve and protect the institution and not its students. The ACLU would not touch this. In the end, the legal fund donations stopped coming in, and at that, the lawyers went away.

One man did stick around. His name was George Frandsen. He was a retired attorney who had attended law school at BYU years prior. He had offered to help me pro bono. He told me he was tired of BYU and the church being allowed to bully people and make their own rules—breaking

246 LAW OF ZERO

them as it serves them. He felt someone needed to hold them accountable and was willing to help me do it.

George poured himself into researching BYU and found several violations that the school was in with the Northwest Commission on Colleges and Universities (NWCCU). He determined that this was the angle of pursuit, and I agreed. We streamlined all his research into a single seventeen-page letter that showcased each violation line by line. We had found several incidents where BYU had allowed the church leaders to decide whether a student was worthy enough to graduate. Per the accreditation standards, it was a violation for any person or entity unrelated to the college to hold influence over a student's education.

A few weeks after I mailed the letter to the NWCCU, I received a response from Dr. Sandra E. Elman, president of the Northwest Commission.

After carefully reviewing both the material you submitted and the documentation of Brigham Young University, the Commission has concluded that the University's actions do not represent non-compliance with the Commission's Standards for accreditation. The Commission now considers this matter closed.

I felt defeated. I realized it was, like so many things, all about money and power. My brother was outraged, telling me that withholding my degree was unfair and constituted a punishment far too severe for the alleged infraction. He was there, taking a stand for me, offering me emotional support, but I was too caught up in my own trauma to see it.

Having been well-versed in the effects of trauma and practiced in the art of revenge, I remember lying in bed thinking: *I could become a vigilante about this. The media was still on my side. I could leverage that and stir up the documentary makers and get them to go after the corruption that exists in the education system in our country. That would work.*

But in the quiet of my space, in the depth of my heart, I didn't want to be that person. I didn't want this to be my legacy. I wanted to let go. I wanted to let go of all of it. I just didn't know how. Eventually, I decided that I didn't need a degree to be successful. I had the education, whether or not I had the paperwork to prove it. That would be enough—that would have to be enough.

Despite my newfound intentions, I still had the seed of revenge germinating within me. I still had my calendars selling like hotcakes. As such, my next move was the BYU Edition of the *Men on a Mission* calendar featuring its alumni, including a centerfold of myself. If that didn't pour enough salt on the wound, we also created a new calendar featuring Mormon mothers titled *Hot Mormon Muffins*, with the following description:

> Twelve beautiful Mormon mothers posing in kitschy vintage pin-up style. Much like the missionary men before them, these sexy moms have dared to step into the spotlight to break down stereotypes and extend a hand of friendship beyond religious and social boundaries. Shot in a centerfold format with oversized imagery, the calendar features the ladies' favorite muffin recipes with a portion of the proceeds going to Breast Cancer research. **All calendars and products are shipped in plain packaging to ensure that others don't covet your muffins.

This venture certainly raised eyebrows as it offered a different view of some of the women in the LDS community. Yes, it's true that most Mormon mothers would not choose to be part of such a project, yet it's also true that there are plenty of faith-filled women who would (and did) find it empowering and liberating to be seen not just as a Mormon, not just as a mother, but as a beautiful, sexual being.

As soon as the *Hot Mormon Muffins* calendar hit the market, the media went into a feeding frenzy with feature stories that plastered news headlines worldwide once again. It even made the Google Hot List as the second most searched item on the web. Amid fielding interview requests from reporters, I got a call about doing a reality show, to which I initially said no. But after their persistence, I eventually agreed to drive out to Santa Monica, California, and meet with a small production team.

The team hailed from Australia, mainly producing documentaries, and they were really forward-thinking. They loved the project as soon as it came across their newsfeeds and felt the networks would easily pick it up. They explained their vision of how the show would follow the lives of a half dozen Mormon mothers running a bakery startup in Salt Lake City with me as their boss, like Charlie from *Charlie's Angels*. The characters would empower their sexuality to build a brand selling muffins and challenge the status quo stereotype in Utah, all while balancing their home life and their personal struggles within Mormon culture.

Sounded brilliant. I would just have to convince the women in the calendar to go along with it, which to my surprise, was much easier than expected. After all, I now had a scarlet letter placed on me, and many models shied away from the project after I was disciplined for it. Unexpectedly, the women featured in our calendar were willing and ready to let their voices be heard.

The next thing I knew, we were knee-deep shooting a pilot, and everybody wanted this show. Reality TV was big then, and we were getting interest from numerous networks. On the top of the list were Bravo, Oprah's Network OWN, and the Food Network. The show had been given the green light at OWN by the network producers all the way to the top. It seemed like we were days away from signing a deal. And then, as suddenly as it gained momentum, it was hit on the head, dead in the water. Once Oprah passed us on, others followed suit until we were bought by the Game Show Network, which seemed like a strange fit, and then shelved and forgotten.

Other things started to fall by the wayside. Our interview with *The*

Daily Show with Jon Stewart was abruptly canceled the day before we were to shoot, and then our slot with *The View* was pushed and canceled.

A follow-up story on *Inside Edition* was filmed and never aired. Montel Williams kept pushing our interview back and then eventually ghosted. The *CBS morning show* flew me all the way to New York City to go live, only to tell me when I got to the hotel they provided for me that my interview had been removed from the lineup and to enjoy my free trip to the Big Apple.

I couldn't figure out how, just as things would be about to happen, they wouldn't. It was like the rug was consistently being pulled out from under me. Then, I got a chilling phone call from my mom.

"Chad, don't call the house phone anymore."

I heard a series of click-click-click sounds on the call.

"Chad, hang up now!" she exclaimed.

I was worried. I called her back on her cell phone and asked what was happening. She said there had been a small crew working on the phone lines outside her home, but they were not from the phone company. She put it together; someone had been listening in on our calls. I had called her all the time to give updates on news interviews and the progress of the reality show.

My mom worked at the Mormon temple. We quickly realized these people were serious and would ensure they stayed one step ahead of me. They took the LDS Church's reputation seriously and were willing to cross boundaries where they deemed necessary. I began to wonder about the intentions of the two men dressed in suits parked outside my house for two weeks after the first news broke. Who exactly were they? Was it all just part of a scheme to scare and intimidate me? To be honest, if so, their efforts were working.

Not only was every door suddenly shut to me, but I was beginning to spiral into a state of paranoia. I was scared that my mom might lose her job or that this would all become the identifying factor of my life.

More than this, I was just tired. This whole thing had just become so toxic and soul-draining. It had all really just started as a prank business born of my hurt feelings. It was a way to strike back against the church and the self-righteous people of St. George for stealing my livelihood and dreams. It had all just snowballed from there. I remember thinking back to my literal and figurative vow I'd made to myself on Utah Lake—that come hell or high water, or both, I intended to go to Vegas and start my team-building company.

I began to think about that single beacon of light that had guided us to safety. Where was that light now? Where was my instinct to know just what to do next? I began to understand how the calendars became a runaway train that ultimately became a roadblock to my dream. My startup company suffered due to my inability to let go of the past. I didn't know much, but I did know this—and this was enough for me to drop the lawsuit George and I were pursuing. I had to find a way back to my dream and, more so, back to myself.

18

CLEARING OUT TRAUMA

After a traumatic experience, the human system of self-preservation seems to go onto permanent alert, as if the danger might return at any moment.

—Judith Lewis Herman, *Trauma and Recovery*

Over the next year and a half, anxiety once again found its way into my psyche, but this time, I could not medicate or meditate it away. I was in real trouble—again. I called my Aunt Cherylee, who had been practicing biofeedback and doing brain training on her clients with anxiety and addiction issues, with positive results. We decided that I needed to start treating the underlying issues of my anxiety.

We began by having a few counseling sessions over the phone. We determined that I would benefit from a trip to the White Mountains in Arizona, where she could conduct a week-long intensive training with her new electroencephalograph (EEG) biofeedback machine.[1] There are various forms of biofeedback. My aunt uses one that monitors your brain waves using an EEG. During the session, you're connected to electrical sensors on your scalp that monitor your brain waves while listening to the waves as tones and musical-sounding notes that mimic brain waves. How my aunt explained it to me is like holding up a mirror to your brain. Similar to when you look at yourself in the mirror to adjust your collar or fix your hair, the machine helps you listen to your brain waves in real time to recognize when it is firing incorrectly. When your brain sees the negative activity, it can find the trauma and create new neural pathways around it.

We needed to rewire my brain, so to speak. This meant stepping into the biggest picture and processing my trauma. If I were to find my way to any form of peace, any fragment of productivity in my daily life, something all-encompassing must occur—and I had to be both willing and all in. I needed to come to terms with not just the actions of others but also with my own.

I was both ready and willing. More than anything, I just wanted to feel safe, secure, harmonious, and most of all, authentic. I wanted to reach the ultimate place of trust—the state of neutrality. I was unwittingly seeking Zero; this was what I so desperately needed in my life.

The twice-a-day therapy began with basic exercises that would ease my brain into flexibility for the treatment to work. Each session, my aunt would hook me up to the machine like a scene from *The Matrix*. With electrodes attached to my head and earphones in my ears, random musical notes would play that sounded like a toddler got its hand on a xylophone as it attempted to follow the orchestra conductor in my subconscious mind. Some sessions, I would just lay there and relax, and others would require my aunt to lead me through a guided meditation with visualizations.

In the first session, she had me recline in a chair to get comfortable and relax. She then instructed me to close my eyes and imagine I was riding a bike on an open road, tracking on the center yellow line. Next, I was to weave outside the line from left to right, increasing the girth of the weave as I progressed. This exercise is created to put a person at ease while getting the left and right sides of the brain to communicate with one another. It was miraculous. I remember feeling both relaxed and exhilarated as I weaved my way forward. I could almost feel the wind on my face and in my hair. I felt like, if I took my hands off the handlebars, the bike would magically continue to weave all of its own accord. When I came out of the meditation, Cherylee said that my brain responded really well, better than most of her patients. She showed me the graph on her computer that looked like a Richter scale, which displayed how my brain waves went from intense to moderate.

As I continued the sessions, one focused specifically on my upbringing, we uncovered a heap of intergenerational trauma stored in my cells. During the session, I felt the emotions and envisioned aspects of my family history that I never remembered learning. The experience is not simple to describe, yet it profoundly impacted me. It allowed me to fully understand the concept of epigenetics as it related directly to me and the connection to my ancestors.

The beauty in the study of epigenetics is that each person has more than twenty thousand genes, and the possible combinations of these genes being switched on or off are astronomical. This means the system itself is malleable.

Such malleability offers a new and exciting application for the law of cause and effect and a fantastic reality for humanity as a whole. These newfound discoveries indicate that, even on a biological level, we may be able to pinpoint specific effects, trace them to their correlating causes, and release them by getting to Zero with them. Once we achieve this state of Zero, we can influence our biology. This is as close as I've come to understanding my claim for the limitless application of the law of Zero. It's precisely what I've experienced in my life.

Besides brain training, there are additional models and strategies for addressing traumatic experiences, and these can, in effect, rewire our Human Story Code as it pertains to particular stimuli or trauma points. Such work is already being done through cognitive-behavioral approaches in trauma-informed therapy. Elements of trauma can be passed down from generation to generation through culture, story, and association, and our biology is impacted too. This is a big deal. It's a big deal because a person's Human Story Code not only takes into account their life and unique experiences but it also includes their specific lineage—all integrated into their unique being—to include their biology. In this context, we can truly identify our place within humanity itself.

If we can trust science this far, perhaps we can trust it a bit more. Maybe we can trust an idea that science can't quite harness just yet. This is the idea that releasing our trauma can create a ripple effect in both directions. Not only does it liberate us to move forward, but it also provides healing for our ancestors in the past.

OUT THE WINDOW

The next day, after I was hooked back up to the machine and comfortable in the chair, I was instructed to visualize a safe place. A space void of discomfort, criticism, fear, harassment, or any form of emotional or physical harm. Soon a lush green meadow appeared in my mind. An encompassing base of tall trees and majestic mountains on all sides surrounded the meadow. A cabin with a front porch and a porch swing was in the middle of the meadow. Intuitively, I stepped onto the porch. As I described the vision to my aunt, she instructed me to sit on the swing and speak to my subconscious mind. I was to ask: "What trauma exists? What needs to be addressed?"

My mind then shuffled through several people and unexpectedly landed on a vision of myself as a child. Looking at the five-year-old version of me, I realized who he was and why he was here. He stood in the middle of the meadow in front of the cabin and was very apprehensive. He didn't want to respond emotionally or physically in any way, so I began to open my heart to him with the vibrational energy of pure love. At this, he approached and followed me into the cabin. Once in the cabin, we found an empty room with a door. Through the door was another empty room that led to a third room. This room was dark and dingy with a neglected, soot-covered fireplace and two windows.

When we entered this space, the child was no longer there, but the trauma he represented was. Memories of my collective childhood birthday parties appeared. I immediately felt this immense feeling of unfairness and sadness overcome me. As a child, not only was I celiac, but I was also allergic to processed sugar and dairy. This meant that I couldn't eat birthday cake at my own birthdays or anyone else's for that matter. I had not realized how something like this could impact a person to the point of causing a root of trauma in their Human Story Code, but it made sense as such realities can cause emotional injuries. If these injuries are only felt and not acknowledged, they do take root.[2]

As I conveyed these revelations to my aunt, she instructed me to focus on feeling my emotions. As I did this, I knew exactly what to do. I scooped up all the energy associated with these emotions and threw them out the window. I then did a sweep of the entire room to ensure I removed everything. Once this was complete, I recreated the birthday party I had always wanted in my head. The party included my very own triple-layered chocolate cake, stacks of beautifully wrapped presents, and pounds of mint chocolate chip ice cream, along with all of my friends and family there to celebrate with me.

As we continued, fragmented pieces of trauma revealed themselves in the most random and abstract ways. All feelings of self-doubt and sabotaging emotions came to the surface and filled the room as words, people, and places. Traumatic experiences would appear like an instant playback in full detail, including the abuse my brother put me through during our adolescent years, being stranded on the lake, negative experiences with family members, being bullied at school, church worthiness interviews and discipline, and entire belief systems that contradicted my authentic self that I still subconsciously clung to.

As each memory presented itself, I would feel the deep-rooted emotional pain attached. It was ugly and heart-wrenching and almost too much to bear. I wanted to rip the electrodes off my head and quit, but Cherylee was there and made me feel safe, encouraging me to be brave and push through. One by one, I threw all of the energy of each trauma out the imaginary window until the dingy, dark room was filled with a brilliant, divine light, and the fireplace illuminated the most beautiful warm glow.

After the session, I learned that my brain had reached an incredible state of quiet. Cherylee said that such a response was astounding. The treatment had gone so well that she insisted I would sleep like a baby that night.

However, this was not the case at all. During the night, I shot straight out of bed as I awakened in the midst of another panic attack. My entire body felt overwhelmed by a sense of fear. My heart raced, and I couldn't seem to get enough breath into my lungs. As my eyes began to focus in the dark room, there at the foot of my bed stood a premonition of the five-year-old me who'd visited me in the meadow. Like a scene right out of a horror film, he walked up right next to me and whispered into my ear: "There is something else I need to tell you." Then, he disappeared. I was dumbfounded, scared, and confused, but the anxiety immediately subsided. I even fell back asleep.

The next morning, I woke up and walked downstairs, where my aunt was making breakfast. She grinned from ear to ear in anticipation of me reporting on how well I had slept. I told her about my premonition of what felt like the ghost of Christmas past. She dropped everything and told me to get back into the chair.

She leaned me back and quickly hooked me up to the electrodes; the strange sounds of the machine fired back up. As soon as I closed my eyes, I was immediately transported back to the meadow. Five-year-old me stood there, waiting. He approached me and grabbed my hand to walk me into the house. The scene shifted to my kindergarten playground. As I looked around, I saw the shadow of a man standing next to the big tree on the other side of the fence. I felt a terrifying sense of fear I had never experienced before. It was dark and evil. I began to cry uncontrollably because it felt as if some demonic force had gripped my heart and began to squeeze hard.

Though I was suffering, the child begged me to stay and watch. My aunt, guiding me, asked for the name of the man, and I blurted out his full name. She asked me what he did to me, but I couldn't remember. What-ever he did was so evil that I had repressed the memory but not the pain.

I begged my aunt to stop the session, and she looked at me with tears in her eyes. She told me I was the most happy-go-lucky child, always laughing and smiling until kindergarten. I went from being very outgoing to suddenly being shy, reserved, and insecure.

The unnamed man was my mom's best friend's husband and a member of our church. I had not thought about or heard about him in years, so it astonished me how he came to mind just as clear as day.

I called my mom that evening, asking if she had ever left me with this man. I could only remember occasionally going to his house as a child, but she told me yes, he would sometimes pick me and my brother up from school and take us to his house until she got off work. As far as she knew, nothing out of the ordinary occurred. Yet the (T)ruth of me said differently.

I don't know what he did to me, but I know something happened. Whatever it was, it was evil, and it changed me. In recognition of this, Cherylee and I continued the training, working through every aspect of my life. We constructed my trauma timeline and worked our way to the present day. There were no stones left unturned.

EXTENDING GRACE

One of the stones we turned was my brother. After realizing there was so much more packed into my trauma, it became clear that my child-hood grievances ran much deeper than mere sibling rivalry. I had spent years, from my early childhood to young adulthood, blaming him for all the misfortunes that plagued my life. I had made him the scapegoat for everything I perceived as wrong with me, unfairly pointing the finger of blame squarely at him. Only then did I start to fathom the depth of this tangled tale.

I considered the reality that, like all of us, my brother suffered his own unique traumas. He had his own fair share of struggles and was constantly being disciplined. Perhaps it was me who changed at age five, and his actions toward me were a response to the shift in my behavior. Even though that does not dismiss or take away the pain I felt, it does solidify the reality that I found myself caught in the crossfire of trauma. His trauma—my trauma. After all, we were both just kids trying to make sense of the world.

I may never uncover the entire truth of what happened, nor do I need to, but this is clear: reality doesn't always align with our perceptions. Our Human Story Codes are persuasive, shaping our narrow world perspective. This is why extending grace to those who trespass against us is crucial. We must recognize that we will never fully comprehend the depths of their stories as they interconnect with ours. Beneath the surface lies a narrative we might never grasp.

Because of trauma, the conditioning of our Human Story Code can lead to ignorance in matters of love. I believed myself so unlovable that I failed to see the pure love emanating from those closest to me. Like my dad, my brother had an unconventional way of expressing his love. As we grew older, he fell short of meeting the expectations of what I felt I needed from him. Sound familiar? So I turned away from any ounce of love he offered me. If I couldn't have it my way, I didn't want it at all. When he showed up on my doorstep with nowhere to go, all I could think about was how much he would be inconveniencing me. Only in hindsight did I grasp the significance of his act of showing up at my doorstep; it was his way of showing up for me. Because deep down, he loved me.

As I nursed my wounds in the aftermath of my battle with the church and BYU, which I created all by myself, many friends and family members shunned me. But not once did my brother turn his back on me. Instead, he became a significant source of support during this time. Witnessing firsthand the anxiety and stress I endured from the harsh punishment I received in retaliation for my transgressions, he chose to formally have his name removed from the church's records to stand in solidarity with me.

Regardless of your stance on the faith or whether you still practice, this was no small thing. Growing up in the LDS Church, the doctrines become ingrained in you, intertwined with every other facet of your identity. He was willing to throw away his promise and excommunicate himself for me. This marked a pivotal turning point, one that not only bridged the gap of our strained relationship but also helped to heal years of pain.

19

THE KEY TO FINDING
AND LOVING YOUR SELF

*By oneself is evil done; by oneself is one defiled. By oneself
is evil left undone; by oneself is one made pure. Purity and
impurity depended on oneself; no one can purify another.*

—Gautama Buddha, *The Dhammapada*

After doing the extensive release work with my Aunt Cherylee, I reflected on the hurricane of a life I had been living. It was no wonder I was in such a state of dysfunction. I was not living the complete life I was made to live. I was undoubtedly not encompassing and embodying the moment at hand. I could then see quite clearly how all the trauma I had gathered within myself (including that which I had self-created) kept me from living out a path of the pure love.

As I continued to search my soul for understanding, I realized I had been given a precious gift all those years ago within the walls of the church I had long wanted to seek revenge against. I reflected back on how powerful forgiveness had been in my life. It was perhaps the greatest gift I'd ever received.

When I looked back on the calendar project, I can remember fantasizing about how it was going to prove me right. It would prove that the church is full of hateful and judgmental people. Well, it's not hard to find what you're looking for in a big wide world such as ours, so of course that's exactly what I found. In the end, I also found that I, too, could be hateful and judgmental. That I, too, could be vengeful and self-serving and choose to only see partial truths to soothe my own pain and appease my own poisons. I had experienced people being divisive again and again throughout my life, and here I was, creating even more division.

I decided that my continued therapy would be to write a tell-all book about my entire experience, and how I discovered the miracle of forgiveness. The more I wrote and released onto the paper from my head and heart, the better I felt. This was it! Release. This was just what I needed. *I could do this.*

So, I kept writing. It wasn't until I got about ten chapters in that wisdom appeared. I began to realize the entire manuscript, every secretive detail, came from a place of pain, just as the calendars had. My life experiences summed up a very salacious story and not much more. It was clear I failed as an expert on forgiveness. I had not fully forgiven the church. I had not completely forgiven my brother. I had not forgiven myself. *I couldn't publish this.* To publish this book would make me a hypocrite and cause more hurt to my family and the people I loved. It would also cultivate more division and allow readers to justify their own traumas and pain into victimhood, as this was precisely what I was doing, unbeknownst to myself.

I needed higher ground. This did not occur in the ways it had to merely circle back and hurt others. With this understanding, I went to wisdom with my concern and questioned, "What now? What do I do?" Straight away, I knew the answer. *Not this.*

Full stop, I put the writings to bed. I knew that this was not the legacy I wanted. It was not the mark I wanted to make on the world. I needed to ask myself how I wanted to live my life. Would I keep plodding forward, striking back again and again to get the world to acknowledge all the wrongs that exist? Is there any particular measure of effort I could put forth that would ever secure the justice I sought, any action I could take to counter my pain?

No. No, there wasn't, and I just wanted to live my life. I wanted happiness, and I wanted freedom. I didn't want to keep scratching and clawing to get people to see my value. I didn't want to crave justice. I didn't want to be vengeful or to live my life with the negative energy that all this sadness, anger, and resentment both created and perpetuated.

In retrospect, this release process did serve me well; it allowed me to get all that pain out on paper. It served me even better to never allow it to be published. Those first writings were my way into awareness. It was in the mapping out of my story in this linear fashion that I was able to see the extensive trauma within me that STILL needed to be acknowledged and brought into the light. Once I was made aware of this, I could take ownership of it—I could actually do something about it. And if my own story had taught me anything, it was that seeking revenge and hurting others to even the score was not the answer.

Through my quest for answers, I recalled healing my body as a child, the miracle of forgiveness, my deck of cards experience, and the magic of Snow Canyon. I recalled swimming out of that lake with the odds stacked against me. I had seen too many miracles in my life to engulf myself in anything that didn't reflect that. Wisdom showed me that I must return to the basics of who I am and reclaim my purpose.

My purpose was bringing people together, team-building, (eventually) writing a book that would help people to heal, and manifesting positive and life-affirming things—and above all, my purpose was happiness. So I decided to let go, to release it all. I chose to lose, as this was the only way I could truly win.

FINDING FORGIVENESS

I tapped the weather app and smiled at the display: a perfect 72 degrees. San Diego's nickname, "America's Finest City," couldn't feel more fitting. I walked into my new office in the heart of Hillcrest, a bright red building shadowed by an oversized rainbow flag—a proud emblem of the community. It was the summer of 2019, four years since I had traded the neon lights of Las Vegas for this coastal paradise, all to grow my team-building enterprise. Life, by all accounts, was splendid.

As I exchanged morning pleasantries with my staff, my phone rang—it was my dear friend Quinn. His voice carried an urgency I'd rarely heard before. "You have to finish that book on forgiveness," he pressed. To underline his point, he and our friend Yayoi made the drive from Los Angeles to San Diego, not just for a casual visit but with a mission.[1] As we settled around my table, the weight of their message became clear. This book wasn't just a project; it was a calling. With time and a new perspective, I felt reinvigorated and ready to resume writing. However, my focus had shifted. I felt what I needed to explore was so much more than forgiveness.

This shift led me to a pivotal question: What is on the other side of forgiveness?

That evening, after they left, I settled into a quiet meditation and allowed myself to be deeply immersed in this question. In that serene space, I asked wisdom for some clarity. And once again, I heard that familiar, gentle voice whisper, "It's called the law of Zero."

At that moment, I knew this was a direct message from the Divine. Forgiveness is the key to unlocking sacred power. But what kind of power? I knew my next venture: I needed to learn what the law of Zero entailed and how it applied to forgiveness. My first discovery was that one can learn to manage virtually any trauma by embracing forgiveness. My second realization was that by holding onto pain, we prevent ourselves from tapping into the full potential of Zero. The third, perhaps most crucial, was the understanding that inauthentic living veils us from the true essence of Zero, keeping us from the core of our being where our power resides. At the time, I didn't fully understand Zero. But I knew that, through forgiveness, we would find a direct path to its power, whatever that might be.

I have learned that there are three primary categories when it comes to forgiveness. There is forgiveness of others, situational forgiveness, and perhaps most significantly, forgiveness of self. I have also learned that, in many instances, more than one of these categories needs to exist.

A significant indicator that forgiveness is needed is rumination. To ruminate is to consider something repeatedly, to continue turning it over and over in your mind, to get stuck on it or in it. When rumination takes hold, you cannot release or move past the grievance—often to the point of embracing it in some strange and dysfunctional capacity. Rumination generally shows up as repetitive thoughts or actions. It can manifest in the reliving or retelling of the painful situation and (especially) its impact, over and over again.

There are other telltale signs of the necessity of forgiveness. Whether or not we recognize them, they often manifest within our bodies. These signs can be emotional, but they might also appear physically. For me, it is both. I react emotionally and physically to pain, whether it arises from situations, others, or even self-inflicted circumstances. It impacts every part of my being, playing a significant role in my struggles with irritable bowel syndrome, anxiety, and depression. These can be manifestations of past and present trauma.

Per the Substance Abuse and Mental Health Services Administration (SAMHSA), there are both immediate and delayed responses to trauma: "Initial reactions to trauma can include exhaustion, confusion, sadness, anxiety, agitation, numbness, dissociation, confusion, physical arousal, and blunted affect. Most responses are normal because they affect most survivors and are socially acceptable, psychologically effective, and self-limited. Indicators of more severe responses include continuous distress without periods of relative calm or rest, severe dissociation symptoms, and intense intrusive recollections that continue despite a return to safety. Delayed responses to trauma can include persistent fatigue, sleep disorders, nightmares, fear of recurrence, anxiety focused on flashbacks, depression, and avoidance of emotions, sensations, or activities that are associated with the trauma, even remotely."[2]

The Immediate and Delayed Reactions to Trauma chart grants us an honest view of why we should all desire the capacity to find our way to Zero and, thus, forgiveness.[3] Recognizing this, I'm now committed to being action-oriented toward achieving a state of Zero concerning grievances and trauma. I rely on its principles as it relates to forgiveness as a vital tool for managing my mental and physical health.

Catherine Ponder, an American minister and founder of Unity Church Worldwide, once said, "When you hold resentment toward another, you are bound to that person or condition by an emotional link that is stronger than steel. Forgiveness is the only way to dissolve that link and get free."[4] These words and Unity's belief system (expressed as The Five Principles) resonate with me.[5]

When it comes to forgiving others, awareness is the first step. This is because interpersonal wounds are not always easy to recognize, especially those that are born of unreleased trauma from the past. Forgiveness begins with exploring how you've avoided or chosen to address the emotion tied to the person, incident, or situation. Looking directly at *your* role in the scenario—even if your role (up until now) is just an emotional response—and taking hold of it with your mind's eye puts you in a powerful position.

This is a crucial component of self-possession, defined as the state or feeling of being calm, confident, and in control of one's feelings and self to be composed. Next, it is essential to acknowledge that merely responding emotionally or developing coping mechanisms *only* is not the answer. It is not a resolution. Neither is ignoring what occurred. Recognize that where there is trauma, forgiveness is not just needed but necessary for true freedom and personal harmony to be found.

Once you've taken a good look at yourself, it can then be beneficial to consider the offender. Think about *their* humanity, *their* trauma, *their* intentions, and *their* circumstances. You must look at the person through the lens of love. Consider the unknown pain and hidden realities of the life they've led. This view can be held when you practice acknowledging that all humans have trauma. There is great value in cultivating this reality. Go ahead. Bring an individual who has offended you to mind and consider them in these ways.

It's not easy, is it? That's okay. This is all preparatory work, a litmus test by design. Stepping into this tender space is an exercise that allows you to assess if you're ready to forgive. If not, that is okay too. Just to consider forgiveness is a step in the right direction. Consideration alone reveals your heart place and mental state, which allows you to take possession of your (T)ruth. This is genuine progress.

Situational forgiveness, though a less commonly discussed concept, plays a crucial role in ensuring that trauma does not strangle our connection to Source. It applies to scenarios in which events, circumstances, or natural occurrences beyond anyone's control cause us harm and leave deep emotional scars. Imagine being a survivor of a devastating natural disaster or war, dealing with the death of a loved one, grappling with a life-changing illness, or enduring the hardships of an economic recession. The frustration and helplessness that arise from such situations can be maddening. These are the moments in films when the protagonist looks up at the sky in despair and cries out, "God! Why have you forsaken me?!" In the absence of a tangible entity to blame, we turn our eyes to the heavens.

The anger, resentment, and bitterness stemming from these unexpected and undeserved events often feel righteously justified. While these emotions are completely valid, choosing to dwell in them and allowing them to consume us is a decision we make. By practicing situational forgiveness, we can start accepting life's unpredictability and fallible nature. This means acknowledging that we cannot always foresee or control these events and choosing to accept unchangeable circumstances. In doing so, we release the pain that hinders our progress, thus paving the way for healing and reconnection with our inner peace and with Source.

Perhaps the most helpful quote I came across while researching forgiveness was one from Ram Dass's most well-known book, *Be Here Now*, where the beloved guru shares an encouraging word: "You've got to go at the rate you can go. You wake up at the rate you wake up. You're finished with your desires at the rate you finish with your desires. You can't rip the skin off the snake. The snake must molt the skin. That's the rate it happens."[6]

These words have been so helpful for me while crafting this book amid a worldwide pandemic and numerous day-to-day struggles. They have helped me to be calm, patient, and understanding—they've also granted me the wisdom to know that I, too, cannot rip the skin off the snake. The process (all processes) takes the time that it takes. Deep trauma, especially, has a way of taking the time it takes to contend with it, and that's okay. It's all part of the human condition.

SELF-LOVE

The process of mastering forgiveness boils down to cultivating a sense of self-love. To do this, we must engage in the art of forgiving Self. It requires a holistic perspective, recognizing our actions as part of a greater whole. We must be able to address our own faults and take ownership over our own behaviors because here's the thing, poor choices are poor choices—no matter the story ascribed to them. If we don't have personal responsibility, what do we have?

The most impactful relationship a person will ever have is their relationship with their Self as well as their relationship with their (T)ruth. Ask yourself these questions: What do I think? What do I feel? Is this true? Do I *really* feel this? Do I *truly* believe this?

Is the most impactful human relationship I have with myself?

There is a powerful reference to the Self in *The Hundred Thousand Songs of Milarepa*, wherein the teacher states, "It is difficult to conquer oneself while vanquishing the outer world; conquer now your own Self-mind. To slay this deer will never please you. But if you kill the Five Poisons within, all your wishes will be fulfilled. If one tries to vanquish foes in the outer world, they increase in greater measure. If one conquers his Self-mind within, all his foes soon disappear."[7]

The five poisons referenced here are also known as the five negative emotions: anger, jealousy, pride, ignorance, and attachment. Time has a grand way of teaching us all sorts of lessons, and interestingly, I have found over time that when it comes to a person's need to forgive themself, there will be at least one of these five negative emotions present.

By recognizing these emotions, I learned that many of my choices were not the path to peace or happiness, and I had to face that reality. I also had to forgive myself for my choices, actions, and divisive hand in it all. Once I did this, I could see how my choices affected my family. Also, how my actions in regard to the calendar project reflected poorly on the very good and beautiful people within the LDS faith—I had to acknowledge the various repercussions that I, myself, had created. In the end, I needed to not only admit to this, I needed to work to rectify it.

The first step was to acknowledge it, learn from it, and forgive myself for it—for all of it. The process of forgiving oneself always includes reflection. You must acknowledge your role within the situation and take responsibility for the trauma you've caused. Next, reflect on why the event occurred, as in which forces were within your control and which were outside of it. From here, you extract the lessons that this particular incident or scenario has for you so you can identify how to avoid such a place or state in the future.

It can be helpful when forgiving yourself to start by focusing on the loving, powerful energy of Source. It can also be helpful to write or to talk it out, as this attaches your past actions to the present moment. Saying "I forgive myself" earnestly and aloud can be so powerful because it grants form to (T)ruth. When you do this, you allow the (T)ruth of forgiveness to take root in a tangible way, not only in your life but in the world.

For the longest time, I became so entangled in the thick of it all, and I was totally unaware that forgiveness of myself was what I truly needed. I was so wrapped up in the constructs of what others deemed "The Way" that "My Way" was a foreign concept with no self-assigned parameters or boundaries. This conundrum manifested into the man in the mirror, a living paradox trapped between these two ways of being. Because of fear, I resisted facing the (T)ruth he represented, which led to my aversion toward him.

As I began to connect and truly engage with his reflection, that disdain turned inward, causing me to despise myself. It was only through learning to embrace self-love that I found the capacity to forgive myself for the self-destructive victim I had become. I had to forgive myself for denying my (T)ruth for so many years. Only then did it become clear that the man in the mirror was not a cautionary tale nor the alluring pied piper working tirelessly to lead me astray. He was and has always been my (T)rue reflection, my (T)rue story, my (T)rue light, my (T)rue purpose. He stood as a beacon, a guiding light, leading me toward discovering my authentic, divine (T)ruth. He showed me the love buried deep beneath my wounds. The love that is Me.

Forgiveness of Self is not an easy endeavor. Suffice to say, it all boils down to one reality. One must learn to forgive oneself of their own wrongdoings if one is ever to be capable of forgiving others of theirs.

This profound lesson hit me full stop when it became clear that the letter I had written my brother years prior did not complete the forgiveness process. It was just the beginning. It took many years for me to discover that I needed to turn inward to relinquish the blame I harbored toward him and to extend forgiveness to myself. In this sacred space of self-compassion, I discovered the true essence of forgiveness.

Alexander Pope once wrote, "To err is human; to forgive, divine."[8] This sentiment aligns with my belief that forgiveness is an act inseparable from love. To know love is to know Zero and vice versa. It takes love to conquer all great difficulties—and forgiveness is not just difficult, it can be downright impossible. But with Zero, it can be achieved. With love, it can be easier.

The key to forgiveness will always be found in the divine essence of love. If you can find love in your heart of your own accord, that's commendable. If not, practice the art of accessing it. If you cannot extend your own human love, even to yourself, practice extending the love of all creation. This loving resource is not only consistent but irrefutably available to you. The love that dwells in all creation is available to you to give and to receive. You can channel it, both for yourself and for others. And if forgiveness feels impossible, that's okay—just know that it *is* possible. Maybe not just yet. Forgiveness takes time. Take what time you need.

When you learn to unlock the sacred power of forgiveness, you enable yourself to heal and move forward with your life. Forgiveness grants empathy, renewal, calm, and peace of mind. It is the key to freedom, happiness, and magic. It grants us passage to Zero.

20

ACCESSING ZERO

He who tastes life as it really is, not as men say or think it is,
is indeed wise with the wisdom of God rather than of men.

—Thomas À Kempis, *The Imitation of Christ*

As the adventure of life marches on, Zero continues to work mysteriously in the context of every person's story. I hope as you've delved through the pages of this book that you've been inspired to reflect on your story. Perhaps you recognized and connected the dots backward to see that Zero has always been at work for you.

It's my heartfelt desire that you've been able to be honest with yourself. And that you've identified the pivotal moments where the threads of your Human Story Code intertwine, shedding light on the aspects of your life that need healing. As you move forward, trust the incredible power of Zero within you to guide you on this transformational journey.

Remember, your will is the only prerequisite to accessing Zero. With this key in hand, you can unlock the sacred power of human potential, release pain and trauma, embrace forgiveness, and create magic. Zero grants access to your individual sacred self. This sacred self is your soul, its consciousness, the birthright of your higher self.

The power contained within the sacred self can shape more than your day-to-day existence. It has breadth, range, and magnitude—it has amplitude. If you let it, it will rewrite your Human Story Code and transform your life. Not only that, but when you are in sync with Zero, your destiny will be revealed, your legacy strengthened, and your world illuminated. The transformation within you will allow you to play a pivotal role in changing our world for the better. Your power will create a world that radiates love and acceptance rather than greed, control, and judgment.

So, how do we go about changing the world?

SACRED POWER

We start right where we are. Small acts of forgiveness and love within our family and friend circles create the ripple effect of Zero. We can work within our communities, churches, and workplaces to be a beacon of light and acceptance. Where there is greed, control, and judgment, we trace our way to the trauma and choose to see it. We recognize the world's pain, suffering, and injustice, and we stand defiant of it with the power of Zero.

As we do this, we recognize the creative power available to us in Zero. We trust that we each possess direct access to it. Harnessing its power for positive change has the potential to reshape the world in a single generation and create a meaningful impact right now.

The challenge is that many view life *only* in terms of the natural world. This limits our resources, believing all we have to work with are the assets we have, be they material, monetary—or mortal. Yes, mortal. Life viewed merely from a mortal perspective is limited. Yet, when we align divinely, learn how to tap the sacred self, and live from our souls, we are so much more with much more available to us.

To be clear, sacred power is the power of Source manifest in life—in the here and now. It is the true understanding that the Source of Creation is part of you, and you are part of it. It is the belief that Source dwells at the core of your existence and is readily available. To enact sacred power is to bring a portion of Source to the natural world by rising into your highest self and cocreating with the power of Source.

This is something my grandfather understood well. He understood how to access and employ sacred power. He understood his own sacred self and how to attune himself to the sacred energy that permeates our existence. I am grateful daily for his example of this, as it was the one thing I could hold onto as I navigated my younger years. No matter what happened, I always understood that magic was real, even when I felt disconnected from it. It just took me half a lifetime to figure out how to get in alignment and access it intentionally in the blink of an eye.

DIVINE AUTHENTICITY

So how do we know if the principles of Zero are being fully realized in our lives?

We subject our Human Story Code to the litmus test of Zero. When there's a disconnect between wisdom, the reality of our lives, and our deepest desires, it signals that we haven't yet fully accessed all five entry points to Zero. This realization isn't a verdict but a call to action, an invitation to delve deeper. There is work to be done.

Since the day that my house of cards metaphorically fell, I've learned that reaching Zero is about putting oneself in *spiritual* positioning *with* Creation. It's intimate. It's relational. And it's possible for everyone. However, it cannot be done while masking, consciously or unconsciously, as this is not a true representation of the authentic Self.[1] Again, one must be prepared (and willing) to come face to face with unresolved trauma. If this does not occur, you cannot reach true freedom. And the boundless potential of Zero remains beyond your reach.

We might tap into aspects of Zero throughout our lives, such as using the law of attraction to manifest things like wealth or meaningful relationships. However, these experiences are limited if we are not wholly aligned with our (T)ruth. This practice often paints an oversimplified picture: "*Believe in yourself, and all your dreams come true!*"

While I've tasted some great success with it, it ultimately didn't bring me the fulfillment and happiness I yearned for. That's because such mantras and promises of manifestation can leave many feeling like frustrated, anxious failures. These fruitless manifestations derive from our self-imposed constraints, personal (t)ruths, and trauma. Perhaps you can relate—maybe you've tried creating vision boards or sticking motivational notes on your mirror, only to find the results are fleeting, much like the temporary success of a fad diet.

Connecting with Zero demands a wholehearted commitment to embracing our (T)rue nature and essence with divine authenticity. When we are authentic, we become powerful, void of limits. However, despite our efforts to tap into its vast freedom and resources, we struggle to align perfectly with Zero. This misalignment arises when our inauthenticity takes hold, and our pathway becomes clouded by (t)ruths. It's easy for this to happen.

We are programmed with uniquely complex Human Story Codes. And we are all incredibly stuck in our own human experiences—as well as the experiences of those around us. We vehemently care about our opinions, ideas, and constructs (or those of our fellow humans), so much so that it can be virtually impossible to hear the still, quiet voice that speaks to each of us alone. And so we align with the noise instead of the magic. We work to manage, maintain, or manipulate ourselves and our lives into the status quo of limitations.

Unlocking your sacred power and becoming limitless requires a developed perspective, self-possession, surrender of control, and, lastly, authentic Self-to-Source alignment. It is here, in this place—at Zero—that sacred power dwells.

Now, a developed perspective is born of the willing mind, but what of self-possession? This brings us deeper into the will as it directly engages choice. A decision grounds each moment in time—and every decision is anchored in choice and personal agency. Each choice then creates a new reality. It all starts and ends with You. Recall the zero exponent rule analogy: the baseline is always You. When raised to the power of Zero, your life story equals You. This places the entire responsibility and accountability for your life's outcome squarely on your shoulders.

I am reminded of a quote from Johann Wolfgang von Goethe, a late eighteenth-century poet, which my mother framed and displayed in our home: "*Choose well. Your choice is brief, and yet endless.*"[2]

Our final Human Story Code, the legacy we leave on earth, is woven from the multitude of decisions we make throughout our lives. Each thought and action casts ripples into the expanse of time, influencing not just our trajectory but also that of future generations. Our life stories, and the struggles within them, can serve as a perpetual source of limitation and pain, or they can transform into invaluable gifts. Our stories can shape our existence, enhance our engagement with the world, and bestow wisdom upon those who follow in our footsteps.

To be self-possessed is to recognize that life itself is an ever-evolving gift. The vision of a self-possessed life is for one to acknowledge their past in the context of their present in pursuit of an aligned future. It is an intentional embrace of one's state of function *and* state of being.

Oscar Wilde says that "*to live is the rarest thing in the world*";[3] this is what we are getting at. The ambition of self-possession is not to strive but rather to thrive! The self-possessed journey is a steadfast yet investigative voyage that requires a person to be willing to seek their own personal (T)ruths, and then to own them. It is to do this with the understanding that, just as our lives evolve, so do our (T)ruths.

Wayne Dyer says, "If you change the way you look at things, the things you look at change."[4] This maxim is valuable insight from the field of quantum physics, as it pertains to our subjective filters and limited perceptions as viewers of "truth." Enter humility. The literal meaning of the Greek word that translates into humility (ταπεινοφροσύνην) means "lowliness of mind." To be humble is not a weakness. Rather, it is a great strength as it opposes selfish ambition and conceit and aligns with the most extraordinary power of all, love.

The world has goals, values, ideologies, precepts, and concepts-a-many.

Self-possession determines which ways of being, frames of thinking, forms of understanding, etc., you align with. To choose the path of self-possession is to embrace the idea that the only way to your (T)ruth is through the willingness to investigate *all* things intimately and personally. It is to discard for a moment what you've been told—what the world has to say—all the "truth" you've received. And regard instead what the still, quiet voice within has to say. What do you know from your very guts to be (T)rue? You cannot find the authentic, divine You without questions such as this.

One of the most beautiful facets of Zero is that it is a judgment-free zone. Zero holds sacred power that, when tapped, enables an individual's sacred being to become virtually limitless. Zero is found with a state of acceptance engaged. What is real, what is (T)rue, and what is authentic is different for everyone—by design—and if a person is busy working hard to be something that they are not, it's virtually impossible for them to find acceptance for themselves or for anyone else.

Again, self-possession is defined as being calm, confident, and in control of one's feelings and self, to be composed. As I look at it, self-possession is more than this when viewed in the context of syzygy. To experience Zero, you must be perfectly aligned to enter the space of no thought and perceive reality without the world or the mind's interference. You must step into the present and fully embrace what is. To fully love, forgive, and accept others, you must first embrace the fact that you deserve those virtues. Zero provides you with a space to bestow those gifts upon yourself. This is what it is to truly live, and this is what it is to find Zero.

LET'S UNLOCK ZERO

The final address is this: How, then, does one reach Zero? How precisely does an imperfect human find alignment with the perfection of Source? And further, how do we tap into the infinite power that dwells thereof?

The extent of this miraculous mystery is something that I will pursue to the end of my days. I will give what I have, share what I know, and continue to align with the understanding that there is an infinite power source we have full access to. And with that power, if handled correctly, it can create a bounty of magic and miracles.

To start, it takes introspection and awareness. You must be willing to take the journey and understand that substantial effort is necessary to master all five entry points to Zero. To open the portal, grab hold of that metaphorical fire hose and point it in the direction of your desires, you cannot be encumbered by the ways of the world. This means healing wounds and cultivating an inner core of self-love, acceptance, forgiveness, and gratitude. Nurturing your internal environment is necessary to forge an authentic and powerful connection with Source. Zero is exacted presence, true freedom, and syzygetic harmony.

Ultimately, you must open each entry point to open the portal to Zero and dip into the wellspring of its power. As I mentioned, Find Awareness and Secure Alignment are similar to the practices taught in the manifestation techniques. But they are only two of five essential steps to grasp the total capacity of Zero. The more arduous entry points, Take Ownership, Release to Receive, and Engage Power, are fundamental.

Zero doesn't just create harmony. It creates *everything*. So it's vital that we judiciously wield its power to create more of what we want and less of what we don't want. Navigating the five entry points may seem especially daunting for those bearing the heavy burden of severe trauma. For these individuals, the path to Zero is not just a mere endeavor but a profound and unparalleled journey that demands courage, resilience, and an unwavering commitment to healing and self-discovery. My grandmother often reminded me that monumental tasks are conquered through persistent, gradual effort—one step at a time. While the path to Zero demands dedication and work, by patiently progressing each day you will eventually find Zero in its fullness.

Numerous practices are available to deepen our understanding of our (T)rue selves and the world around us. I would like to leave you with some practical tools as well as a visual worksheet that represents the portal to Zero. These tools can aid you in unlocking the five entry points to Zero and facilitate your journey toward profound power and transformation.

PORTAL TO ZERO

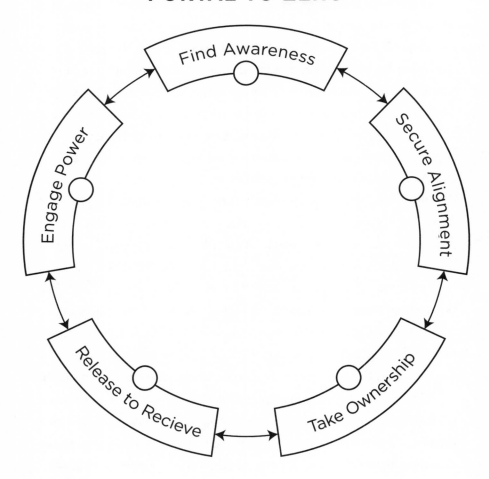

Write in the center a goal, a statement of your desire, or a question you want answered. Do the work to open the entry points. Once you feel clear and neutral with each one, color in the circle green. Once all five entry points are green, prepare for the magic of Zero!

⠐ Find Awareness

I believe that creating a visual map of your trauma timeline is one of the most effective methods to unlock the gate to the *Find Awareness* entry point. Transcribing these pivotal experiences onto paper aids in comprehending the significant events that have shaped your life and understanding their impact on your Human Story Code. By visualizing and reading your timeline, it becomes tangible and permutable. Rather than simply sifting through triggering memories as they come to you, a trauma timeline provides you with a bird's-eye view of the events that shaped who you are. Thus begins the unraveling process, allowing you to assess your core values and behavioral patterns to instigate positive change.

Besides mapping out traumas, getting on the awareness superhighway requires introspection about what truly matters to you in different areas of your life, whether it's relationships, career, or personal growth. To start, honestly ask yourself these basic questions:

- *Who am I at my core?*
- *What are my deepest desires?*
- *What is my life purpose?*
- *What are the beliefs that define me?*
- *Am I satisfied with the life I'm leading?*

Reflecting on the answers to these questions free of judgment can illuminate aspects of your life that perhaps have remained unexamined. Authentic growth requires courage to uncover (T)ruths buried deep within that struggle to find the light.

Awareness can come through mindful meditation where wisdom can whisper (T)ruth. If meditation isn't your cup of tea, immersing yourself in activities that demand your full attention, like exercise or painting, can profoundly increase your attunement to your inner thoughts and feelings.

Journaling is another powerful tool, a way to record and reflect on your thoughts, emotions, and experiences. It uncovers patterns and triggers, providing valuable insights.

Seeking professional guidance through therapy or counseling is beneficial in exploring and managing your emotions, aiding in making decisions that resonate with Self. Equally important is seeking honest feedback from people you trust, which can offer external perspectives on your life. It's essential to be in the company of what I fondly refer to as "Zero Heroes"—individuals who are on their own paths to discovering their (T)rue selves and harnessing the power of Zero. Surrounding yourself with like-minded people offers mutual support and encouragement as you each navigate your unique journeys. This camaraderie enriches your experience and creates a shared space of transformation.

Dedicating time for silence and solitude, especially in the tranquility of nature, can significantly deepen your connection with your inner self. This became my saving grace on countless walks through Snow Canyon in Southern Utah. This sacred place has become a sanctuary of reflective inspiration. A space for reaching Zero and connecting with Source.

At its core, the roadmap to awareness is about creating a harmonious alignment between your authentic, divine Self and the nuances of your human experience. It's about forging a deep connection with your innermost desires and unlocking the innate magic that dwells within.

Secure Alignment

Activating the *Secure Alignment* entry point is found through various unique (and powerful) modalities. These modes are different for everyone. It could be a direct connection with nature and the splendor of the outdoors. It might manifest through intellectual pursuits or studying various doctrines, theologies, and cultures. Perhaps alignment is best found in intense solitude and sensory deprivation or through symbols and sacraments.

Is your most significant connection with Source found in communion with loved ones or maybe in connections with strangers? It doesn't matter whether you find alignment while pulling weeds in the garden, moving your body, singing a song, or performing a ritual of your own accord—or even one passed on to you—the *what* is not what matters. What's important during this stage is to reflect upon *where, when,* and *how* you feel the most *you.*

Which aspects of your daily, weekly, monthly, or annual routine do you feel align the most with the energy within you? How often does this occur? How can you expand this or build upon it? While reflecting on your mode(s) of connection, take a minute to consider the happiness, harmony, and contentment they bring, and then consider whether these connection points are receiving the time and space they deserve in your life.

Securing alignment can also be effectively achieved through goal setting and mindfulness. Drawing from the wisdom of my grandfather, I learned the significant power of putting goals onto paper. Writing down what we want is a decisive first step in transforming abstract ideas into tangible realities, setting the stage for actualizing our dreams.

Visualizations play a crucial role in this process. They help in aligning our mental and emotional energies with our objectives. When we vividly imagine achieving our goals, experiencing the related emotions, and visualizing the necessary steps, we are programming our subconscious to align with these outcomes. This mental practice prepares our mind and body to work harmoniously with our goals.

By practicing mindfulness, you can respond to life's cyclones more thoughtfully rather than reacting impulsively, which can quickly lead to misalignment. Coupled with this is the development of emotional intelligence, understanding and managing your emotions, and recognizing and empathizing with the emotions of others. This dual practice of mindfulness and emotional intelligence leads to more harmonious relationships and decision-making that ensure alignment with our core values, effectively keeping those emotional storms at a manageable distance.

Perfect alignment, like the balance and neutrality of a solar eclipse, can be achieved through less-known practices. My sister introduced me to the Cellular Alignment Technique (CAT), which combines tapping and breathing exercises to neutralize negative emotions and facilitate emotional and mental alignment.[5] In just one session, I achieved getting to Zero with some persistent negative beliefs, or "parasitic (t)ruths," that were embedded in my Human Story Code.

"Tapping," a key component of CAT, is often associated with the Emotional Freedom Technique (EFT), a practice supported by numerous studies for its effectiveness. CAT enhances this technique by adding breath work, which my sister describes as "EFT on steroids." The method involves tapping over the top of the head, engaging all the meridians used in traditional Chinese medicine. Individuals can release emotional blockages by gently tapping with their fingertips on the governing meridian and following a specific breathing pattern while focusing on a particular issue or emotion. This process is believed to balance the energy system, leading to reduced stress, anxiety, and emotional distress, particularly those stemming from trauma.

Prioritizing self-care and activities that nourish your mind, body, and soul is crucial in sustaining alignment with your personal goals and reaching Zero.

Take Ownership

Opening the *Take Ownership* entry point requires us to fully embrace responsibility for our actions and life circumstances. This moves us toward a more proactive and accountable approach to life. This practice involves seeking self-acceptance, acknowledging our role in our experiences, and celebrating personal achievements.

We are aligned with a place of honesty and authenticity when we take ownership of the totality of our lives. The practice is twofold. First, it entails taking complete accountability for what we have created in our lives, past and present, and recognizing and embracing our strengths and weaknesses. Now, this isn't about resignation, but rather acknowledging our current state without judgment.

The second aspect of seeking acceptance involves embracing the things beyond our control, including our past traumas. Our most significant traumas often occur in childhood, when we are most vulnerable. We tend to carry these traumas into adulthood until we are ready to confront and take ownership of them. By coming to terms with what happened to us, we gain the power to change what happens to us.

Acknowledging our role in our experiences is crucial in shifting from a victim mindset to ownership and accountability. It's about understanding how our actions, decisions, and responses have contributed to our current life circumstances. This doesn't mean blaming ourselves for everything; rather, it's recognizing that we are active participants in our life story. This change in perspective from seeing oneself as a victim to recognizing oneself as a survivor can be transformative.

Life inevitably presents us with unforeseen and uncontrollable challenges. In these cyclone moments, the one thing we have complete authority over is our reaction. The way we engage with these cyclones is a choice. You have the agency to choose how you react and act in different situations. Acknowledging our role and how we manage our emotions when life throws a curveball grants us the power to make choices that align with our higher self.

Celebrating your achievements, no matter how small, is vital. Each step forward is a marker of progress and a testament to your journey. Recognizing and celebrating these milestones boosts confidence and motivation. It's a reaffirmation that you are moving forward, taking ownership of your path, and actively shaping your life. Taking ownership is about embracing self-compassion, accountability, and recognizing your power—all crucial steps in carving out a life that is authentically yours.

⠇ Release to Receive

Unlocking the *Release to Receive* entry point is about understanding the need to let go of roadblocks, negative influences, and energies that hinder your path to achieving your deepest desires. This practice of releasing is not just about creating space; it's about inviting new, positive energies and opportunities into your life, fostering growth, and opening the door to new possibilities and of course, magic.

If, during your awareness journey, you find answers to those questions that leave you unsatisfied, it's crucial to delve into the reasons why. Often, not achieving what we want in life is tied to our reluctance or inability to let go of what holds us back. This manifests from a myriad of reasons, ranging from various false beliefs intertwined into our Human Story Code to toxic relationships or even a reluctance to let our (T)rue selves emerge and be seen.

Think about it. How often do we wear masks to fit into roles that don't feel right? We need to release those ill-fitting aspirations so we can receive the authenticity that we are denying ourselves. Imagine breaking free from those fears and pain we often hold on to without realizing it.

This is where the power of forgiveness plays a pivotal role. Learning to forgive neutralizes negative emotions and experiences associated with our traumas, stripping them of their power over us. Doing this allows our authentic, divine light within to shine through the darkest corners of our being. You'll recognize that this transformation has occurred when you can reflect on or discuss these traumas without feeling triggered or pained, almost as if you're narrating someone else's story. This state of neutrality is "Getting to Zero."

When you are at Zero with your trauma, you attain a state of neutrality where the boundless resources of Zero can effectively work in your life. I vividly remember experiencing this when I symbolically released my deck of cards in my house on the hill. And when I wrote that letter to my brother, freeing him from all the pain. And again, on my walk through Snow Canyon. Those moments were a profound turning point, unleashing a series of events that propelled me through my incredible journey of self-discovery.

⬡ Engage Power

Activating the *Engage Power* entry point marks the dynamic shift from preparation to action. After laying the groundwork through the first four entry points, the focus turns to translating this foundational work into tangible steps forward. It's about embracing the spirit of initiative and discarding passivity. Rather than waiting for life to unfold, it involves actively seeking solutions and forging opportunities.

This entry point is characterized by a proactive approach, where you understand and leverage your capacity to direct the course of your life. It's a journey of cultivating trust in your ability to wield this power effectively. Overcoming challenges becomes more manageable as you learn to overcome fear and embrace authenticity.

Here, the power you engage is not just about action; it's about informed, purposeful action that aligns with the Awareness, Alignment, Ownership, and Release to Receive you've developed. Utilizing these four entry points as a foundation, you harness the power of Zero. Engage Power is not just a single step but a culmination of your journey. It's a point where your newfound understanding, alignment, and resilience converge, propelling you toward your (T)ruth with confidence and clarity.

Setting healthy boundaries is essential for engaging and maintaining our power. These boundaries help us define what is acceptable regarding how others treat us and how we manage our time and energy. This practice requires us to say no to situations that cause us to cyclone, or to distance ourselves from individuals who do not align with or support our highest authentic selves. It's common to encounter relationships that are mentally or emotionally draining. While the people in these relationships with you may appear to have good intentions, they can drain your resources and deplete your personal power. In such cases, setting boundaries might mean limiting the time spent with these individuals or choosing not to engage at all.

I've developed a valuable tool to handle life's cyclones effectively, ensuring I keep my power fully engaged. Recognizing the triggers that spark these emotional whirlwinds is the first step. Once identified, create a "cyclone escape plan." Remember the fire drills we practiced in grade school? It's that but for emotional emergencies. The plan involves predetermined actions to take when a cyclone hits. For instance, if certain people or situations tend to stir up turmoil, have a strategy to disengage and seek shelter from these individuals or situations until the emotional storm passes. Instead of confronting the storm head-on, practice redirecting its energy. This could mean stepping out for a brisk walk or channeling emotions into a physical activity that diffuses the intensity and clears the mind. Another practice is visualizing scenarios where challenging situations are handled gracefully and effectively. This mental rehearsal builds resilience to better manage real-life situations.

Music has the power to alter moods dramatically. Curate playlists with songs that evoke calmness, happiness, or empowerment, depending on what is needed to combat your emotional cyclone. Become armed with positive affirmations tailored to counter specific triggers. When a storm is brewing, repeating these out loud fortifies a positive mindset, turning your spoken affirmations into a shield against negative emotions. Another great escape plan is to practice gratitude. When a cyclone hits, take a moment to list things you are grateful for. This can help shift your energy from distressing emotions to a positive outcome. By deciding on these actions beforehand, we avoid making impulsive decisions that disrupt our alignment. This approach keeps emotions in check and ensures we remain in a position of power, calmly and purposefully navigating life's storms.

Engaging your power involves profoundly understanding and believing that you are worthy of all the magic and abundance that is all around you. To engage power means accepting who you truly are. This means shedding the layers of societal expectations or roles that don't resonate with your genuine self. You must stop attempting to be something you are not. Stop chasing a dream that was never meant for you. I had to release my white picket fence fantasy to engage the power of who I authentically am, to unapologetically be the man in the mirror. I invite you to embrace your (T)rue being without fear and without limits.

THE GIFT OF ZERO

We must trust in each of these five entry points if we want to use Zero to change our lives in a literal or material fashion and on a cellular level. Like anything worth having, this requires daily practice and dedication. If anything does not align with our (T)rue selves, we must surrender it by raising it to the power of Zero. This modifies our genetic and experiential predispositions, allowing us to trust in our power with unfailing capacity. This is the beauty of a life lived from trust rather than one lived through trauma.

If I am to claim anything of what Zero has taught me in my journey thus far, I believe it would be these three simple truths:

- Every person inherently possesses value granted to them by the Source of all Creation. No person, entity, religion, social structure, or law of man can dictate an individual's own ability to explore and realize their (T)rue identity and life's purpose.

- Just as Source has crafted each of us uniquely in our ways of doing and being, Source has established a distinct path within us to connect with the world and the greater universe. Through this connection, we can relate to everything that exists, has existed, or will exist. This universal connection is Zero.

- Zero grants access to the power of all creation itself. This is the promise of Zero; the (T)rue promise of our full potential that is inherently ours—our absolute birthright. This mighty power can be claimed and directed when our (T)rue Self fully aligns with Source. Then and only then will it be granted in the light of unadulterated, unconditional Love. At Zero—harmony simply is, (T)ruth expands, and wisdom dwells. Here, everything aligns in perfect, divine order.

Wait, we better make that four simple truths because there is one more thing Zero has taught me, and this is something I believe must be learned again and again—and again—ad nauseam.

- Life doesn't necessarily get easier with Zero. It just gets easier to manage. The difference is that, rather than working desperately to maintain a status quo or manipulate life to our favor, we surrender all. We access Zero and step into neutrality. We release what does not serve us. We receive what aligns with our higher self. We accept that we are an imperfect being imperfectly living an imperfect life—and so is everyone else.

Currently, this is what I have to offer by means of a prescriptive measure. I implore you to take what is useful and receive only what resonates. I ask that you move into this according to the promptings you receive of your own accord—and that is all; as my way is mine, your way is yours. If you embrace nothing else in your search for Zero, please remember that finding Zero is about seeking your place in the context of all creation. This means that for Zero to be found, you must first welcome an awareness of *Self*.

The primary gift of Zero I received was the understanding that my way of being was not just okay but beautiful and celebrated—and that this *way* had more to do with my soul than it would ever have to do with my human expression. Beyond this, something I had always innately known was now perfectly and beautifully clear. Everyone's story matters as they are all an integral part of the grand consciousness. To negate a story, devalue a person, or reject an individual's life path is perhaps the greatest of all wrongs.

The most exquisite (and valuable) elements of humanity are our unique differences and our individual expressions. Recognizing this (of oneself and others) is what it means to live authentically—to live at Zero. This is why getting to Zero with the world we live in (and its traumas) is so important. It is also a realization that must be embraced to be happy and live the measure of our creation.

In retrospect, I understand this is what the law of Zero both grants and governs. The law of Zero, like all laws of nature, is indisputable. It has no agenda and offers absolute neutrality. Once you reach Zero, you are in perfect, irrefutable alignment with who you are, and this state of being is the epitome of true joy.

The power accessed at Zero is a personal, present-tense, creative affair. It comes together just as every single letter of this page, this chapter, and this book. It comes together like the greatest of all things, one micro-moment at a time, and when trust and the catalyst of surrender are engaged—what a ride! All possibilities are at your fingertips. Any world can form—just as any word can. This is the beauty of potential and the very premise of the law of Zero. This is the essence of its promise.

As I reach the end of this exploration and reflect on its beginnings, I'm reminded of those childhood nights spent under the stars. I recognize that curious boy within me, filled with belief in all things magic. In the busy hustle of adulthood, I still find moments on moonless nights to lay on my back and stare into the heavens. I now know the promise of possibilities are out there. The vast number of stars no longer makes me feel small; instead, they fill me with a sense of power and a deep connection to the universe. I understand now that what lies out there is a part of me.

The magic that the universe whispered to me as a boy continues to whisper now. But with Zero, I comprehend its message. With Zero, I don't just dream; I act. Zero has not just been an adventure; it has been an awakening, a realization that the magic I believed in as a child is the same force that drives me forward today.

CONCLUSION

I f you are indeed ready to engage yourself fully in the pursuit of Zero, consider making today the day that everything changes. Make today the day that you choose unencumbered exploration. Harness this very moment and make it yours. Choose to pursue all possibilities for yourself and your life.

If it's helpful, write a vow along the following lines. You can use my words if you'd like, or you can craft your own. This is *your* journey. There are no rules here. This book exists merely to share my (T)ruth and my pathway to Zero. If the following words are helpful in any way, please receive them.

Today, (date), I engage my will in an effort to release all that impedes my mind, my heart, and my spirit. I'm willing to venture into the unknown, and I'm ready to search out the life I'm meant to live—the life I'm made to live. I won't let my ego, pride, position, or past impede the possibility that lives within me.

I will not allow others, despite their position or relation, to determine my life's path, and I will no longer give my power away to anyone or anything as today, (date), I reclaim the sacred power that is my birthright.

I am here to seek Zero.

I am ready to unlock the sacred power that dwells within.

I choose to release all trauma touchpoints from my life, moving throughout the span of time, past, present, and future. I'm willing to step into forgiveness for myself, for others, for our world, and for the benefit of future generations.

I will not carry my trauma forward nor pay it forward to my family, my friends, and those around me. My trauma, pain, and shame stops with me. I trust in myself and my capacity to do all things.

I commit my will to the journey from trauma to Truth that I may seek, embrace, and know Zero.

Today, (date), I reclaim my sacred power.

ACKNOWLEDGMENTS

First and foremost, a heartfelt thank you to my dear friends Quinn Coleman and Yayoi Swapp, who braved the traffic from Los Angeles to San Diego and back to encourage me to write this book. Without your divine intervention, the words of these pages would not exist.

Momala, thank you for being a constant light in my life and for bestowing upon me the gift of discernment. Your encouragement to question everything and seek the Truth is the reason this book exists today.

A tremendous appreciation for Emily Daves, who joined me in the deep dive headfirst into understanding the law of Zero. Thank you for three diligent years of exploring, researching, and shaping my thoughts into text during our weekly Zoom calls throughout the pandemic. Your wisdom and dedication were instrumental in transforming my life lessons and stories into the pages of this book.

Monique Soltani, my friend of over two decades, has been with me every step of this journey into the law of Zero. Through daily texts, reflective discussions written on cocktail napkins, and beach sunset conversations over champagne, you helped me test and refine Zero with each of its entry points. Thank you for your friendship.

Lisa Feellove, our creation walks in Snow Canyon sparked the magic that turned our spoken words into tangible realities—thank you for walking this path with me.

My sister, Cherylyn Carpenter, your magical tapping techniques were instrumental in helping me experience true alignment in my body. Thank you for grounding me in Zero with recognizing how it feels to be completely neutral.

To my Jerri Eckert, you will always have a piece of my heart. Your unwavering love has been my rock, especially during times when I felt unworthy of your love.

Angel (AJ) Chavero, thank you for showing up in my life when I truly needed you. You are and will always be my angel.

Thank you, Pedro Roberto Melo Rodriguez, for always taking care of my (our) pup Cooper. You're always one step ahead to make sure I am taken care of. Everyone (especially my mother) loves you.

David Roetto, thank you for exemplifying authenticity in a time when it felt impossible to do so, inspiring me to live my (T)ruth courageously.

To Lora Fudale, whose belief in me as a young entrepreneur sparked an adventure from being my first team-building client to becoming a cherished friend and confidant. Your support and advice have been invaluable.

Wayne Scholes, thank you for encouraging me to step into the world of entrepreneurship. Your advice and example of living life fearlessly created a lasting ripple effect.

To my "wives," Karla Anderson and Cinthia Gambino, who have witnessed (and participated in) countless shenanigans since our childhood days. Your unwavering friendship and love have been my anchor, always reminding me of where I come from and keeping me grounded.

I am forever grateful to all my teachers who have shaped my path. Mark Tomlinson, Rosemary Mallet, and Richard Reed, you recognized something within me that I couldn't see through the weeds of insecurity. Your encouragement to develop my talents during my formative years gave me the courage to shine. Russell Bice and Elizabeth Bossard, your faith in me opened doors I never imagined possible. Thank you for "giving me a chance."

It took many hands to bring law of Zero to these pages. Thank you to Brannan Sirratt for your expertise in guiding me through the book writing process. To Laura Taylor, fate brought us together for you to share your invaluable guidance as an author. Thank you for believing in me.

Theresa Hunt-Stell, thank you for your sharp skills and intuition that brought this book across the finish line.

A special thank you to Cassondra Martinez, Tiffany Berg, and everyone at Greenleaf Book Group—Morgan Robinson, Benito Salazar, Jeanette Smith, Laurie MacQueen—your collective efforts have turned the *Law of Zero* into a reality, and a huge shoutout to Dee Kerr for being one of the first self-proclaimed Zero Heroes.

And finally, I am nothing without my family—my parents, siblings, grandparents, aunts, uncles, cousins, nieces, nephew, and the friends who have become just as dear. Each of you has shaped the person I am and the words I write. Thank you for your unending love and support.

NOTES

INTRODUCTION

1. Robert K. Beshara, "The Chakra System as a Bio-Socio-Psycho-Spiritual Model of Consciousness: Anahata as Heart-Centered Consciousness," *International Journal of Yoga—Philosophy, Psychology, Parapsychology* 1, no. 1 (January 2013):29–33, https://doi.org/10.4103/WKMP-0041.123289/.
2. This is known as perennial wisdom born of perennial philosophy.
3. Richard Lyman Bushman and Joseph Smith, *Rough Stone Rolling* (New York: Knopf, 2005), 87–88.
4. Source is the root of all creation, a force synonymous with deity. Consider Source to represent your Higher Power: God, Allah, Buddha, Universe, etc. A power both outside of oneself but accessible within oneself.

CHAPTER 1

1. The concept of the law of attraction can be traced back to the nineteenth century during the New Thought movement first appearing in *The Great Harmonia*, written by the American spiritualist Andrew Jackson Davis. The modern interpretation of the law of attraction gained popularity in the early twentieth century through books like *The Science of Getting Rich* by Wallace D. Wattles and *The Master Key System* by Charles F. Haanel. It further gained widespread attention in the early twenty-first century through the self-help book and movie *The Secret* by Rhonda Byrne.
2. "Nirvana" is a term found in the texts of all major Indian religions to include Hinduism, Jainism, Buddhism, and Sikhism.
3. In Japanese culture, the *ensō* is often drawn on washi (thin, white paper) with sumi (a black ink wash), yet it can be drawn on various surfaces, including dirt, walls, or even the air.

4. The golden ratio, often represented by the Greek letter φ (phi), is a mathematical constant approximately equal to 1.61803. It is a number that represents a proportion considered to be aesthetically pleasing in various forms of art, architecture, and nature.

5. In 2014, physicist Max Tegmark released the book *Our Mathematical Universe: My Quest for the Ultimate Nature of Reality*, which included his concept of the Mathematical Universe Hypothesis (MUH). This concept proposes that the entire physical universe is fundamentally a mathematical structure. It posits that everything that exists can be explained entirely through mathematical concepts.

6. The book *Feelings Buried Alive Never Die* by Karol K. Truman was originally published in 1991. This nonfiction text emphasizes the importance of addressing buried emotions and unresolved feelings, suggesting that these emotions can significantly affect one's physical, mental, emotional, and spiritual well-being.

7. Steve Jobs, "'You've Got to Find What You Love,' Jobs says," Stanford Commencement Address, June 12, 2005, https://news.stanford.edu/2005/06/12/youve-got-find-love-jobs-says/.

CHAPTER 2

1. The law of attraction is a philosophical and spiritual concept suggesting that the energy of one's thoughts, emotions, and beliefs can directly influence and shape one's reality. At its core, this law posits that like attracts like, meaning positive thoughts attract positive outcomes, while negative thoughts attract negative outcomes. This idea is encapsulated in the belief that by focusing on positive or negative thoughts, a person can bring positive or negative experiences into their life.

2. Alice is the main character in *Alice's Adventures in Wonderland*, a widely beloved British children's book by Lewis Carroll, published in 1865. In 1951, this story was adapted by Disney into an animated film.

3. "Syzygy" is defined as a conjunction or opposition, particularly in reference to the moon with the sun.

4. The lunar nodes are the two points where the moon's orbital path crosses the ecliptic, the sun's apparent yearly path on the celestial sphere.

CHAPTER 3

1. "What Is Trauma?" Trauma-Informed Care Implementation Resource Center, March 2020, https://www.traumainformedcare.chcs.org/what-is-trauma/.

2. Donald E. Brown, *Human Universals* (New York City: McGraw-Hill, 1991). A cultural universal is a pattern, trait, or institution that is common to all human

societies. The entire body of cultural universals at work is otherwise known as the human condition.

3. As stated by Ordinance 38.6.16 in the *General Handbook of The Church of Jesus Christ of Latter-day Saints*, the church affirms that marriage between a man and a woman is essential to the Creator's plan for the eternal destiny of His children. The Church also affirms that God's law defines marriage as the legal and lawful union between a man and a woman. Only a man and a woman who are legally and lawfully wedded as husband and wife should have sexual relations. Any other sexual relations, including those between persons of the same sex, are sinful and undermine the divinely created institution of the family.

4. Joseph Smith, *Doctrine and Covenants* (1835) 88:33–35.

5. Sherry Hamby et al., "Recognizing the Cumulative Burden of Childhood Adversities Transforms Science and Practice for Trauma and Resilience," *American Psychologist* 76, no. 2 (2021): 230–242, https://doi .org/10.1037/amp0000763; V. J. Felitti et al., "Relationship of Childhood Abuse and Household Dysfunction to Many of the Leading Causes of Death in Adults: The Adverse Childhood Experiences (ACE) Study," *American Journal of Preventive Medicine* 14, no. 4 (May 1998): 245–258, https://doi.org/10.1016/ s0749-3797(98)00017-8.

6. Large-T trauma is a classification of traumatic events that are (generally) undeniable from a rational perspective. This includes significant, identifiable events such as physical abuse, sexual assault, illness, a natural disaster, car accident, terror attack, etc.—basically, any event of great negative impact that can be singled out. Large-T traumas can leave a person feeling utterly powerless and in a position where they have little to no actual control over their environment. This results in extreme helplessness, and it is this state that impacts a person deeply.

7. "About the CDC-Kaiser ACE Study," Centers for Disease Control and Prevention, https://www.cdc.gov/violenceprevention/aces/about.html/.

CHAPTER 4

1. In Mormonism, the concept of mortal divinity teaches that humans have the potential to become gods through spiritual progression and obedience to God's commandments, with the belief that God Himself was once a mortal. This belief underscores the idea of eternal progression, where individuals aim to become more like God in character and attributes.

2. Joseph Smith Jr. was the founder of the Latter-day Saint movement and a key figure in the early history of Mormonism. He claimed to have been visited

by God and Jesus Christ in the early nineteenth century, leading to the publication of the Book of Mormon and the establishment of the Church of Christ, later known as The Church of Jesus Christ of Latter-day Saints.

3. It was the King James Version Bible, including the Old and New Testaments, as well as the *Book of Mormon*, *Doctrine and Covenants*, and *The Pearl of Great Price*.

4. *Priesthood Ordinances and Blessings*. It's taught that this is the same priesthood that Jesus held and that this priesthood was passed on to Joseph Smith by John the Baptist in Ghost form. It was this very priesthood that was then eventually passed on to my father and would someday be passed on to me.

5. John 3:5, *KJV Bible*; Joseph Smith, *Doctrine and Covenants* (1835) 33:11. A person becomes a member of the church only after the ordinances of baptism and confirmation are both completed and properly recorded.

CHAPTER 5

1. Then these words were spoken, a cold shiver ran down my spine as if I were in grave danger.

2. The husband who is laid off from work comes home to take it out on his family. A kid who is abused at home magnifies ants in the sun and gives the chubby kid a wedgie on the school bus.

3. We've to look no further than Nazi Germany, slavery, and even the Salem witch trials to know the truth in this. The visceral experience of control, of having it and exerting it over the reach of one's domain—be it the highest office in the land or the school playground—makes a person feel like a god: My will be done.

4. The powers that be (sometimes initialized as TPTB) is a phrase used to refer to those individuals or groups who collectively hold authority over a particular domain.

CHAPTER 6

1. Ricks College transitioned to the name Brigham Young University—Idaho on August 10, 2001.

2. Mairi Levitt "Perceptions of Nature, Nurture and Behaviour," *Life Sciences, Society and Policy* 9, article 13 (December 2013): https://doi .org/10.1186/2195-7819-9-13.

3. Andrea Ganna et al., "Large-Scale GWAS Reveals Insights into the Genetic Architecture of Same-Sex Sexual Behavior," *Science* 365, no. 6456 (August 30, 2019): https://doi.org/10.1126/science.aat7693.

4. Walter H. Bucher, *The Deformation of the Earth's Crust: An Inductive Approach to the Problems of Diastrophism* (Princeton, NJ: Princeton University Press, 1933).

CHAPTER 7

1. "Quick Facts," BYUI.edu, archived from the original on May 8, 2011, https://web.archive.org/web/20110508105533/http:/www.byui.edu/admissions/quickfacts.html/.

2. A quick lesson in LDS Culture 101 taught me that "preemie" meant I was not an RM, or "returned missionary," and therefore, not marriage material—which meant getting a date just became twice as hard. Mish was short for "mission" and FHE stood for Family Home Evening. Being in a church congregation of nothing but single students, we were assigned to a small group that became our "family."

3. In the Church of Jesus Christ of Latter-day Saints, Family Home Evening (FHE) or Family Night is a weekly event, typically on Mondays, where families gather for religious instruction, prayer, and bonding via games and other activities to reinforce gospel principles and familial love.

CHAPTER 8

1. In the Church of Jesus Christ of Latter-day Saints, once a person accepts and is approved by members for a church calling, they are "set apart" by one or more Melchizedek priesthood holders through a ritual or priesthood action to formally bless them for that specific responsibility.

2. Imagine getting a letter signed by the Pope or the President of the United States. This was a big deal.

3. "Endowment," The Church of Jesus Christ of Latter-day Saints Library, https://www.churchofjesuschrist.org/study/manual/gospel-topics/endowment?lang=eng/. The endowment ceremony, conducted in temples of The Church of Jesus Christ of Latter-day Saints, is available to its worthy adult members. It encompasses teachings on the Creation, the fall of Adam and Eve, and the path of redemption through Jesus Christ, aiming to guide participants back to God's presence. This ceremony involves making sacred covenants that enhance one's commitment to live according to divine laws of obedience, sacrifice, chastity, and consecration, promising blessings of power, purpose, and protection in daily life. Faithful adherence to these covenants also opens the way to eternal marriage and eternal life, fulfilling God's promise to endow His people with divine power.

4. "Marriage," The Church of Jesus Christ of Latter-day Saints Library, https://www.churchofjesuschrist.org/study/manual/gospel-topics/marriage?lang=eng/.

Marriage and sealing is a religious ceremony within The Church of Jesus Christ of Latter-day Saints where a couple is joined as husband and wife for eternity. During this ceremony, the couple forms an eternal bond, and any children they already have can be sealed to them, ensuring the family unit remains intact forever, contingent on living according to God's commandments. Children born after the couple's sealing automatically become part of this eternal family. Additionally, children who are adopted into the family at a later date can also be sealed to them through a separate sealing ceremony, without the need for another marriage ceremony. This practice underscores the belief in families being together eternally.

5. "Sealing," The Church of Jesus Christ of Latter-day Saints Library, https://www. churchofjesuschrist.org/study/manual/gospel-topics/sealing?lang=eng/. Sealing to parents is an ordinance for children who were either born before their parents' marriage and sealing or who have been adopted. This ceremony integrates the children fully into their family, as though they were born into it after the sealing had already taken place. It establishes an eternal connection between the children and their parents, affirming their place in the family unit in the afterlife.

6. "Baptisms for the Dead," The Church of Jesus Christ of Latter-day Saints Library, https://www.churchofjesuschrist.org/study/manual/gospel-topics/ baptisms-for-the-dead?lang=eng/. Baptisms for the dead is a religious ordinance performed in the temples of The Church of Jesus Christ of Latter-day Saints, wherein church members are baptized on behalf of those who have passed away without the opportunity to receive the ordinance themselves. This act is based on the belief that baptism is essential for salvation, and performing it by proxy allows those who have died to accept or reject this baptism in the afterlife. It underscores the church's teaching on the universality of salvation and its commitment to ensuring that everyone has the chance to accept church doctrines and teachings, regardless of when or where they lived.

7. "Plan of Salvation," The Church of Jesus Christ of Latter-day Saints Library, https://www.churchofjesuschrist.org/study/manual/gospel-topics/plan-of-salvation?lang=eng/. The Plan of Salvation, as taught by The Church of Jesus Christ of Latter-day Saints, outlines a framework for human existence, including pre-Earth life, mortal life, and post-mortal existence. According to this plan, all human beings are spirit children of God, who lived with Him before being born on Earth. Earth life is viewed as a crucial stage where individuals gain a body, make choices, undergo trials, and grow from their experiences, all with the ultimate goal of returning to live with God. After death, spirits go to the spirit world to await resurrection and judgment. Faithful adherence to the gospel of Jesus Christ, which includes acceptance of His atonement, adherence to His commandments, and participation in sacred ordinances, is believed to lead to

eternal life in the presence of God and eternal families. This plan emphasizes the eternal nature of individual and family relationships and God's desire for His children to progress and achieve divine potential.

CHAPTER 9

1. Marion G. Romney, "Trust in the Lord," speech given in April 1979, https://www.churchofjesuschrist.org/study/general-conference/1979/04/trust-in-the-lord?lang=eng/.

CHAPTER 10

1. Mormon missionaries follow a "Missionary Handbook" that advises against swimming due to safety concerns and to maintain focus on their spiritual work. This prohibition also helps ensure modesty and cultural sensitivity and avoids distractions from their primary purpose.

CHAPTER 11

1. I have since learned that such all-encompassing messaging is termed "social constructionism," a theory that recognizes that various aspects of the world around us are not real in and of themselves, but rather, they exist or don't exist as reality due to social agreement.

CHAPTER 12

1. *The Secret* is a self-help documentary film released in 2006, based on the best-selling book of the same name by Rhonda Byrne. It explores the "law of attraction" and how positive thinking and visualization can manifest one's desires and success.

2. Imposter syndrome, also known as impostor phenomenon or fraud syndrome, is a psychological pattern in which an individual doubts their accomplishments, skills, or abilities and has a persistent fear of being exposed as a "fraud" or as someone who doesn't deserve their success. People experiencing imposter syndrome often attribute their achievements to luck, timing, or external factors rather than recognizing their own competence and hard work.

3. "Smiles," words by Daniel Taylor.

4. "Sabbath Day Observance," The Church of Jesus Christ of Latter-day Saints Library, https://www.churchofjesuschrist.org/study/ensign/2014/01/sabbath-day-observance?lang=eng/.

CHAPTER 14

1. A kangaroo court is an unofficial court held by a group of people in order to try someone regarded, especially without good evidence, as guilty of a crime or misdemeanor.

2. "Mountain Meadows Massacre Memorial," https://www.atlasobscura.com/places/mountain-meadows-massacre-memorial/.

3. Intergenerational trauma refers to the transmission of the effects of trauma or adverse experiences from one generation to the next, affecting individuals who did not directly experience the traumatic events. It can manifest through emotional, behavioral, cultural, and even biological factors, impacting the descendants of those who suffered the trauma.

4. Reeya A. Patel and Donna K. Nagata, "Historical Trauma and Descendants' Well-Being," *Ethics* 23, no. 6 (2021): 487–493, https://doi.org/10.1001/amajethics.2021.487.

5. Martha Henriques, "Can the Legacy of Trauma Be Passed Down the Generations?" BBC, March 26, 2019, https://www.bbc.com/future/article/20190326-what-is-epigenetics/.

6. Snow Canyon State Park is a 7,400-acre scenic park boasting incredible sandstone cliffs and majestic views. If you've ever experienced the canyonlands of Utah, you will understand the natural healing properties that can be found in the interplay of light and shadow.

7. Although I didn't know it at the time, I was, in this moment, releasing to and receiving from Zero. I was in full surrender and had made myself completely available to the creative and capable power of the Source of all creation.

8. John C. Maxwell has used the quote "Change is inevitable, growth is optional" in various speeches and writings, but it isn't linked to a specific book or speech that made it famous. It's a piece of his broader teachings on leadership and personal development, which he has shared across numerous platforms, including conferences, seminars, and in his published works. This quote is often cited in motivational contexts to highlight the importance of choosing to grow amidst life's inevitable changes.

CHAPTER 15

1. "Hypothermia," Mayo Clinic, https://www.mayoclinic.org/diseases-conditions/hypothermia/symptoms-causes/syc-20352682#/. Hypothermia occurs when the body gets cold and loses heat faster than it can make it. Your body temperature can drop to a dangerous level if you are in 60°F to 70°F water (or colder) for an extended period.

2. It turns out that the lake experience strengthened Cherylyn's resolve to go on her mission, find her companion, and become a mother. All of this came true—not to mention that she met her husband on a trip to Las Vegas.

3. Roger Allers and Rob Minkoff dirs., *The Lion King*, 1994, Walt Disney Pictures, https://www.disneyplus.com/movies/the-lion-king/1HqwiEcje6Nj/. The scene opens with an adorable little mouse scurrying about and preening in the light. Suddenly the score shifts, the mouse becomes frightened, and a large lion paw swoops in and catches the mouse. Dissonant low music ensues, and the scene shifts to Scar holding the squeaking mouse by its tail as it struggles to be let free. "Life's not fair, is it? You see I—well, I . . . shall never be King. {exhales lightly} And you . . . shall never see the light of another day . . . Adieu . . ." Scar then begins to place the mouse on his extended tongue. In proper Disney fashion, Zazu swoops in to give the mouse its escape and provide the perfect comedic relief, "Didn't your mother ever tell you not to play with your food?"

CHAPTER 16

1. Shams-i Tabrīzī was a Persian Poet and the spiritual advisor of Rumi. More can be learned of him through his writings and those of Rumi, specifically, *Maqalat-e Shams-e Tabrizi* (Discourse of Shams-i Tabrīzī) and *Divan-i Shams-i Tabrizi.*

2. Before writing this book, I released the domain mormonsexposed.com and I am no longer affiliated with the site or any future iterations of it.

3. James worked at Chippendale's in Las Vegas prior to becoming a contestant on the twenty-first season of *The Amazing Race* in 2012 and later becoming a correspondent for *Celebrity Page* and *The Talk.*

4. California's Proposition 8, backed heavily by members of the LDS Church from Utah, was being put on the ballot to reverse marriage legality (which was passed in 2008), and Mitt Romney, a prominent Mormon, was in the spotlight while running for the US presidency.

5. A victim impact statement is a spoken or written statement made during the sentencing phase of a trial by the victim of a crime describing the harm and suffering experienced as a result of the defendant's acts.

CHAPTER 18

1. Biofeedback is a form of brain training (also known as cognitive training) that is often conducted in physical therapy clinics, medical centers, and hospitals. However, a trained practitioner is also able to conduct it in-home.

2. I now know that there is no hierarchy in suffering. There is no qualifying pedestal of pain, nor a degree to which one must be hurt in order for it to count. Trauma doesn't work like that.

CHAPTER 19

1. Yayoi was Ms. August in the 2010 *Hot Mormon Muffins* Calendar.

2. *Trauma-Informed Care in Behavioral Health Services* (Rockville, MD: Substance and Mental Health Services Administration, 2014).

3. "Immediate and Delayed Reactions to Trauma," NCIB, https://www.ncbi.nlm. nih.gov/books/NBK207191/table/part1_ch3.t1/?report=objectonly/.

4. Catherine Ponder, *The Dynamic Laws of Prosperity: Forces that Bring Riches to You* (Radford, VA: Wilder Publications, 2011).

5. The Five Principles: (1) God is all there is and present everywhere. This is the force of love and wisdom that underlies all of existence; (2) Human beings are divine at their core and therefore inherently good; (3) Thoughts have creative power to determine events and attract experiences; (4) Prayer and meditation keep us aligned with the one great power in the universe; (5) It is not enough to understand spiritual teachings. We must live the Truth we know.

6. Ram Dass, *Be Here Now* (New York: Harmony, 1971), 57.

7. Garma C.C. Chang, *The Hundred Thousand Songs of Milarepa* (Boulder, CO: Shambhala, 1962), 279. Jetsun Milarepa was a highly accomplished and famous Tibetan disciple and spiritual poet. He was a student of Marpa Lotsawa and is most known for having been a murderer in his youth before turning to Buddhism.

8. Alexander Pope, "An Essay on Criticism."

CHAPTER 20

1. This practice is termed masking in psychology and is a process wherein a person "masks" parts of their natural self in an effort to conform to various environmental factors such as social pressures, abuse, or harassment.

2. Johann Wolfgang von Goethe, "Symbolum," *Goethe's Werke*.

3. Oscar Wilde, "The Soul of Man Under Socialism" (1891).

4. Wayne Dyer, *The Power of Intention* (Carlsbad, CA: Hay House, 2004), 287.

5. My sister, Cherylyn Carpenter, is a CAT method practitioner and works with individuals every day to find their alignment and reach Zero. Visit her website to learn more: https://www.joyfully-resilient.com/.

ABOUT THE AUTHOR

Raised as a devout member of the Church of Jesus Christ of Latter-day Saints, Chad Michael Hardy found himself at a crossroad with his faith when he made international headlines for being excommunicated and stripped of his degree from Brigham Young University. But this was not the crushing setback you might think, rather it fueled his long-standing passion for personal development.

Since his discovery of the law of Zero, Chad has channeled the multitude of personal challenges and triumphs of his life into helping others find their authentic joy and their True Self. His narrative is a testament to the power of authenticity in a world that often demands conformity. His path is one marked by profound introspection, spiritual awakening, and a relentless quest for Truth. This pursuit led him to authorship, where he invites you to contemplate your own journey, encouraging you to break free from the status quo and embrace your vulnerabilities as gateways to growth and enlightenment.

Chad has a proven track record of building people up and bringing people together by producing community and corporate events. An award-winning entrepreneur, he founded a flourishing team building company, AdVenture Games Inc. With nothing more than a credit card and a prayer, Chad transformed his vision from a humble Las Vegas startup into a nationally recognized enterprise, partnering with Fortune 500 companies like Amazon, Google, and Microsoft.

Chad divides his time between two of the happiest places on earth—San Diego, California, and Orlando, Florida. You will often find him soaking up the sunsets and giving impromptu cocktail napkin sermons about Zero and the magic that he calls life.